Informal and incidental learning in the workplace

International perspectives on adult and continuing education

Edited by Peter Jarvis
University of Surrey

Consultant editors: Chris Duke and Ettore Gelpi

Informal and incidental learning in the workplace

Victoria J. Marsick
and
Karen E. Watkins

London and New York

First published 1990
by Routledge
11 New Fetter Lane, London EC4P 4EE

Simultaneously published in the USA and Canada
by Routledge
a division of Routledge, Chapman and Hall, Inc.
29 West 35th Street, New York, NY 10001

Typeset by
NWL Editorial Services, Langport, Somerset TA10 9DG
Printed and bound in Great Britain by
Biddles Ltd, Guildford and King's Lynn

British Library Cataloguing in Publication Data
A CIP catalogue record for this book is available from the
British Library.

Library of Congress Cataloging in Publication Data
Informal and incidental learning in the workplace / Victoria J.
Marsick and K.E. Watkins.
    p.   cm. – (International perspectives on adult and
continuing education)
Includes bibliographical references.
ISBN 0-415-03141-9
1. Employees – training of. 2. Adult education. 3. Learning.
I. Watkins, Karen E., 1946–   . II. Title. III. series:
International perspectives on adult and continuing education
(Routledge (Firm))
HF5549.5.T7M29   1990   90-8359
658.3'124 – dc20   CIP

Contents

Figures and tables

Tables

Series editor's note

The Routledge Series in International Perspectives on Adult and Continuing Education brings to an English-speaking readership a wide overview of developments in the education of adults worldwide. Books are planned for the series of four different types:

a. about adult education in a single country
b. having a comparative perspective of two or more countries
c. having an international perspective
d. symposia of papers for different countries following a single theme.

This book falls into the first category and it is an important contribution to the literature of adult education since it focuses upon an area, adult learning, which is important to both adult education and human resource development. In fact, this book should be of interest to students and practitioners in both of these overlapping fields.

Victoria Marsick, who is a professor at Teachers College in New York, has already edited one successful volume on adult learning – *Learning in the Workplace* – and this develops many of the themes that occur there. Karen Watkins, a professor at the University of Texas, is well known in the fields of adult education and human resource development, having published a number of papers in these areas.

Peter Jarvis
Series Editor

Acknowledgements

Karen and Victoria wish to acknowledge the following people, without whom this book would not be possible. First and foremost, we would like to thank our families – Tanya and Tyson Watkins, Karen's children, who have been as patient as young people can be when working parents work; Peter Neaman, Victoria's spouse, and Adam Neaman, his son; Karen's parents, William and Elizabeth Carncross; and Victoria's parents, Edwin and Marie Marsick.

Second, we would like to thank our colleagues in our Departments, Oscar Mink and Jack Mezirow, respectively of the University of Texas, Austin, and Teachers College, Columbia University, for their support and inspiration. We are also grateful to Peter Jarvis for his advice and guidance in this effort.

Finally, thanks go to our doctoral students, who have listened to our ideas, proof-read our work, and inspired us to keep going because of their own interest in the topic.

Victoria's special appreciation goes to the following students from Teachers College who have helped her in various ways: Pat Cusack, who proof-read an early version of this book; Kathleen Dechant, whose own work on the informal learning of managers parallels Victoria's interests; "the Grapevine Gang," a group of doctoral advisees who are collaboratively researching informal learning in different work settings – Diana Baule, Jennifer Foster, Maria Fressola, Chris Kelly, Barbara Larson, Michele Shapiro, Karen Stevens, and Marie Volpe; and the Adult Education Guided Independent Study cohort IX, some of whom have contributed to the "stories" told in Chapter Five and all of whom have been especially supportive while she has been writing this book.

Karen's special appreciation goes to the following students from the University of Texas who have helped her in various ways: Renee Rogers, who co-wrote Chapter Six, and Bert Wiswell, who worked with Karen on some early research on incidental learning; Bonnie

Blackburn and Tom Broersma who proof-read parts of this book; and last, but not least, Olivia Becerra and Nancy Treffler-Hammonds who helped type parts of this manuscript.

Part one

Introduction

This book is written for those who are interested in informal and incidental learning in the workplace, which we contrast with more highly structured workshops, seminars and courses that are often referred to as training and development.

We are particularly interested in reaching people who work in human resource development because we believe that informal and incidental learning, which are difficult to organize and control, represent a neglected, but crucial, area of their practice. However, we also believe that learning is everyone's responsibility in the workplace even though human resource developers should know more about helping to facilitate learning wherever it occurs, be it formal, informal, or incidental. One could use the point-of-sales analogy further to describe why this is important. When a product is sold, information is needed at the time the transaction takes place. The customer is at no time more motivated to learn than at the point-of-sale. The same is true for learning. People are obviously ready to learn when they are at the point-of-sale, so to speak, yet training and development is often treated as a commodity for which employees are scheduled at the convenience of the organization. By focusing on informal and incidental learning, we believe that employees will develop skills to facilitate more effectively both their own learning and that of others, at the point-of-sale, when they are experiencing a situation that demands learning.

Learning vs. training

In the pages that follow, we describe briefly what we mean by informal and incidental learning, and why we believe it to be so important to human resource developers. We also provide an overview of this book. We start by looking at training vs. learning.

As Marsick (1987a) describes elsewhere, training and education are delivery systems. By contrast we define learning more broadly as "the way in which individuals or groups acquire, interpret, reorganize, change or assimilate a related cluster of information, skills and feelings. It is also primary to the way in which people construct meaning in their personal and shared organizational lives" (p. 4). Learning might be limited to a specific change or reinterpretation, or it might take place over a longer period of time. Learning is sometimes identified through measurable changes in behavior or it may represent a change in an internal viewpoint that is difficult to quantify.

By emphasizing learning rather than training, we do not intend to devalue the importance of appropriate structured learning activities. However, we believe that an overriding interest in how best to organize learning through training has taken attention away from the natural opportunities for learning that occur every day in a person's working life. Training usually refers to short-term activities that emphasize practical skills immediately applicable to the job. Training is sometimes, but not always, distinguished from longer-term courses that develop generic abilities and developmental activities.

By virtue of the fact that trainers design short-term activities, they typically select a discrete array of knowledge, skills, and attitudes that experts deem most appropriate to a topic the organization believes is important for its employees to master. The model most frequently used for training design in the United States, Instructional Systems Design, reflects this controlled focus on demonstrated performance with respect to desired behaviorally described objectives. The model works well when employees share an interest in the topic and can relate to the examples on which they practice.

However, learning then deals with situations out of one's natural context. Employees may demonstrate that they have learned new knowledge and skills at the end of a training activity, but they find it difficult to transfer this learning to their normal work environment. We believe that people learn in the workplace through interactions with others in their daily work environments when the need to learn is greatest. Of course, people do not always learn from their experience and often, when they learn in this way, they may reinforce inaccurate ways of doing things. However, the potential exists to help people learn more effectively in the workplace by focusing on real life rather than on prescriptions, examples, and simulations.

In this book we highlight and describe informal and incidental learning, which has been left out of many definitions of the scope of training and development. In so doing, we reexamine linkages with training and with other functions in the organization that play a key role in learning outside the classroom. We are not advocating the elimination of training activities, but seek ways to enhance its linkage with informal and incidental learning.

The human resource learning circle

As Watkins (1989a) describes, a profession and a field of practice have grown up around workplace learning, usually referred to as training and development, but sometimes also called by the term human resource development, a broader umbrella term that encompasses a wide range of activities concerned with hiring, maintaining, and retiring an organization's personnel pool. Training and development has grown from humble origins into a big business.

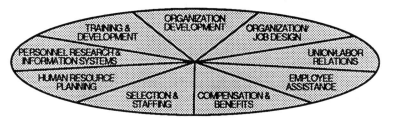

Figure I.1 The human resource wheel

Source: P. McLagan (1983). Reprinted with permission. All rights reserved.

Watkins explores the burgeoning growth of the field, the definition of which is still subject to controversy. Watkins notes a movement away from the early definition provided by Nadler (1983) which emphasized organized, job-specific learning activities toward a broadened identification with the full spectrum of human resources, illustrated in McLagan's (1983) nine areas of practice in the human resource wheel (Figure I.1). As we see in Figure I.1, training and development is one small segment of the human resource wheel. By contrast, we take the position that learning is a primary function of all of these sectors. Learning, for example, plays a role in contract negotiations or provisions to be made to assist employees who suffer from debilitating diseases such as alcoholism or drug abuse.

Figure I.2, the human resource learning circle, illustrates the relationship of learning to various areas of practice. The shape of the inner circle, formal learning, varies with the need for learning in different organizations and times. The learning pie is subdivided to

5

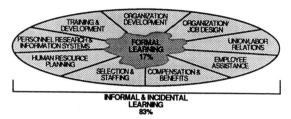

Figure I.2 The human resource learning circle
Source: Adapted by V. J. Marsick and K. E. Watkins from P. McLagan (1983).

show the approximate percentage of time and money spent on informal and incidental learning (83%), as opposed to formal learning (17%), based on annual estimates in Carnevale (1984).

Preview of part one

Learning can take place in many situations: formal, informal, or incidental. In this book, we focus on informal and incidental learning to shed light on the phenomenon of learning, as seen from the learner's point of view, rather than training, as seen from the trainer's point of view. In Part One of this book, we define and describe informal and incidental learning, and discuss what we see as an emerging rationale for a renewed interest in learning in training. In this section, we provide an overview of key ideas introduced in these two chapters.

Informal and incidental learning

In Chapter One, we define and illustrate the concepts of informal and incidental learning by contrasting them with formal learning. Figure I.3 summarizes characteristics that are then explained in Chapter One.

Informal and incidental learning both speak to learning outside formally structured, institutionally sponsored, classroom-based activities. As a result, both informal and incidental learning often take place under non-routine conditions, that is, when the procedures and responses that people normally use fail. In such cases, people may become aware of many tacit, hidden, taken-for-granted assumptions. In the process of doing this, people often reframe the problem they are experiencing, that is, they realize that a particular situation can be defined and solved in many different ways.

Informal and incidental learning, however, are not exactly the same. Incidental learning is defined as a byproduct of some other

Definitions

Informal learning: is predominantly experiential and non-institutional.
Incidental learning: is unintentional, a byproduct of another activity.

Differences from Formal Learning

Informal learning: differs by degree of control exercised by the learner, location (not classroom-based), and predictability of outcomes.
Incidental learning: differs by degree, since it is a subset of informal learning. It is tacit, taken-for-granted, and implicit in assumptions and actions.

Examples

Informal learning: self-directed learning, networking, coaching, mentoring, performance planning, and trial-and-error.
Incidental learning: learning from mistakes, assumptions, beliefs, attributions, internalized meaning constructions about the actions of others, hidden curriculum in formal learning.

Delimiters

Framing: how individuals selected the problems to which they attend and relate them to the context as they explore interpretations.
Capacity: ability to project learning over a long time period and over many separate learning outcomes.

Enhancers

Creativity: different ways of seeing problems and generating solutions.
Proactivity: process of actively seeking out learning in everyday experiences in various ways, e.g. meeting routinely with colleagues to reflect on experiences or keeping a journal.
Critical reflectivity: taking the time to look deeply at one's practice to identify values, assumptions, and beliefs that govern actions.

Figure I.3 Informal and incidental learning: a summary

activity, such as task accomplishment, interpersonal interaction, sensing the organizational culture, or trial-and-error experimentation. As such, incidental learning is never planned or intentional, whereas informal learning can be planned or intentional, as for example, in self-directed learning or help consciously sought from coaches or mentors.

An example might illustrate the distinction between informal and incidental learning. Informal learning can include many situations outside the classroom that are not designed in any detail, but that are planned. Susan may know that she needs skills in running meetings. To gain these skills, Susan might read about how to run meetings, might consult with her manager who seems to run meetings well, and might then seek out opportunities to practice these skills. Informal learning might also be accidental. Susan might participate in a quality circle that includes training in running meetings, or she might run into Robert who mentions an effective technique he has learned. Incidental learning, however, is never intentional and seldom explicit. It is serendipitous or coincidental with some other activity, and largely buried in the context of other tasks. For example, Susan might have had to give a report at a meeting of department heads, which she normally would not attend, that was not at all run well. Her incidental learning might be that it is not important to run meetings well.

Incidental learning is always delimited by the nature of the task that spurred its creation. For example, Susan might not be able to inquire into whether or not the meeting of department heads was always run in that fashion because her main purpose for participation was reporting on a specific project. It is always tacit, whereas informal learning may be more or less tacit; and success in this kind of learning always depends on the ability of the person to frame the problem appropriately. Incidental learning is also delimited by the work capacity of the individual, which is described in Chapter One in terms of Jaques's (1988) work on goal-directed behavior in everyday work.

Finally, experience with successful informal and incidental learning suggests that it is enhanced by proactivity, critical reflectivity, and creativity. Proactivity refers to a readiness to take initiative in learning. Critical reflectivity is related to the surfacing and critiquing of tacit, taken-for-granted assumptions and beliefs that need to be examined in order for people to reframe problems. Creativity refers to the capacity of people to see a situation from many points of view, and to use new perspectives and insights to break out of preconceived patterns that inhibit learning.

There is no formula that guarantees learning, whether it is formally organized or not. People may or may not learn when they are on-the-job, in classrooms, observing others, or participating in structured or unstructured conversations. We can understand formal, informal, and incidental learning, as illustrated in Figure I.4, in terms of the degree to which learning is characterized naturally by action or reflection. As described in this book, we find that learning takes place through an ongoing, dialectical process of action and reflection. To reflect, people must consciously become aware that they are learning. This involves a degree of intentionality. However, if reflection alone is emphasized, formal learning tends to be theoretical. Reflection is enhanced by the active application of concepts in practice. Informal and incidental learning, on the other hand, take place without much conscious reflection.

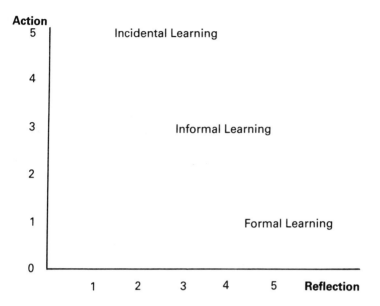

Figure I.4 Action and reflection in types of learning

Overview of this book

In Chapter One, we begin to develop a theory of informal and incidental learning. In Chapter Two, we step back and put this theory into the context of current developments in training and in human resource development so that we can better illustrate the value of a learning perspective in the field. We also introduce what we call the human resource learning cone as a framework for understanding various levels of formal, informal, and incidental learning in organizations. Building on the human resource learning circle, the learning cone is used to examine learning at the following four levels: 1) the individual, about whose learning we know the most; 2) the group in which many people naturally work; 3) the organization itself, influenced by top-level managers; 4) professional groups, whose learning is greatly influenced by norms set outside the organization.

Learning can take place at one of these four levels or, in many cases, at several of these levels simultaneously. The field of human resource development has paid more attention to individual learning, usually through formal classroom-based activities, even though the very nature of work in organizations argues for learning in groups and for organizational learning led by those who influence larger collective units. Professional learning is another growing, powerful force in workplace learning. We are particularly interested in the way in which human resource professionals learn since they influence greatly the strategies for learning that are open to others in the organization.

Each author introduces Part Two and Part Three with a preliminary description of the section's focus and the way in which chapters fit together within it. The chapters are arranged to highlight one of the above levels of learning. We also illustrate different characteristics of informal and incidental learning as they are relevant to the information in the chapter and relate our findings to the theory presented in Part One.

Marsick, in Part Two, examines informal learning. In Chapter Three, she looks at the way in which individuals – managers in companies in Sweden – learn through fairly unstructured projects that are part of an innovative strategy for management development called action learning. Chapter Four focuses on the way in which educational field workers learn how to facilitate informal learning in communities. Chapter Five is concerned with professional adult educators in the workplace. She analyzes the way in which they have learned from their own experience and influence that of others.

Watkins, in Part Three, examines incidental learning. In Chapter Six, she looks at the incidental learning of individuals, in this case, professionals who examine the way in which their experiences as children growing up in alcoholic families have influenced their responses to working and learning in the workplace. In Chapter Seven, Watkins focuses on learning at the organizational level by looking at the way in which key leaders in postsecondary institutions respond to change and innovation. In this chapter she describes the way in which incidental learning takes place under non-routine conditions when innovations are introduced for which there is no preferred, known way of managing. In Chapter Eight, Watkins addresses the professional level of learning by describing the way in which human resource developers are influenced by the assumptions they hold about learning. These professionals learn incidentally as they begin to highlight tacit beliefs and challenge them through critical reflection.

Table I.1 shows the primary level of learning addressed by each of these chapters as well as the key dimensions of informal or incidental learning, discussed in Chapter One, that are illustrated by that chapter. The reader will note that Part Two (Chapters Three to Five)

Table I.1 Dimensions of informal and incidental learning, by learning level, emphasized in Parts Two and Three

Learning level	Informal learning	Incidental learning
Individual	Chapter Three:	Chapter Six:
	Learning from experience Non-routine conditions Reframing Critical reflectivity by challenging of norms	Learning from experience Non-routine conditions Reframing Tacit dimension Critical reflectivity
Group and/or Organizational	Chapter Four:	Chapter Seven:
	Learning from experience Non-routine conditions Proactivity Creativity	Learning from experience Non-routine conditions Work capacity Creativity
Professional	Chapter Five:	Chapter Eight:
	Learning from experience Non-routine conditions Proactivity Critical reflectivity	Learning from experience Tacit dimension Critical reflectivity Reframing

addresses most directly several dimensions shared by both informal and incidental learning, specifically learning from experience, non-routine conditions, and factors that enhance learning. Part Three (Chapters Six to Eight) highlights dimensions more likely to be found in incidental learning because of its unique character as a by-product of other learning.

Finally, in Part Four, we highlight key ideas that emerge from our research. We also discuss strategies for enhancing informal and incidental learning at the individual, group, organizational, and professional levels, as described here in terms of the human resource learning cone, and consider ways in which informal and incidental learning can be linked more effectively with training.

Chapter one

Toward a theory of informal and incidental learning

In this chapter we develop a theoretical framework for understanding informal and incidental learning that, while not empirically tested, is, at least in part, empirically derived. We first describe informal and incidental learning and provide additional examples that illustrate and differentiate between the two types of learning. We then contrast our definitions and concepts with those of other key writers in this field.

Overview

We define informal and incidental learning by contrasting them with formal learning. Formal learning is typically institutionallys ponsored, classroom-based, and highly structured. Informal learning, a category that includes incidental learning, may occur in institutions, but it is not typically classroom-based or highly structured, and control of learning rests primarily in the hands of the learner. Incidental learning, a subcategory of informal learning, is defined by Watkins as a byproduct of some other activity, such as task accomplishment, interpersonal interaction, sensing the organizational culture, trial-and-error experimentation, or even formal learning. Informal learning can be deliberately encouraged by an organization or it can take place despite an environment not highly conducive to learning. Incidental learning, on the other hand, almost always takes place in everyday experience although people are not always conscious of it.

People can learn informally from their interactions with others but, as Jarvis (1987) points out, they do not always do so. They may not be open to change and to seeing things from new points of view. Jarvis describes potential non-learning responses to a situation, that is, times when adults rely on presuppositions without questioning the need to do anything differently, not considering the experience as an opportunity for learning, or simply rejecting the option of learning. At worst, no learning takes place; at best, people are aware of a need to learn but, even then, they may learn errors that fit in with their existing view of the world or that reinforce erroneous beliefs.

Incidental learning includes learning from mistakes (including how people frame experiences as mistakes), learning by doing (including trial-and-error experimentation), and learning through a series of covert interpersonal experiments ("I test my limits with a new boss by asking for things and then waiting to see what gets a yes"). Mistakes are potent tools for learning, in part, because individuals so often feel brittle about making them. As a result, they will be more likely to reflect on the mistake to determine its causes and to prevent its repetition. Neumann (1988) studied the mistakes of college presidents and found that they reported mistakes of four different types: (1) Errors of omission: "I should have done something"; (2) Substantive errors of commission: "What I did was wrong"; (3) Process errors of commission: "How I did it was wrong"; and (4) Action errors of commission: "I should not have done anything."

Individuals also often learn from their successes. People draw on these models when they judge a new situation to be similar. However, past experience can also bring distortions. Kelly (1955) found that our experiences are "channelized" or interpreted through personal constructs, subjective filters tied up with how we see ourselves.

Informal and incidental learning take place along a continuum of conscious awareness. The degree of conscious awareness of one's learning plays an important role in the clarity of learning. This may be especially true for incidental learning because the person's attention is turned elsewhere. At times, for example, someone stumbles on something extraneous to the task in which he or she is engaged. He or she must consciously pursue the discovery instead of moving ahead with the task at hand, as, for example, with the discovery of penicillin, a green mold that was interfering with the successful growth of cultures in other experiments. At other times, a person learns incidentally by paying attention to what is apparently extraneous.

Many times these learnings are unintended consequences, as illustrated in part by the old adage, "Do as I say, not as I do." Two trainers, for example, might learn informally about a development coaching workshop by talking to many people with skills in this area, by reading, and by working together. As they work, they might use the opportunity to explore one another's thinking about how people best coach others. At the same time, conscious, explicit learning might take place when they incidentally discover they have different learning style preferences that influence their vision of the flow of the workshop. The trainers might talk about these differences and examine the way in which these differences show up in alternative training designs. Unconscious, undiscussed learning might also take place if the person who subsequently conducts the workshop does not practice effective consultation with the learners about their needs and preferences, active listening, and reflective dialogue to assess learning needs.

Informal and incidental learning are thus similar in that they both take place in the normal course of daily events without a high degree of design or structure. Incidental learning differs from informal learning, however, in that the messages that are being conveyed are often buried in the interaction. Attention is needed for people to learn both informally and incidentally, but a different kind of attention is needed in the latter. People must shift their attention to these byproduct messages and see them clearly before they can learn. Skruber (1987, p. 58), in an article on organizations as learning environments, provides an example of a problematic conversation between a manager and his subordinate that illustrates the differences between informal and incidental learning. The manager tells Mary she is "a good worker" but must "be more assertive" to be promoted. However, "statements such as these (1) are unaccompanied by any information to substantiate Mary's 'need', (2) lack any attempt to have Mary reflect on her learning needs, (3) are minus a concrete link between Mary's performance and her chances for success, and (4) are missing a plan for helping Mary to learn new strategies for success." Thus, Mary does not know how to be more assertive, or even if that is the problem.

Mary has learned informally that she is not doing something right, in what should be a coaching interaction, but she is not sure what "right" is. Mary might also have incidentally learned that people who get ahead in this organization are not direct in their communication and do not have to tell employees the truth. She might also attribute her lack of success to gender or other personal characteristics, which may or may not be true. Mary's manager might have learned incidentally that Mary is not assertive, even if he had simply made this up as an excuse not to tell her why she was really passed over, since she simply accepted his explanation without further questions. Learning might have taken place, but the learning could be full of errors because neither Mary nor her boss clarified their perceptions and assumptions.

It is clear that incidental learning can take place almost anywhere and at any time. The same is true for informal learning. However, some organizations provide structure and design to what otherwise would be considered informal learning. For example, an organization might initiate a mentor program, designate certain recognized experts as coaches, or institute a career development system that includes planning for learning outside the classroom. These activities can be informal learning when they take place naturally in the course of human interaction, or even when the person sets out to work with someone with whom he or she periodically interacts. But a mentoring program might include predesigned meeting times scheduled by the organization, not the learner, whether or not they are needed; or a coach may be asked to follow a highly prescriptive process. It is difficult for trainers to structure or predesign informal and incidental learning, but it can be enhanced, as we discuss in our last chapter.

Definition and characteristics

In the next sections of this chapter, we further describe defining characteristics of informal learning, that is, that learning is experience-based, non-routine, and often tacit. We also describe conditions that delimit or enhance informal and incidental learning.

Learning from experience

A central feature of informal and incidental learning is learning from and through experience. We do not mean the kind of experience-based learning promoted in various models that are used to design formal educational activities. Kolb's work (1984), which is discussed below, is an example of just such a formal learning model. Many trainers are also familiar with Pfeiffer and Jones's experiential learning cycle (1983), which is analogous to Kolb's, and is used to describe the phases in a learning activity. We also distinguish our use of the term from the work of the Council for the Advancement of Experiential Learning (CAEL) which is concerned with the way in which institutions incorporate experience into education, as, for example, in cooperative education, internships or the field practicum. By learning from experience we mean the way in which people make sense of situations they encounter in their daily lives. A proverb might illustrate this: "Nature is the hardest teacher. She gives the test first and the lesson later." We are concerned with how we extract these lessons so that each experience adds to our knowledge instead of simply being a repetition of the same mistakes.

Learning from the context

What we learn, and how we go about learning from experience, depend on a number of factors. When people learn in the workplace, they are highly influenced by the context, that is, the particular situation in which something happens. Zuboff (1988) suggests that many types of workers – whether they act on machinery or act with other people – are context-dependent. This is as true for laborers, who want to tinker with machines when they break, as for managers, who rely on personal knowledge often gathered in face-to-face settings to make decisions. Some types of work, of course, are less dependent on context, such as work with computers and other technology requiring abstract thinking. We believe that context is more important to learning from experience when the nature of the task is interpersonal or social in nature, and thus subject to a greater number of differences in interpretation. On the other hand, even when people learn in a highly technical environment, context plays a role since many decisions about data are dependent on the judgment of people and are taken through some kind of collaborative, social interaction.

There may be a relationship between sensitivity to the context and certain cognitive learning styles as suggested by Witkin's work on field-dependence and field-independence (Witkin, 1949, 1950; Witkin and Goodenough, 1977). Field independents seem more able to separate an object and its context, more analytical in nature, and more oriented to internal frames of reference. Field dependents seem more influenced in their perceptions by the context, more social in nature, and more oriented to external frames of reference. Brookfield (1986), however, found that field dependence and field independence are not mutually exclusive in self-directed learning. Likewise, successful informal learners may draw on both sets of skills as relevant.

Dewey and Lindemann

Learning from experience is widely lauded, but the dynamics of such learning are still unclear even though much of the education system in the United States is based on the work of John Dewey (1938), who wrote extensively on this subject. Dewey felt that education must address the notion of reflective thought. Reflective thought begins with an ambiguous situation which in some way presents a dilemma to an individual. From this "felt difficulty," the individual locates and defines the problem. The third step is a consideration of solutions with analysis of their many angles. This leads to observation and experimentation and, finally, to a decision to act or not on these suggestions. Dewey's notion of reflective thought is clearly similar to the scientific method as it is applied to everyday experience and action.

Eduard Lindemann (1926), building on Dewey's thinking, defined adult education as a cooperative venture in non-authoritarian, informal learning, the chief purpose of which is to discover the meaning of experience; a quest of the mind which digs down to the roots of the preconceptions which formulate our conduct; a technique of learning for adults which makes education coterminous with life and hence elevates living itself to the level of adventurous experiment.

[Lindemann, 1926, p. 546]

Lindemann (1961) further assumed that education is life; that the approach to adult education will be via the route of situations, not subjects; and that the resource of highest value in adult education is the learner's experience. Lindemann's vision seems clearly focused on informal and incidental learning.

John Dewey's pioneer work shaped the thinking of several theorists on whom we draw in this book, for example, Argyris and Schön's ideas about action science (Argyris, 1982, 1985; Argyris and Schön, 1974, 1978; Argyris et al., 1985; Schön, 1983, 1987). We describe action science in the next section since it forms the basis for our work on learning from experience.

Action science

Aside from Dewey, the intellectual roots of action science can be traced to Kurt Lewin's approach to uniting theory and practice, that is, action research, which is also based on the scientific method. Usually facilitated by an outside consultant, action research is a tool of organization development practitioners that has also been used in education. Action research is a cyclical process by which a group of people jointly identify a problem, experiment with a solution, monitor results, reflect on the process, and use the resultant information to reformulate the problem, which leads to another cycle of research.

Argyris and Schön are interested in improving practice. They believe that no one ever sets out deliberately to create error, but despite our best efforts, error does take place and often recurs persistently. Argyris and Schön suggest that a gap occurs between the formulation of plans and their implementation, a gap of which we are often unaware and which we frequently cannot eliminate even when we try. They describe this gap as the difference between our espoused theories and our theories-in-use. Simply put, our espoused theories are what we think we do, while our theories-in-use are what we actually do. One reason for our difficulty in correcting our errors is that we do not dig deeply enough into the underlying variables governing our actions. Of course, this kind of deeper analysis is difficult because governing variables are often taken-for-granted. Argyris and Schön (1974) borrow the notion of single-loop and double-loop learning from Ashby (1952), described by the example of a household thermostat, to explain the difference between surface causes and governing variables. Single-loop learning refers to the way in which the thermostat adjusts the temperature to a pre-set level; in double-loop learning, one asks whether or not the temperature is set at the right level in the first place. Single-loop learning works well in most ordinary situations where our assumptions about cause and effect are correct. Double-loop learning is needed when expected results are not achieved.

Argyris and Schön note that we learn from experience by drawing inferences from what people say and do. They introduce "the ladder of inference" to illustrate this process. The first rung of the ladder represents the directly observable data of what is said and done in a situation. As we move to successively higher rungs on this ladder of inference, we impose personal, social, cultural, and organizational meanings on the directly observable data. We make errors because we jump from the directly observable data to higher-level inferences which we assume are accurate and upon which we then act. Error can be reduced if we illustrate our inferences with directly observable data and then inquire of the other persons in the situation as to the accuracy of our assumptions. When we do this, we make explicit the reasoning that is implicit in our thinking and that of others in the situation. This allows all parties to test publicly the accuracy of assumptions, evaluations, and judgments, which leads to double-loop learning or the identification and examination of values that govern our action, including our reasoning and learning.

Argyris and Schön bring several important dimensions to our definition of informal and incidental learning. First, they suggest that learning takes place under conditions of surprise, the non-routine circumstances that require heightened attention, experimentation, and determination of the nature of a problem. Second, they point out that critical reflection is called for in these circumstances, that is digging below taken-for-granted beliefs and assumptions so that one can reframe the situation. Finally, Schön points out that professionals learn more than technical rules that are unilaterally applied; professionals must learn to "think like an ..." architect, lawyer, doctor, etc. Professionals exercise judgment when they encounter new experiences that do not completely fit those governed by known rules. In learning to think like a professional, whatever the profession, people do not only learn certain skills for certain tasks; much background or contextual learning takes place, consciously or unconsciously, that shapes their perceptions. This background learning bears some similarity to incidental learning.

Argyris and Schön also address the organizational context for

18

learning in their discussion of how to develop a climate conducive to inquiry. They describe two different organizational learning climates which they label Model I and Model II. Model I climates are characterized by values such as unilateral control, secrecy, and win/lose thinking. Model II climates, by contrast, help people make their assumptions and beliefs public so that their thinking can be examined. Such public inquiry cannot take place in an atmosphere of extreme defensiveness and control.

We illustrate these concepts with an example provided by a graduate student at Teachers College, Sharon Scully, as she reflected on the role of college financial aid practitioners. In some college settings, these practitioners are expected to "follow the rules and keep the enrollment steady" and "not 'make waves' by questioning too deeply whether the regulations work for students." This is a Model I climate. The financial aid officer has control over the resources and often obscures the basis for these kinds of decisions. The student must "submit a great deal of confidential information without knowing exactly why and with no assurance of receiving the money; there is no public scrutiny of the formulae involved in determining eligibility, and there is no trust between the student and the administrator." Scully shifts this to a Model II climate: "I brought my assumption that the regulations were not written with the adult undergraduate in mind into public scrutiny by first discussing this with my financial aid colleagues" and with students. "With both sets of people I discussed, as openly as possible, the values underlying my view" and the way in which "the current political and social atmosphere affect these programs." The problem was eventually resolved through open inquiry.

Alternative experiential learning theories

Perhaps the best-known perspective on learning from experience in the United States is that of Kolb (1984). Kolb draws on Dewey, Lewin's *Gestalt* psychology, Piaget's developmental psychology, therapeutic psychologists (Jung, Erikson, Rogers, Perls, and Maslow), and the so-called "radical" educators, especially Freire and Illich. Kolb suggests that people apprehend and transform their experience differently. Some apprehend through concrete experience (CE), and others through abstract conceptualization (AC). Some transform through reflective observation (RO), and others through active experimentation (AE). These two dimensions interact, resulting in both a typology of learning styles and an experiential learning cycle that moves from experiencing to observing to conceptualizing to experimenting and back to experiencing. Some educators follow the learning cycle sequentially and others simply make sure that all learning needs are taken into consideration.

While the formulaic way in which Kolb has been interpreted may not accurately represent reality, his theory provides those who wish to be more learner-centered with a starting point for thinking about their practice. Kolb also underscores the importance of some kind of dialectical interaction between action and reflection, and between direct experience and its opposite. While critiqued by Jarvis (1987) and others as too simplistic, Kolb's work has been espoused by many as a useful framework (Byrne and Wolfe, 1980; Keeton and Associates, 1976; Lewis, 1986; McCarthy, 1987). Kolb, however, is still used to address individual learning in formal classroom situations.

An alternative to Kolb's theory is that of Cell (1984), whose conceptual framework is psychological in its orientation and based on the work of Carl Rogers. Cell identifies four levels of change in people, each of which can involve a different domain of experiential learning, and each of which builds on the previous domain: response learning focused on behavior change, situation learning involving interpretation, transsituation learning centered on autonomy, and transcendent learning leading to creativity. Cell brings to informal learning theory a greater reliance on the way in which learners ascribe meaning to their experience and highlights the multiple perspectives needed to interpret experience. His emphasis on autonomy and creativity for higher levels of change is relevant to the conditions, discussed below, that can enhance informal learning.

While differing in their orientation, Kolb and Cell emphasize several dimensions relevant here to informal learning. Both oppose a behavioral definition of learning, suggesting instead that meaning – which is difficult, if not impossible, to observe and measure behaviorally – plays a central role in learning. Meaning is derived through reflection on experience. Kolb, however, looks at learning primarily from the individual point of view, which is not sufficient to explain learning within the organizational context. Cell does address the organizational context. He suggests that "our pictures or maps of organizational life and of ourselves in it contain assumptions that unduly limit our control of our life in the organization" (p. 163). Cell's assumptions are fairly common among educators, who often see the organization as a totalitarian force that oppresses individuals. Cell believes that individuals in the workplace must struggle to maintain autonomy in the face of pressing socialization, and when this does not succeed, must minimize the psychological damages of survival tactics they feel forced to adopt. Informal learning under such circumstances is an essential means to discern the subtle ways in which the individual may have changed as part of the organizational socialization process and to alleviate disorientation that can result from this largely tacit "adjustment learning."

Non-routine vs. routine conditions for learning

We believe that informal and incidental learning are needed most when individuals experience a situation as non-routine. Learned responses and habitual ways of acting are least likely to work under these conditions. The situation might be completely new and thus fully non-routine; or it might be potentially routine, but treated as non-routine for some reason. We believe that trainers typically deal with non-routine situations. No matter how often they have given a course or how closely they are following scripts in a packaged curriculum, trainers always have to deal with many "unknowns" because of differences in the learners and the group's dynamics.

In the workplace, one might argue that productivity is increased through routine since it is inefficient continually to invent new responses to daily task demands. On the other hand, too much routine can lead to boredom and errors, a case that is argued by proponents of increased worker participation and of job redesign on the assembly line. Stimulated by the early theoretical work of Herbert Simon (1965), the concept of routine vs. non-routine work has enjoyed a long intellectual tradition. Simon's administrative decision-making theory states that individuals have a bounded rationality which leads to "satisficing" in decision-making. Given the large quantities of information we deal with, we place boundaries on the scope of data to which we will attend. We often use heuristics or rules of thumb which experience tells us lead to acceptable solutions most of the time; hence they "satisfice." But these heuristics may also limit our search for solutions.

Simon suggests that managerial behavior has four parts: (1) stimuli that require a decision response; (2) a series of execution steps; (3) both factual and value-based inputs; (4) outputs. Managerial activity is both programmed and unprogrammed. Programmed activity is an automatic response, similar to the concept of non-learning described by Jarvis (1987). In such cases, a manager recognizes a situation as similar to a previous one and simply replicates the previous response. Unprogrammed activity occurs when there is no tried-and-true method for handling the problem either because it is a new situation, its nature is elusive and complex, or it is so important that it deserves a customized response.

The unprogrammed nature of an activity may lie in the actor, the situation, or the social context. Schön (1983) suggests that experts question seemingly routine situations and examine the way in which problems are formulated so that creative solutions can be sought. Yet, people also have a much larger, more fluid repertoire of previous solutions to draw upon as needed. Watkins (1989a) asserts that the human resource developer's work is increasingly non-routine and unprogrammed. Human resource developers must thus develop skills in handling non-routine situations, particularly given the multiple ways in which an activity may be unprogrammed as described by Simon.

Simon described three stages in unprogrammed activity: (1) intelligence activity in which the individual searches the environment for conditions calling for a decision; (2) design activity in which the individual invents, develops, and analyzes courses of action; (3) choice activity. This process closely parallels informal learning. Although informal learning is often said to lack design, it is more accurate to say that it lacks design imposed by others. Rather, it can be thought of in terms of the artistry of expert practitioners described by Schön (1983) in their "reflective conversation with a situation."

Other theorists have further developed the concept of routine and non-routine activity. Berg and Ostergren (1979) distinguish between system-consistent and system-divergent innovations. They contend that systems should have a much higher capacity than they do now to embrace system-divergent innovations. Davies (1979) studied 22 process innovations in the United Kingdom and classified them as either technically simple and cheap (routine) or more complex and expensive (non-routine). The non-routine innovations took longer to take hold but seemed eventually to surpass the routine innovations in rate of adoption. More interesting was the fact that there was ample evidence of learning-by-doing. Later trials were more productive than earlier versions. This work again emphasizes the importance of the design phase in relatively unprogrammed activity.

Perrow (1967) furthered Simon's distinctions by theorizing that the nature of the raw material with which one works will determine the relative routineness of the technology. When the raw material is fairly predictable, the technology is routine and logical search procedures are in order. When there are many exceptional cases, the technology is non-routine and the search procedure is largely intuitive. Thompson (1967) has also found that there is a fundamental press toward routineness in organizations. Sutherland (1975) points out that some activities may have an intrinsic analytic floor below which no level of effort or resources can move them toward routineness. To a large extent, working with people is a task that fits Sutherland's description. "Most technologies for changing human behavior are non-routine and indeterminate" (McDaniel and Morris, 1978, p. 16).

22

Keen and Scott-Morton (1978) distinguish among structured, semi-structured, and unstructured tasks. They emphasize that the context may be a sufficiently confounding variable to alter the classification of the task. Juggling three balls, for example, is a routine task for a juggler until you ask one to do it while standing in the aisle of a speeding train passing over uneven tracks. Similarly, give this same task to an amateur, and it is again non-routine.

Informal learning, by definition, is non-routine because it occurs in an indeterminate, unsystematic, uncontrolled context. The task of learning for a work assignment may be made more or less routine by the presence or lack of a systematic learning-how-to-learn process. Nevertheless, the nature of the process of inquiry remains "messy, multivariate, back-forth-many-stages-all-at-once" (McClellan, 1983). It is this persistently non-routine characteristic of informal learning which produces the need for skill in critical reflection among informal learners, as discussed later in this chapter, and the need to make explicit the tacit knowledge we bring to the task, which we discuss next.

Tacit dimension of knowledge

In formal learning, a person's attention is directed to certain abstracted principles. Tacit knowledge typically resides in the context, outside of a person's main focus of attention, and is thus a fertile ground for informal and incidental learning.

Schön (1983) draws on Polanyi (1967) in describing reflective practice. Inkster (1987) explains the thrust of Polanyi's thinking based on a reading of his major works (Polanyi, 1962, 1967; Polanyi and Prosch, 1975). Not surprisingly, Argyris and Schön share Polanyi's concern with the deficiencies of logical positivism. Unlike Argyris and Schön, however, Polanyi was trained professionally in chemistry. Inkster states that Polanyi found "what he and other scientists did – the mental acts they performed – in the course of their professional work ... totally inconsistent with the popular view of how scientists do science" (p. 114). While science was supposed to be value-free and totally objective, Polanyi found that his career and that of other scientists were "full of every variety of subjective emotion, including curiosity, exhilaration, frustration, anxiety, and an intense persuasive passion or need to convince others of the correctness of the interpretation of the phenomena he observed." Polanyi called this *"the ubiquitous personal coefficient in all knowledge"* (ibid., Inkster's italics).

As Inkster points out, most instances of tacit knowledge are intangible. In any given complex situation, when our attention is being pulled to a specific task, we must decide what to include or exclude from our interpretation of a situation. We draw on our past experience and, most importantly, we typically draw on frameworks for understanding that which we have already developed because we do not have time to build a new framework from scratch. It is only when we think that the framework does not match the experience that we will develop a new framework. In most work situations, there are a lot of reasons for trying to use our existing mental frameworks since we are being pushed to carry out assigned tasks and reach assigned goals. However, many of our errors occur because we have put our attention in the wrong place or excluded important signals from the context that would lead us to different inferences.

Zuboff (1988) draws on Polanyi to understand the knowledge associated with action-centered skills, those skills used by workers of many levels when they act on machinery or equipment or act with other people. Action-centered skills rely on tacit knowledge because the active use of the mind is combined with an almost subconscious or unconscious use of the body. As novice–expert studies have shown, in fact, the expert would lose facility in doing things if conscious of every act (Dreyfus and Dreyfus, 1986). Zuboff suggests that tacit knowledge "is too layered and subtle to be fully articulated" and that this accounts for the need to teach action-centered skills through experience: "Actions work better than words when it comes to learning and communicating these skills" (p. 188). Zuboff suggests that abstract skills, which she calls "intellective", "must be made explicit in the learning process and can only become tacit when an individual has attained a high level of expertise" (p. 190).

Zuboff believes that many action-centered skills can remain tacit and never be made explicit. While we agree that this often happens in informal and incidental learning, we also argue for the same reasons that tacit learning can easily result in error because inaccurate reasoning is never brought to light and examined. It would be, of course, impossible and inefficient to make everything we do explicit.

Delimited nature of informal and incidental learning

Informal and incidental learning are delimited in a number of ways, but these delimitations are clearest in incidental learning. Incidental learning is delimited by the primary activity being undertaken. For example, when incidental learning is coincident to task accomplishment, the nature of the task defines the substance, purpose, time available for learning, and criteria for success. When it occurs as part of an individual's internalization of organizational culture or policy, the degree of discussibility of that culture and its clarity delimits

24

learning. This contrasts with formal learning, which is also delimited, but typically by an instructor making decisions about the logical and feasible parameters of learning within the constraints of a given situation. These are educational decisions based on educational goals, educational considerations, and the educational context. Other delimiters include the way in which the situation, of which it is a part, is framed and the learner's work capacity since the open-ended nature of learning influences the way in which people approach the task.

Problem framing

A critical factor that delimits incidental learning is the way in which a person frames or sets the problem since the messy nature of reality does not easily lend itself to the scientific purity of laboratory conditions. Schön (1983) calls this the interactive process of naming the focus of our attention and framing the context in which a problem is understood: "we select what we will treat as the things of the situation, we set the boundaries of our attention to it, and we impose upon it a coherence which allows us to say what is wrong and in what directions the situation needs to be changed" (p. 40). Schön depicts the process of problem setting as a reflective conversation with the situation in which the practitioner draws on his or her experience to understand and frame the situation, suggest action and then reinterpret the situation in light of the consequences of action. Action may be taken in fact, or it may be understood hypothetically through discussion of what might happen in a "virtual world, a constructed representation of the real world of practice" (p. 157).

Problem framing is crucial for incidental learning. People can focus solely on the task at hand, or they can widen their vision to include aspects of the context in which the problem rests and thus open themselves to both multiple definitions of the problem and to an examination of other learning-related concerns. People used to believe erroneously that, when they read, they had to focus their attention on individual words. Speed reading specialists showed how people could widen their view and take in the entire page at a time. Likewise, an excessively tight focus in a complex situation can lead people to define problems prematurely.

Problem framing also influences the lens by which people interpret their experiences. For example, Inkster (1987) noted that Polanyi reanalyzed many of the classical studies conducted by the behaviorists from a different perspective and found different results: "Where the behaviorists had seen conditioning, Polanyi saw intelligent learning, even in life forms as primitive as worms" (Inkster, p. 117). Problem framing is particularly appropriate to trainers who often have to deal with what Schön (1983) calls "situations of uncertainty, instability, uniqueness, and value conflict" (p. 50).

Problem framing is also addressed by Culbert and McDonough (in Cell, 1984) in terms of organizational indoctrination in which a framer paints a complex picture of some aspect of the organization to serve his or her self-interest. To a certain extent, Culbert and McDonough share the slang meaning of the term in the sense of "I've been framed." By thus framing a problem, a person can manipulate the way in which other people might frame the situation through careful image management, thereby creating a sense of reality distortion.

Framing a problem can be a fairly powerful shaper of perception. Schön suggests that individuals make their tacit framing explicit to determine the extent to which it may be limiting their perceptions. Culbert and McDonough describe the way in which the framing of problems by others may limit our perceptions. Thus, problem framing is clearly a potential delimiter of incidental and informal learning.

Work capacity

A further delimiter of informal and incidental learning is intellectual capability. Elliot Jaques's concept of work capacity explains this phenomenon. Jaques (1988) refers to intellectual capability as the ability of individuals to engage in goal-directed behavior in problem solving and in everyday work (p. 108). Jaques has conducted extensive research studies on time span of discretion (the amount of time supervisors permit subordinates to work autonomously), felt fair pay (how much workers feel they should be paid given their capabilities), the number of strata in the "accountability hierarchy" (Jaques's term for bureaucracies), and how the number of levels of a hierarchical system correspond to the previous variables. The most significant of Jaques's findings was that individuals vary considerably in their time frame or work capacity: capacity "comprises a person's cognitive power and psychological tools and orientation. Cognitive power is the mental force a person can exercise in processing and organizing information and in creating a complex world; it is measurable in what I call time frame" (p. 111).

Work capacity is measured in terms of the longest period of time that a person can conceive of a project (in operational terms) and act toward its eventual accomplishment without needing feedback. Jaques has found a 0.86–0.92 correlation between a person's time span and their felt fair pay. Therefore, by knowing what a person thinks they should make for what they do and comparing it to the work capacity and salary chart Jaques developed, one could determine a person's work capacity. Work capacity varies among normal adults from one day to 50 years and beyond. "The temporal horizon sets the limits of the world of purpose and intention within which people live and construct patterns and organize their active lives and aspirations" (ibid, pp. 127–128). Table 1.1, adapted from Jaques in Link (1988), outlines these time periods.

Table 1.1 Time periods involved in work capacity

Stratum	Time Period	Description	Employee Category
VII	20 yrs+	Extrapolative development of whole system	Basic scientist, 5-star general
VI	10–20 yrs	Defining whole systems in the wide world	Executive vice-president
V	5–10 yrs	Shaping whole systems	Chief Executive Officer of corporate branch
IV	2–5 yrs	Transforming systems	Brigade commander, junior professor
III	1–2 yrs	Task extrapolation	Specialist, professional
II	3mo.–1yr	Task definition	1st line supervisor and one level up; some professionals
I	1 day–8 mo.	Concrete shaping of things	Factory worker to 1st line supervisor

Jaques noted that although most people work within Stratum I, most people think in Stratum II. This leads Jaques to call for widespread restructuring of work and of organizations. Jaques finds that a gap of two strata may lead to extreme psychic anxiety if the work demands a higher capacity than the individual has; or frustration and even sabotage if the individual's capacity exceeds that demanded by the work. Individuals at Stratum VII often need individuals around them at Stratum VI or V to "interpret" their goals to lower stratum workers. These and other findings suggest to Jaques that organizations should be structured, as the Army is almost naturally, in terms of time span. But, as an individual's cognitive power matures, the work may still become too limiting even when it is so structured.

From the perspective of informal learning, individuals will vary widely in their ability to conceive of the scope of the learning task.

Perhaps the "natural progression" often noted in self-directed learning (Tough, 1979), in which individuals move from one learning activity to another based on prior activities, is in reality a description of the learning practices of a Stratum I learner. Although Jaques does not believe that work capacity can be developed (it "matures" like people grow taller), it would seem that encouraging people to design learning projects over longer periods of time would aid in maturation. If his theory is correct, a person's work capacity would seriously limit the informal learning projects of which he or she could conceive.

Enhancing informal and incidental learning

In this section, we describe conditions which we have found enhance the effectiveness of informal and incidental learning, that is proactivity, critical reflection, and creativity. These characteristics are not essential to all types of learning; however, their presence influences the quality of learning, whether it be formal or informal.

Proactivity

Proactivity refers to a readiness to take initiative. Its opposite, reactivity, suggests a victim-like, almost fatalistic stance toward events in which one lets circumstances dictate one's response. Learning often starts as a reaction to a set of events, especially in a changing environment. A proactive person will quickly take charge of his or her learning once pushed into the learning cycle. Proactivity bears a relationship to two other terms discussed in the adult education literature, "autonomy" and "empowerment." Brookfield (1986) links empowerment to autonomy, which he sees as the heart of self-directedness and which he defines as an internal, mental disposition. He draws on Chené (1983, pp. 45–46) who suggests that autonomy is not simply "the adult's independence from all external constraints and the ability to make choices in harmony with self-realization;" autonomy is governed by one's ability to learn how to learn and by an awareness of the norms of society that limit choices.

Empowerment, a term with political connotations, was introduced into the adult education literature by Freire (1970) who worked with illiterate adults, originally in Brazil. Freire contrasted what he called the "banking" approach to education, in which knowledge is poured into passive recipients, with a liberating approach that he calls conscientization. Freire's method of dialogue and problem posing involves people in a critique of their own taken-for-granted reality so that they can reexamine what they believe to be problematic in their lives and take action, usually with a group, to change the underlying conditions that have shaped their beliefs. Freire's methods have been adopted and adapted by many educators who are not political, and who contend that conscientization and action can take place without the kind of revolution needed in South America.

"Empowered" can easily be interpreted as a personality trait. Freire reminds us that powerlessness is a social issue, which requires structural solutions. For that reason, empowerment in the workplace is typically associated with organizational changes that allow workers greater participation in decision making and access to the benefits of their labor. Power issues can make learning difficult when people hold on to their points of view and are unwilling to subject them to critical scrutiny and public testing. From the point of view of learning, empowerment involves the opportunity to examine and test social norms on which expectations are based. Empowerment is thus an internal stance, but it is shaped by social forces. Empowerment is a precondition for proactivity although people can feel empowered in some areas of their lives, while being powerless in others.

Critical reflectivity

Mezirow (1985, p. 25) has defined critical reflectivity as follows: "the bringing of one's assumptions, premises, criteria, and schemata into consciousness and vigorously critiquing them." Critical reflectivity is distinguished from a simpler level of reflection in which people think back over what worked or did not work, try to identify observable sources of error in cause-effect relationships, or simply let their attention wander back over an event. Critical reflectivity requires that people check out their assumptions before blindly acting on them, pay attention to surprising results and inquire into their meaning, ask probing questions, and reframe their understanding of what a problem might be. Action scientists, as discussed earlier, explain the difference between simple and critical reflectivity in the concepts of single-loop or double-loop.

When we are critically reflective in organizations, we pay attention to, and inquire into, what is commonly known as the organization's culture, "the way things are done around here." Acculturation is informal learning that typically involves a kind of "blind" socialization of workers, in part because organizations must socialize a large number of people with very different ways of looking at the world into a body that is sufficiently homogeneous to accomplish its goals. New employees learn the ropes by observing others and following them. Employees may ask how things are done but, many times, they perceive norms to be undiscussible, which they may be in many organizations, and hence do not ask questions. This leads to

29

practices that may be unnecessary, at times harmful, and devoid of personal or organizational learning.

Merlin Lewis, a graduate student in the adult education doctoral program at Teachers College, discussed critical reflectivity in a paper on a county probation office. People came in without appointments, causing time management difficulties. In a workshop, he helped staff examine the norm "that people must be serviced the moment they walk through the door." Staff remembered that the norm was set by a former director, now retired. They wondered "how bad it would be if they changed this in some way" and speculated that "the anger from the public would be too great." The director agreed that people could be asked to wait so that staff had more control over their time; they would revert to their former routines if the public complained. Lewis notes, "So they changed it, and never got one complaint!"

Creativity

The final enhancer to informal and incidental learning is creativity, which enables people to think beyond the point of view they normally hold. Srinivasan (1977), who bases her self-actualizing method of nonformal education on creativity, defines creativity as "the full use of imagination, going beyond the cold and rational analysis of facts" (p. 56). Schön (1983) speaks to the value of creativity in a process that he calls "*seeing-as*" (Schön's italics) or "the perception of similarity before one can say 'similar with respect to what'" (p. 182). Schön gives us the example of a group of product-development researchers who were trying to improve a paintbrush with synthetic bristles. The usual types of experiments had not improved the way in which this synthetic brush delivered paint "in a discontinuous, 'gloppy' way.... Then someone observed, '*You know, a paintbrush is a kind of pump!*'" (p. 184, Schön's italics). This observation led to new experiments that operationalized this generative metaphor and to an improved product. *Seeing-as* has a life cycle of its own. At first, one might see some similarity without being able to explain it clearly. Eventually, "one may come to be able to describe relations of elements present in a restructured perception of both A and B which account for the pre-analytic detection of similarity between A and B. Later still, one may construct a general model for which a redescribed A and a redesigned B can be identified as instances" (p. 186).

Creativity is an important condition for informal and incidental learning because it helps a learner break out of preconceived patterns that do not allow him or her to frame the situation differently, or even to see a situation as in need of reframing. Creativity also allows people to "play" with ideas so that they can explore possibilities without censoring themselves or being censored by others.

Creativity is the basis for training strategies such as "brainstorming" or "synectics" in which people are allowed to free associate and contribute ideas that are not criticized or judged until a later stage of the process.

We believe that people are more likely to play creatively with ideas in informal and incidental learning because they are not locked into the roles they experienced in their former school experience where teachers were authority figures with the right answer to problems they could only solve in one right way. This authority image is often transferred to corporate classrooms where trainers are supposed to provide expert-based solutions. The authority image might even interfere with learning on the job when the coach or supervisor sees himself or herself as the enforcer of company policy and procedures. By contrast, when people learn informally, they can try out many different definitions without the disapproval of others, as long as the organization permits and rewards this kind of creativity.

For example, DeGeuss (1988) talks about the role of play in "institutional learning, which is the process whereby management teams change their shared mental models of their company, their markets, and their competitors" (p. 70). One way in which planners helped Shell Oil Company prepare for changes in oil prices in 1984 was through creatively "playing" with Shell's possible responses to different oil price scenarios. DeGeuss says, "We didn't feel we could go to executives who run some of the biggest companies in the world and say, 'Come on, let's have a little game'" (p. 73). None the less, planners continued to use games by involving managers in creating and playing with various models. Consultants interviewed people, came back to management with a model of what they found, and used that model as a springboard to play with ideas, sometimes using computers. Computer models had several advantages. They allowed people to play with a few key variables at a time, to see how effects could be caused by events that took place much earlier than people would imagine, and to find out what information is relevant in a particular situation. The models helped people make their tacit thinking explicit: "When people play with models this way, they are actually creating a new language among themselves that expresses the knowledge they have acquired" (p. 74).

This section described informal and incidental learning as used in this book. In the next and final section, we compare our definitions of informal and incidental learning with those of other selected authors.

Other definitions

Coombs and Ahmed (1974), Mocker and Spear (1982), and Jarvis (1987) have distinguished informal learning from formal and nonformal learning or nonformal education. Unlike these other authors, we do not use the category of nonformal education. According to Coombs and Ahmed, this term describes organized activities that take place outside the formal educational system, primarily in the developing world. The reason for this distinction is less obvious in the United States, which has always had nonformal learning activities, as, for example, citizenship classes or various farm youth clubs. In countries where education is more difficult to access and frequently tied to social class, nonformal education was often introduced as a "second chance" for credentials, credibility, or knowledge and skill development.

When nonformal education became a recognized force in development activities in the 1970s, early discussions centered on the meaning of "nonformal." While there was general agreement on its essential character as a parallel system to formal education, its advocates often added a second layer of meanings to the term. Nonformal education often connotes an informal, highly participatory learning design. Even when such activities are run by the government, their nonformal character allows departures from the traditional lecture format. It is this dimension of nonformal learning that Kerrigan and Luke (1987) pick up on when they write about its influence on innovative approaches to management development in the third world, or when Srinivasan (1977) analyzes the way in which nonformal curricula can be used to encourage participatory learning.

We include the nonformal learning dimensions of innovation, creativity, participation and freedom from the hierarchical nature of much formal education in our discussion of informal learning. However, the essential defining characteristic of whether or not learning takes place through a formal educational channel does not seem relevant to workplace learning.

For Mocker and Spear (1982), the organizing definition of degree of formality is the extent to which a learner has control over both the objectives and the means of learning. According to their model, in formal learning, institutions have control over both objectives and means. In nonformal learning, the learner controls the objectives, but the institution still controls the means because institutions organize delivery systems. In informal learning, the institution controls the objective, but the learner controls the means; while in self-directed learning, the learner controls both objectives and means. This matrix is of less use to us because of the way in which we define informal and incidental learning, where control of objectives and means is primarily salient for intentional learning activities. Moreover, we are less concerned with who organizes a specific activity or teaching process, and thus controls inputs, than with understanding how people learn using informal approaches. It is true that learners do need to exercise choice in these activities, but they may not set out intentionally and explicitly to accomplish particular ends through preplanned means as described by Mocker and Spear. Often, their choices evolve from their interaction with others in an activity in which they find themselves. Sometimes they become fully conscious of these choices; at other times, they remain somewhat unaware.

Finally, Jarvis (1987) also defines formal, nonformal, and informal learning. His criterion is the type of social interaction that influences learning: "Formal situations are bureaucratic, non-formal are organised but not necessarily in a bureaucratic environment and informal situations are ones where there are no pre-specified, although there are always covert, procedures of interaction" (p. 70). A social perspective, rather than psychological or organizational perspective, is used here because Jarvis is concerned with how people construct meaning. Drawing on Mead and Dewey, Jarvis explains that meaning derives from interaction with significant others, through which people compare individual interpretations with a "generalized other" that is representative of organized society. Our definition of informal and incidental learning also starts with the social setting. We are also concerned with the way in which people make meaning in their individual and collective lives. However, Jarvis's theories are a reaction to Kolb (1984) and are focused on developing a general typology of learning for individuals. We draw more on action science and are focused particularly on the workplace setting which, because of the group-oriented nature of organizations, involves people in a unique joint-learning venture.

Incidental learning

Numerous authors have used the term "incidental learning." Most agree that it is learning which occurs as a byproduct of something else. In 1942, McGeoch defined incidental learning as "learning which apparently takes place without a specific motive or a specified formal instruction and set to learn the specific material in question" (in Postman and Senders, 1946). Nadler (1982) defines incidental learning as learning from experience – from living and adapting to our environment. This learning interacts with intentional learning, resulting in performance. Watkins and Wiswell (1987) conclude that performance presumably can therefore be either enhanced or inhibited by learning that occurs without intention, perhaps because of incidentally acquired notions that are incorrect. Stokes and Pankowski (1988) define it as the "acquisition of facts or information that occurs by chance while one is engaged in another activity" (p. 89). Jarvis (1987) sees it as a form of non-reflective learning which is largely reactive. Jarvis interprets Beard (1976 in Jarvis, 1987) to include an individual's internalization of experience as the nature of incidental learning. Jarvis concludes that the significance of this form of learning "should not be minimized since this is a major part of the process whereby people learn and acquire their culture and by which it is maintained through taken-for-granted behavior" (p. 32).

In the 1960s, writers spoke of a "hidden curriculum" in which students "psyched out" teachers and learned unstated values by the interpersonal actions, climate, and classroom practices of teachers. Students were said to have "built-in crap detectors" (Postman and Weingartner, 1971). Ironically, these largely tacit incidental learnings by students were based on largely tacit, taken-for-granted behaviors by teachers. Astin (1977) found that learners gained more from being on campus through incidental learning than formal learning because of their interaction, in college or student activities, with bright peers. Cross (1988) reinforces this conclusion: "Ironically, perhaps, we seem to know more about how students change through incidental exposure to the college environment than we do about change from what we deliberately try to teach in the classroom." (p. 5).

Finally, Reischmann (1986) differentiates between intentional adult learning (the province of adult education) and unintentional adult learning or learning "en passant" – a planned event in which learning is not the main purpose, but rather an offshoot of life routines. He notes that learning "en passant" may lead to intentional learning but that intentional learning always has unintended learning consequences. Learning "en passant" has these characteristics: it is integrated, holistic, not compulsory, individualized, uses a wide variety of support, builds on previous learning, can be a basis for further learning, and, important to this discussion, it can be especially identified by looking back, i.e., by reflection.

Chapter two

Understanding learning in training

Informal learning is not our invention. As early as 1950, Malcolm Knowles wrote a book entitled *Informal Adult Education* which described much of what we now call adult education as informal. Dr. Harry Overstreet heralded Knowles's pioneer work in the Foreword:

> There are, as you know, two kinds of adult education, formal and informal. The first adopts the methods long established in our going educational institutions. *The second creates its methods* [our italics]. Each type has its place in the scheme of adult life. There are times when a formal course of instruction, given in the regular way of teacher, textbook, recitations, examination, and credit, is precisely what an adult must have if he is to fulfill certain requirements of his later life. There are, however, other times – and these more frequent – when what he most needs is not and could not be found in any formal course of instruction.
>
> [Overstreet in Knowles, 1950, p. v]

Like Knowles, we find ourselves describing the unpatterned learning needs of adults in the workplace. Like Knowles, we also draw on the experiences of practitioners and venture forth on new ground, with success or failure hanging in the balance. Unlike Knowles, we do not see informal learning as predominantly a matter of educational method, although we do believe that trained facilitators can help people enhance their learning skills, both in and outside the classroom. Unlike Knowles, we also view learning as something that does not take place only for individuals. Workplace learning involves a social contract among individuals who work together to achieve higher-order organizational goals. The degree of mutuality and conscious control in goal-setting varies among people and organizations. None the less, individuals learn and work in social units where interactions are not typically subject to design and control by trainers.

35

In this chapter, we describe trends that speak to the increased prevalence and necessity of a learning perspective in training. We also examine the different social levels at which workplace learning must take place – individual, group, organizational, and professional. Based on this broadened understanding of workplace learning, we conclude Part One with a description of the human resource learning cone, which forms the conceptual framework for our thinking in this book.

Trends toward learning

Watkins (1989a) notes an emerging interest in informal learning in the workplace, citing a report by Carnevale (1984) that estimates 180 billion out of 210 billion dollars spent annually on informal learning. Carnevale includes the following in his definition of the latter: supervision, observation of fellow workers, learning from one's mistakes, reading, self-study, and other unstructured ways of acquiring learning in the course of doing one's job.

As Miller (1987) notes in tracing the history of the field, industrialization has influenced the field's growth as technology took some of the "art" out of jobs, making it possible to specify exactly what was expected of workers and thus design activities that reduced the error inherent in experimentation. Concurrently, the demographics of the workforce pushed toward work simplification, standardized jobs, and detailed, teachable procedures to which employees had to adhere strictly. Ironically, technology, which made formal training necessary, may now push the field back, full circle, to revisit its origins in the apprenticeship and guild systems. People became apprentices because many skills involved "art," so to speak, and could only be learned by doing. Technology standardized jobs and learning, and has eliminated and de-skilled many jobs. But technology has also created new jobs that require judgment and creativity, and has thus brought workers back to learning the "art" of their work, once more, from experience.

A recent report from the Work in America Institute (1985) describes learning as an everyday part of the job with employees responsible for learning all of the tasks in their work units. Employees are expected to understand how each part works together to form the whole and how their work units fit in with the organization. An active, non-hierarchical form of interaction is encouraged among work teams, managers, and trainers along with peer learning among co-workers. This approach signals a growing recognition that the enormous demands for learning in the workplace will require increasingly informal learning processes that are common to the entire organization even though the work of each unit itself will define the content.

The half life of education for many jobs is shorter and shorter. Danchak (1987), for example, reported that in 1986 the half life of education for a software engineer was 2.5 years; for an electrical engineer, it was 5 years; and for a mechanical engineer, it was 7.5 years. He recommended the use of knowledge maintenance contracts to attract engineers and forestall obsolescence. The pervasive theme reflected above is a need for continuous learning on-the-job.

Research on training confirms this trend and offers additional insights into the changing nature of workplace learning. Lakewood Research group annually conducts an industry status report for *Training* magazine. Feuer (1988) reports that 39.6 billion dollars were budgeted for formal training in 100 + employee organizations and that 37.5 million people received employee-sponsored training. However, Gordon (1988) noted that these figures do not capture the enormous "hidden investment" in informal learning which "occurs whenever a senior technician walks over to help a junior technician who hits a snag with some project. It occurs constantly in the normal interactions between supervisors and subordinates, and in the give-and-take among peers" (p. 52). Information on instructional methods also points in the direction of an increase in learning outside the classroom. One-on-one instruction was ranked third, and over 31% of the organizations surveyed use non-computer-based self-instructional programs.

In a speech at the Texas Conference on Organizations (April, 1988), W. Richard Scott suggested that training constitutes a meta-organizational form, found throughout society, which connotes a set of roles (teacher/student). He predicted that training departments will look more and more like schools. Just as the district office enables a school system to be lean administratively, training departments will be centralized. Credits and courses enable an educational system to be rationalized because they allow standardization across domains. Thus, training departments are apparently becoming "corporate classrooms" (Eurich, 1985). Scott also finds that government regulations, increased professionalization of trainers, and mandatory continuing education are driving training departments in this direction. Scott thus predicts that training in the 1990s will be diffuse because this leads to flexibility. Figure 2.1 illustrates diffuse vs. specific training by looking at outcomes and at who benefits from training, the individual or the organization. Scott also believes that training will increasingly be seen as a way of socializing people to perform as the organization wants without the need of bureaucratic controls. Education contributes to common professional viewpoints and can increase loyalty to the corporate mission. As such, training should lead individuals to act in predictable ways to unpredictable stimuli, thus replacing the need for other types of controls.

Despite Scott's prediction of more, rather than less, formalized training, we believe that a need for continuous learning in the workplace also requires renewed attention to informal and incidental learning. The American Society for Training and Development (1987) suggests that Americans may expect on the average to change jobs three or four times in their careers. By the year 2000, they note, 75% of all workers will need retraining. Formal training, conducted within businesses or outside them, can assist employees in some of this learning. However, much learning can take place informally, in part because of the sheer volume of the need, and in part because it is more relevant to non-routine problem situations in which workers find themselves.

Benefits to:	*Organization*	*Individual*
Training that is more specific	Problem Solving	Therapy
more diffuse	Team Building	Play

Figure 2.1 A model for describing training in organizations
Source: W. Richard Scott. Reprinted with permission.

Learning levels: overview

In this book, we look at learners as integral parts of many social units, some of which directly relate to learning in the workplace, and others of which function as shadow social networks with which individuals are affiliated. Learning is continually influencing, and influenced by, the way in which people construct meaning. Social networks play a role in that process. However, these personally constructed meanings may or may not be accurate. People may falsely attribute their own projections and beliefs to someone else whom they believe represents the organization, especially a manager. Employees may not have access to a manager to check out these assumptions; they may not think they can discuss such things; or they may be accustomed to operating on taken-for-granted assumptions without checking them out.

In November 1984, Gordon Lippitt spoke to graduate students at the University of Texas about his vision for the future of the field of human resource development. He spoke to the need for "a new organizational culture that performs like a learning system" in which people can more easily learn new roles, take risks despite uncertainty, and share information across boundaries. People must be able to communicate more effectively, "using intuition and feelings as valued information." Similarly, Knowles (1985) has suggested that human resource developers are in danger of being little more than logistics arrangers unless they reframe their role to that of an organizational consultant teaching the organization to function like a learning system.

Lippitt and Knowles point to learning at a collective level, not just at the individual level. It is much more difficult to document collective learning or to understand how it influences individual learning. None the less, we believe that collective learning may be the distinguishing feature of workplace learning, and that it plays a particularly strong role in informal and incidental learning because people learn through interaction in bounded social groups that are connected by common organizational goals.

We start our discussion with a look at individual learning. We then move to learning within small groups and then to the organizational level which represents a collection of work groups, but yet has its own identity that is frequently shaped by the organization's most powerful figures. Finally, we examine professional learning. Professional networks have a great deal of influence on what people do within certain segments of organizations. Professionals network between organizations, and thus represent a source of influential, external ideas. Some companies are dominated by a single profession, for example, engineers or accountants. Learning strategies in those companies are likely to resemble those used by the professional schools and organizations of the dominant group. In other cases, professionals are one of many work groups; however, their training often puts them in positions of visibility and control. Human resource developers, as professionals, can play a particularly significant role because of their influence on the design of learning in organizations.

We use the Johari Window to discuss learning levels. As we do so, we show the vital role played in learning by processes of feedback and disclosure, processes to which we return in our final chapter when we discuss strategies for enhancing informal and incidental learning.

Learning at the individual level

We begin with the Johari Window (Figure 2.2), developed by Joseph Lufts and Harry Ingram (1961), which suggests that individuals grow by being open to others.

Through feedback they learn how others see them. Through self-disclosure they open themselves to the potential of more intimate relationships and also subject more of their perceptions about themselves to public reflection. In this process, others may help shape and affirm their self-understanding.

The upper left quadrant represents the open area of the self which is known to the individual and openly shared with others. The upper

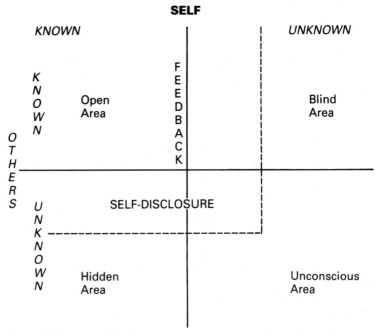

Figure 2.2 The Johari Window: a model for understanding individual learning
Source: J. Lufts and H. Ingram (1961). Reprinted with permission.

right quadrant is the blind area which is that part of ourselves which others observe, but about which we are unaware. The lower left quadrant is the hidden area, that part of ourselves we choose to keep to ourselves. It includes our secrets, and often our dreams. Because of the nature of the workplace, where personal and professional concerns are frequently kept separate, many meaningful concerns related to personal social networks remain in this quadrant.

The final quadrant, the unconscious, refers to that part of the self that is not presently known to oneself or others. Many concerns relevant to our personal social networks probably fall in this quadrant as well; if anything, taboos against discussing these concerns in the workplace heighten their importance because we cannot even name them, let alone examine them. Using the Johari Window, growth can be seen as a process of learning about oneself, reflecting on what has been learned, and making incremental changes based on discoveries acquired through processes of feedback and self-disclosure.

Learning at the group level

It is easier to grasp the notion of an individual's learning since we have all consciously experienced this. It may be harder to think of group learning, but we can probably all recall experiences where a group acquired an identity of its own. In groups, we as individuals think and learn differently as a result of our interaction with others.

Groups learn when they monitor the effectiveness of the process of group interaction while simultaneously attending to getting the task done. As illustrated in Figure 2.3, the group also confronts potential dysfunctions through processes of feedback and disclosure. The upper left quadrant, when all is reasonably well, represents normal group processes visible to all. The upper right quadrant includes what is known to individuals, but not acknowledged and dealt with by the group as a whole, such as "group think" (Janis, 1972). In "group think," the pressure to conform to group norms is so great that individuals form strong common values and bonds that do not allow them to subject ideas to a thorough hearing or a true critical test.

In the lower left quadrant are situations where all group members agree on something privately, but individuals do not own up to this when they are together, as in the Abilene Paradox (Harvey, 1974) in which everyone knows they are on a "trip to Abilene" but are unwilling to express the truth because of perceived risks. Finally, the lower right quadrant represents unconscious states at the group and individual level, as for example in the theory of Basic Assumption Mental States (Bion, 1961). Unconscious states pull the attention of group

41

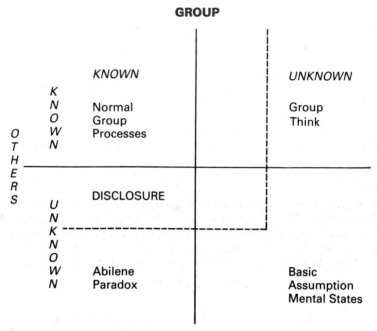

Figure 2.3 Adaptation of the Johari Window: a model for understanding group learning

Source: O. Mink, University of Texas, Austin, Texas

members off the task. These states include fight, flight, pairing, and dependency.

Learning at the organizational level

Organizational theorists distinguish between the way in which individuals go about their own learning and the way in which a larger collective unit learns to function in its environment. In both cases, individuals are involved. However, when organizations learn, individuals become agents who in some way influence the way others in the organization think, act, and learn.

There has been little empirical research on organizational learning, perhaps because this concept is more easily grasped as a metaphor than a reality. Based on a review of the research, Shrivastava (1983) identified four schools of thought on organizational learning: those who emphasize adaptation, those who focus on assumption sharing, those who identify an organization's ability to build a knowledge base of action–outcome relationships, and those who look at institutionalized experience. Organizations as collective units become conscious of what they have learned (for example, outcomes, learning curves, or stored memory) as well as how they go about learning (for example, by insight from outside, by environmental jolts, through systematic mergers and acquisitions, or by training). Fiol and Lyles (1985) also distinguish between organizational learning, or the ability to learn from experience, and organizational adaptation, or the ability to make adjustments as a result of goal or environmental changes.

Using the Johari Window (Figure 2.4), we can examine organizational learning in terms of the interaction between what is known to the organization and what is known to others in the environment. The productive work state, represented by the upper left quadrant where something is known to both an organization and the environment, is depicted as an open system. Central to this concept is the idea that a learning organization is productive, but it is also open to

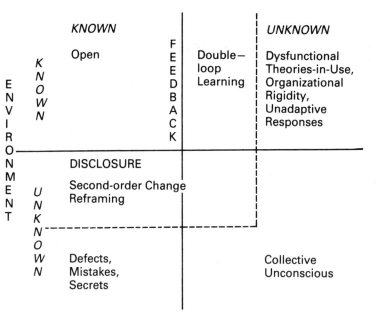

Figure 2.4 Adaptation of the Johari Window: a model for understanding organizational learning

43

learning from internal and external feedback from its environment. Double-loop learning permits adequate feedback (Argyris and Schön, 1974, 1978); second-order change or reframing (Watzlawick *et al.*, 1974) encourages disclosure.

But what is an organization's psychic blind side, found in the upper right quadrant? Argyris and Schön point to dysfunctional theories-in-use (1978) and single-loop reasoning, discussed in Chapter One. Staw *et al.* (1981) note that organizations respond to threat with self-defeating, rigid responses. However, a lack of an institutionalized adaptive response to environmental jolts (Meyer, 1982), or its incapacity to manage surprises, might also be considered part of the organization's blind side. And what about an organization's hidden side, found in the lower left quadrant? Perhaps the organization hides its defects, its mistakes, and its secrets.

Finally, there is the collective unconscious in the lower right quadrant. This area might include the embedded values of the organization's subcultures and unstated interpretations of the organization's experiences. Mitroff (1983) refers to these collective myths and legends as "stakeholders of the organizational mind."

Bateson (1972) suggests another level of learning that transcends what goes on at the individual, group, and organizational levels. We are most likely to see transcendent learning during organizational decline when organizations choose to negate who they currently are in order to reconfigure themselves around the perceived common good.

Learning at the professional level

Benveniste (1987) calls attention to the differences between professionals and other kinds of workers. Professionals are not as easily socialized into the organization because they have learned to think independently. They are more likely to question orders rather than execute them with obedience. They draw on an extensive knowledge base which they update by reading, interacting with colleagues through professional associations and journals, and participating in seminars or other continuing education offerings. Professionals monitor their own collective practice, using standards and codes of ethics that may differ from those of the organization. Sometimes they must be independently certified or credentialed. Professionals want recognition by their peers more than the organization, even though they may occupy significant management positions in the hierarchy. Professionals "are not trained to espouse a narrow organizational perspective" (Benveniste, p. 49). They usually prefer to be autonomous, self-organizing, and self-directed.

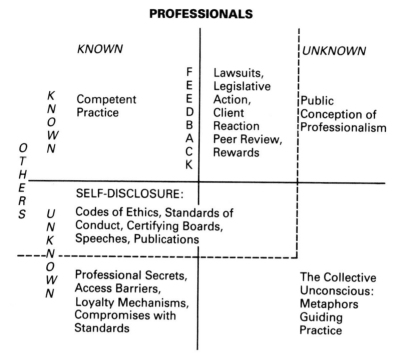

Figure 2.5 Adaptation of the Johari Window: a model for understanding professional learning

When we look at the Johari Window and professional learning (Figure 2.5), we see that external professional standards, norms, and practices influence learning patterns within the organization. Feedback and disclosure are central to learning at this level as well. In the upper left quadrant, we have the area of competent practice that is publicly acknowledged and the ideal toward which the public expects professionals to strive. However, the public has increasingly become disenchanted with professionals who fall short of this standard. The professional's image has become tarnished, as evidenced in the upper right quadrant by the only way in which people can speak back, that is, lawsuits, pressure for laws to curb professional misconduct, and word-of-mouth reactions discussed with others by clients. On the other hand, professionals have their own mechanisms for feedback, as, for example, in peer reviews or public professional rewards.

The lower left quadrant represents the profession's attempt to regulate itself by disclosing inappropriate practice and "punishing" members within its ranks before the public has to take action. Public speeches, publications, and public admissions of error are mechanisms for self-disclosure about both successes and failures. In this quadrant we also find professional secrets, mechanisms that limit entry into the ranks and enforce loyalty, and acceptable compromises negotiated between members and the profession that may often be undiscussed in public. Finally, in the lower right quadrant, we find myths and metaphors that, unbeknownst to the professional, guide practice.

We believe professional learning is central to much informal and incidental learning in organizations. Professionals are already motivated to learn, and have developed a set of procedures for going about that learning. They use one another, and the body of knowledge produced by the profession, as reference points in learning. Because standards are set outside the organization, professionals can create a higher-order set of norms, practices, values, and attitudes that influence the culture and practices of an organization from the outside. Sometimes these standards conflict, but professionals are always ready to ask questions that others in the organization might not consider or may be unwilling to raise because they are in conflict with standard operating procedures.

The Human Resource Learning Cone

Figure 2.6, the human resource learning cone, illustrates the way in which informal and incidental learning permeate all other human resource activities within an organization. It is based on the human resource wheel introduced in Chapter One, but added to it are the various interacting levels at which learning often takes place. Individual learning is most frequently discussed in training and development circles. However, all individuals are part of larger social groups, both within and outside organizations. At the minimum, people function within defined work groups and often network with other work groups across functions. It is clear that individuals seldom act solely on their own behalf in the workplace.

The professional level of this cone can be interpreted in two ways. First, workers in many occupations are becoming professionalized even though they may not be considered professionals in the strictest sense of the word. Professionalization involves the communication of a body of specialized knowledge, through training, to help practitioners distinguish between rule-governed solutions and situations that call for judgment. As Benveniste (1987) points out, profession-

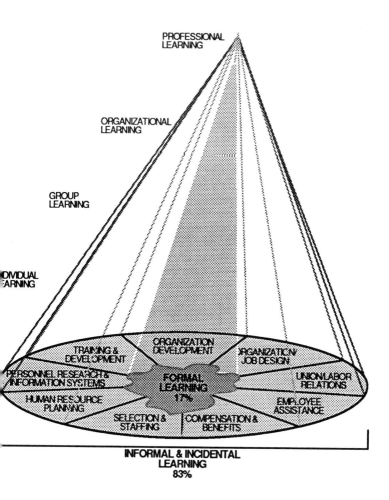

Figure 2.6 The human resource learning cone
Source: V.J. Marsick and K.E. Watkins, based on the Human Resource
Wheel from P. McLagan (1983)

alization brings to the job a level of independence that may conflict
with norms set by line managers. Learning takes place at this level as
well, both for individuals alone and for groups. This learning can influence the profession when people interact within specialized

47

networks, just as the shared knowledge from networks can be taken back into the workplace.

A second dimension of this professional level stems from the fact that human resource development itself is increasingly regarded as a profession, despite the fact that human resource developers often have little specialized training. Watkins (1989a) reports data (Lee, 1985) showing that only 8% of human resource developers have academic training in human resource development. Other fields represented were education (18% of undergraduate and 31.6% of graduate credentials), business or management (16% of undergraduate and 18.6% of graduate credentials), psychology (10% of both undergraduate and graduate credentials), and communications (4.4% of undergraduate and 2.4% of graduate credentials). Over 17% of the trainers surveyed had been either school teachers or college instructors. Watkins concludes that, despite controversy over credentialing, this group is becoming more professionalized. The learning that takes place at the professional level in human resource development is thus highly relevant to both the organization within which such specialists work and the development of the profession itself.

Part two

Informal learning

In Part Two, Marsick examines informal learning. Chapter Three is a discussion of what and how Swedish managers learn from experience as they work in teams on real-life projects and problems. Chapter Four is a look at the learning of educational field workers promoting health and family planning in communities in Nepal and the Philippines. These field workers are being trained to use informal learning to help others learn; the training programs that prepare them for their work are also designed around the kind of informal learning that the field workers will use in their jobs. Chapter Five is a discussion of how a small group of adult educators learned aspects of their work informally and how this has influenced their practice as professional educators in organizations.

Each chapter also highlights learning within one of the levels described in the human resource learning cone in Chapter One. Chapter Three focuses on individual learning; Chapter Four on learning within groups and organizations; Chapter Five on the learning of professionals. However, while the focus is on one or other level, linkages are also explored among levels.

All three chapters involve situations that fall outside one's routines. Chapter Two looks at non-routine problems that managers face in times of change and turbulent environments. In Chapter Three, village-level educational workers are learning a set of tasks for which there are no prescriptions, that is, talking to villagers about changes in their lives and work with which the villagers are not comfortable. In Chapter Four, professional adult educators in work situations reflect on the way in which they have learned informally when they were faced with new challenges. These non-routine circumstances make it difficult to design a prescriptive training program. The circumstances prompt a need first to understand the situation from many viewpoints and then often to reframe the problem. Learning requires digging below the surface to identify and examine values and assumptions that govern the way situations are understood and addressed. Workers in these circumstances cannot rest back on proven solutions, but must proactively and creatively seek new responses.

These chapters, taken together, address the central question of how people can be helped to learn more effectively from their experience. Training models are typically limited in the way in which experience is incorporated. For example, many models presume that learners have life experience that is relevant to the problem at hand and that learners can, on their own, make the connection between concepts that are distilled from experience and applications outside the classroom. Other models go a step further and provide a common experience or practical exercises which learners can work through together, for example, case studies, simulations, or step-by-step activities on which learners are then given feedback. These experiences are selected because the designer perceives them to be relevant to the learners. Moreover, time may be spent following the activity in discussing the application of these lessons to real-life situations.

However, research on practical reasoning (Scribner, 1986) suggests that it is not always easy for workers to make the application between the classroom and the job since people depend on cues in their normal work environment to understand and solve problems. Training, in a sense, turns the tables around by starting with an abstract principle which must be first understood and then adapted to the normal work environment. Action planning and other exercises are often used to help people think through these principles in terms of their own context. However, it is more natural to start by helping people analyze the context in which they experience a problem and then to help them look at the solutions they identify in light of principles that might help them do their work differently. Turning the tables in this fashion avoids the resistance encountered because learners believe the solutions offered do not apply since they were "not invented here."

The drawback of this kind of learning, however, is that the activity cannot be as nicely packaged. Learners feel uncomfortable with the ambiguity involved when they have to analyze their own problems. They may like the conceptual clarity of someone else's framework even though they often resist solutions that are not perceived as applicable to their own problems. Years of training in schools, where learners memorize and repeat someone else's formula, take over as learners look to the trainer to give them the answer, if only so that they can then disagree with it. In these chapters, we enter into the fourth quadrant of Kolb's (1984) experiential learning cycle, which is seldom done in training, because we leave the classroom where we can more easily reflect on experience, talk about theories, and practice within clearly defined guidelines. We enter, instead, the quadrant in which we must experiment in real life where there are no clear answers, where we must analyze our own situations, and build our own solutions which we can then further examine in light of what others know.

Workplace learning is commonly thought of in terms of instrumental, task-related skills. Part Two illustrates that a theory of workplace learning goes beyond this simple focus on observable behaviors, even though the ultimate result is increased competence in the workplace. Elsewhere, Marsick (1987a, 1988c) draws on Mezirow (1981, 1985) to develop a theory of workplace learning that integrates three different learning domains. Mezirow, basing his work on the critical social theorist Jürgen Habermas, differentiates among three domains of learning: instrumental, dialogic, and self-reflective. Instrumental learning refers to task-oriented problem solving, a common focus in the workplace. Dialogic learning refers to creation of consensual norms, which in the workplace are reflected in the organization's culture. Self-reflective learning refers to the way in which people learn to understand themselves. Self-understanding is shaped through social interaction and, therefore, involves many beliefs, perceptions and values of others that have been internalized. While it is possible to learn in any of these three domains separately, in the workplace, learners often set out to solve a task-related, instrumental problem and end up encountering both organizational norms and self-perceptions, which may also involve norms carried over from family, church, and ethnic background. Many times, especially in informal learning, people do not delve into these norms, and yet such norms influence the way in which people perceive, question, probe, evaluate, interpret and judge their experiences. Hence, all three learning domains must be addressed if learning is to be as far-reaching as possible. This perspective on learning provides a framework for chapters in Part Two.

Part Two also illustrates informal learning that is related to change. The managers in Chapter Three, while not described as change agents, forge new ground in their companies, in part because of new business conditions imposed by the globalization of the marketplace. While informal learning can take place anywhere at any time, motivation to learn seems to be higher when people are confronted with new challenges that accompany change. Learners in Chapters Four and Five describe how people become change agents. The field workers in Chapter Four are being trained for this role; for educators in Chapter Five, this professional focus develops over time.

53

Finally, as a group, these chapters illustrate linkages between informal and formal learning. Chapter Three, for example, describes the formal and informal components of Action Learning programs; Chapter Four focuses on experience-based training programs; and in Chapter Five, the adult educators described often work as trainers. It may seem contradictory to suggest that informal learning, the essence of which is its ad hoc nature, be designed. The assumptions in the efforts described in this section, however, are two-fold: that change is better managed if not left solely to chance, and that informal learning can be made more effective if some aspects of it are linked to a forum for the critical examination of informal learning and the enhancement of skills in learning how to learn. The second half of the book thus moves the reader toward responses to questions raised in the previous section about how to facilitate incidental and informal learning: responses that are explored more fully in the last chapter of the book.

Part Two examines models in which people learn from their experience in real-life situations so that we can better understand how to help others learn in this way. While the focus is on informal learning, the chapters also explore connections with training programs. Part Two thus touches on questions of how training can be designed to enhance and facilitate informal learning – questions to which we return in our last chapter.

Chapter three

How managers learn from experience: a Swedish experiment

Informal learning, as described in Chapter One, is organized around real-life experience. This chapter describes the way in which managers learn informally from their experiences. Such learning is often left to chance and, as such, frequently leads to frustration and even to reinforcement of errors. This chapter is a case study of a program in Sweden, based on Action Learning, that joins formal and informal learning to enhance the likelihood of learning and to help people acquire skills in this kind of experience-based learning that they can apply outside the classroom.[1]

Action Learning programs, described more fully below, combine work on a real project in small teams with structured activities relevant to the projects and with seminars for reflecting upon, and extracting lessons from, experience. In the past, people who learned from experience came primarily from the shop floor. White-collar workers learned in the classroom. However, as ambiguity replaces the "one right answer" and as information continues to grow exponentially, employees at all levels must learn on the job. However, there are few systems in place that help people extract lessons from experience, thus reducing high trial-and-error rates.

The focus of this chapter is primarily on individual learning. However, because of the team focus of Action Learning, group learning is also involved, and for those managers participating as part of an organization's strategy for change, learning moves into the organizational level as well. Learning takes place under non-routine conditions in which managers must actively probe and experiment with problems, leading them often to reframe their understanding of the situation. They often find themselves challenging deeply-ingrained personal beliefs and organizational norms.

The chapter begins with a discussion of Action Learning, followed by a report on what managers learned from experience and how their work in project teams facilitated this learning. In the concluding section, these findings are examined in light of informal learning.

Action Learning

The Action Learning model described here has been designed by the Management Institute in Lund, Sweden (MiL) for top-level executives and is more fully described elsewhere (Marsick, 1988a, 1990; Marsick and Cederholm, 1988). Action Learning is best articulated by Revans (1971, 1982) although MiL and other people using this strategy do not strictly follow his approach, nor even knew of his writing at the time they got started. During the nationalization of the coal industry in the UK, Revans discovered that he could help people learn effectively in teams working on real-life problems. Revans, however, was not a manager or a "human resource developer," a field that was not known by that name at that time. He was a successful physicist. He and his colleagues – whom he called "comrades in adversity" – found that they learned best by regularly gathering as a team to help whoever was obviously failing at his work. In other words, failure was an opportunity for learning.

Revans went on to develop his ideas as a system for management development in England. He gained international repute when his strategy was rejected by a British university and embraced by a Belgian inter-university program in 1956. Revans emphasized personal values, combined with a study of information flow, systems logic, decision-making theory, inference and uncertainty, and learning/adaptation. Managers were helped to examine values that predisposed them to act or interpret reality as they did. Action learning focuses on practice, not just abstract theory. The key to this kind of learning is the right kind of questioning. Revans expands on this notion through a comparison of "P" learning, that is, programmed knowledge handed down through books, and "Q" learning, that is, the wisdom of "questioning insight."

MiL's action learning programs

Figure 3.1, which shows the relationship between "P" and "Q" learning, is used by MiL staff as the rationale for their program. Training often focuses on helping managers to polish familiar skills in their current job environment (lower left cell), to develop skills for new tasks in the same environment (top left cell), or to practice the same task skills in a new environment (lower right cell). In such cases, it is relatively easy to build on known "P" expertise because some facet of the situation is familiar. However, managers often find themselves in

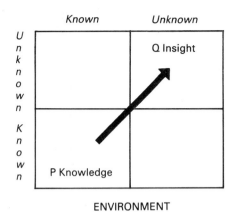

Figure 3.1: Nature of top management tasks

Source: Adapted from handouts used by Management Institute, Lund, Sweden.

situations where both the task and environment are unfamiliar (top right cell). This is what managers typically face as they move from functional areas of expertise – marketing, finance, engineering, or other specialties – to positions of general management where problems are increasingly vague, complex, future-oriented and not amenable to known solutions. Hence, the focus on "Q" learning.

General management problems typically involve judgment and are often based on intuitive "gut feelings" about what should be done, even though managers usually do their "homework" before making decisions. Personal development – an enhanced understanding of oneself – is thus considered central to effective management development. Managers are helped to go beyond their own limited professional, personal and organizational experience. They see situations from multiple perspectives to gain a "helicopter view."

Over the years, a flexible framework has evolved in MiL with three main program components: the projects, seminars, and back-home experience. Project experience runs parallel to seminars and is, at least ideally, drawn upon in the seminar discussions. The same is true for back-home experience since these real concerns faced by managers in their daily work often surface in the project work. MiL's programs can thus be envisioned as three parallel blocks: a project block lasting approximately 20 days, a seminar block lasting approximately 20 days, and a back-home block that runs the duration of the program, which is typically from seven to nine months. Program activities are thus "sandwiched" in between regular work activities.

Through these three components winds a "Red Thread" or "Red Line," the English translation of a Swedish word meaning "central theme." Red Threads, for example, have included becoming a generalist, isolation vs. connection, creativity vs. stability, organizational culture, service management, or working internationally. Staff do not all place the same degree of emphasis on this theme, but they use it as an organizing principle and some arrange special activities around it, such as trips to neighboring countries during which participants are given ambiguous assignments similar to those they might face in their work, such as a new market analysis.

Action Learning is thus based on the old adage that people learn best from their experience. However, MiL has found that experience alone is not sufficient for learning. Thus, while the projects form the backbone of the programs, they are combined with reflection seminars in which facilitators help the groups learn from both the task at hand and their own learning process, including group interaction. Special content-oriented seminars are also arranged on topics relevant to the issues facing companies, such as working across cultural boundaries, service management, or strategic planning. A personal development week, reported by most participants as having the most significance for them, deals with conflict and cooperation in groups. This week, typically led by a psychologist with a background in Transactional Analysis, provides an opportunity to delve deeply into one's hopes, dreams, and patterns of behavior while receiving valuable feedback.

Managers are expected to bring daily work problems into program and group discussions, although some staff felt this was hard to do and often got lost in the process. One facilitator relayed the story of a woman whose husband had been transferred to Algeria as an example of how valuable this integration could be. As a professional, it would be difficult to leave her job, so her husband's boss agreed to send her on the same assignment. The group then helped her think through a strategy for her new job. Such real-life problems reflect concerns that managers often face for themselves or with their staff. MiL's Action Learning programs are thus integrated, holistic, and interactive. Each program component is reinforced and complemented by others.

Learning from experience

Action Learning projects vary, but they share some common features. They are not puzzles with a pre-determined right answer. They are dilemmas that often require outside consulting assistance. They are typically complex and touch on different parts of the entire organization. For example, they involve decentralization, corporate identity, relationships among different operating units, or the discovery of new markets. The problem as originally stated is often reformulated as the group works on it. Table 3.1 lists examples of such projects, and a brief description of how problems were reformulated or refined.

Table 3.1: Some reformulated projects

Problem as originally stated		*Problem when it was reformulated*
1.	Expanding export capacity for fertilizer that was affected by government environmental policy	1. Dealing with "internal politics" that obscured issues and with management threatened by changes
2.	Increasing sales by 400% in a "high tech" pharmaceutical branch	2. Expanding and reorganizing the company
3.	Getting store chiefs defined by top management as lacking in courage to decentralize	3. Getting top management to reconcile discrepancies between what they say and do
4.	Developing new paper products	4. Identifying market preferences
5.	Determining the location for a central paper storage plant	5. Identifying the best way to transport paper from mill to market
6.	Redefining business strategy to deliver energy services	6. Getting marketing and distribution to work well together
7.	Instilling a service orientation	7. Resolving conflict between parent company's ideas and daughter company's needs
8.	Developing a training program operated by Human Resources	8. Involving line managers in their own staff's development
9.	Improved product distribution system	9. Resolving discrepancy between what CEO says and does
10.	Recreating connections between R & D and marketing	10. Identifying project host as obstacle to communications

How do managers go about learning from their experience in the projects? The ideal process, as encouraged and envisioned by MiL, involves a cycle somewhat like that described by Schön (1983, 1987) and discussed further in Chapter One of this book. Schön bases his thinking, in part, on a continuous, iterative action research strategy which successfully works through phases of problem identification, solution exploration, solution testing, monitoring, and problem reformulation. Action research is the basis of many organization development interventions and, in fact, MiL's founder and many of its key staff have theoretical and applied backgrounds in this field.

Over time, the action research cycle has been used in many programs. However, at least in the United States, the first step – variously called problem finding, problem identification, or problem formulation – has become a quick stop in the cycle, a necessary jumping-off point for problem solving. It may be that this focus on doing things, rather than finding out what one should be doing, is part of the pragmatic US preference for taking action that shows up in a proliferation of quick, prescriptive recipes for success such as the "one-minute manager." As such, it is both a strength and a weakness. It prevents wallowing, Hamlet-like, in indecision. On the other hand, it facilitates a faddish search for new answers when the issue may be an inaccurate problem formulation. The emphasis given to action research by Schön and to Action Learning by Revans and the MiL program is not problem solving, but problem finding. This focus is further discussed in the next section.

Problem reformulation and active experimentation

Managers frequently want to jump immediately to solutions. One manager, who had worked on the problem of "the future of a school that no longer met the needs for which it was founded," described the time his group spent on framing the problem. He reflected, "when we got our project, we first of all wanted to solve this problem, but [our advisors] taught us how to analyze before you solve the problem. And I don't think we believed them.... But when we had been working with the program for some weeks, we understood [they] were right."

Managers, on the whole, noted that they were not encouraged to simply reflect on the problem and "do reports." They described a systematic set of interventions, using an approach much like one organization developers would use, in which managers took a problem definition, at whatever stage it was, and experimented with it through some kind of action. One typical intervention, for example, took place around an electricity company's desire to "go from selling electricity to an energy service company." The company thought these changes would have to take place primarily at the periphery of the organization. The project team found through interviews that these workers were more oriented to handling electricity than interacting with customers. So the project group talked to "the eight chiefs of different districts," each of whom had very different viewpoints. The team was surprised "to find in several meetings how the situation could change from the first meeting." So they reflected on these findings, fed them back to those interviewed, and examined them further with this group. But they decided "the problem was maybe not at this level, so we went another step higher up ... at the level of the Divisions" and found the primary problem was between the marketing and the distribution divisions.

So the problem ended up being redefined as a need for "marketing (to) be a service organization to distribution," which called for a reorganization at the top level. This manager saw two similarities between his project and the others. One was that the problem was often caused by someone at the top of the organization, even though it was initially defined as something else. And secondly, a goal was defined, but it was not communicated well throughout the organization. This example also illustrates the role of reflection during various stages of problem reformulation. The group continually examined the problem in light of new findings.

As already noted, Table 2.1 provides other examples of the way in which problems became redefined as managers sought the opinions of different stakeholders. Problems are often initially defined in technical terms, and seem solvable through consultation with experts, but they usually end up being defined in people terms, as, for example, communications, power struggles, personality quirks, or distorted perceptions. The reformulation takes place because managers take action as they would if they were implementing a solution. In doing so, they uncover misperceptions, norms, and expectations that were often hidden, both to the people holding these viewpoints and to others in the organizations. These hidden perceptions, once picked apart and examined, make it possible to uncover errors-in-the-making.

Many managers reported on the value of the action orientation of these programs. As one manager noted, good management does not take place by rationally analyzing the problem, waiting for the perfect moment and writing reports, but by taking some action around the problem, using these results to reassess the situation, and by dealing with difficulties that arise. He learned this through the project experience, finding that when "you collect information, you analyze it at the same time, and you can't collect information in all fields at the same time.... Reality is happening around you ... and if you don't grab these opportunities the situation is lost." Reports may not even be necessary and, if they are prepared, they can note that the recommendations were already being implemented. This manager used this strategy in various projects of which he was in charge while he was in the program "and I found one of the reports that I did finish was totally unnecessary. All the things were already happening."

Another staff member described a project in which managers had to handle conflict between two departments. He suggested the group "let the production department make pictures of the other [and vice versa]. And they also made pictures of what they thought the development department thought about them." The project group brought the two departments together to look at these differences. The group did not write a large report, but through action learned "to have the courage to go into the relationship, to work with it, even if they were engineers and controllers or people not working so much with other people."

Challenging norms

Action can lead to challenging norms. One manager, who worked on the reorganization of a savings institution that was bought by new owners who were eliminating many layers of middle management, pointed out that, "Very often, more than before MiL, [I] question 'why?' 'Why am I working like that today? Why is my organization like this today?' That is new for me." He finds himself "put[ting these] questions to myself or instead more to the managers at the next level, in this bureaucratic organization. I have found myself that I'm not afraid to put this question to the leaders."

One of the clearest examples of norm challenging was a project with a consumer cooperative involving the decentralization of authority to the heads of retail stores in the cooperative. Headquarters had framed the problem in terms of a lack of courage on the part of retail store owners, but the store owners said that policy instruments (for example, budgets and regulations) did not allow them to take full control. The project group interviewed ten store owners, and then brought the store owners and headquarters together for feedback sessions. As a result, headquarters said the store owners could do anything they wanted as long as it was legal. So the project group, supported by their advisor, decided to challenge this. For example, they stopped giving figures to headquarters on which they never received feedback. They also ordered different products, such as a popular beer produced by a competitor, which they had delivered with publicity such as photographs in the company's internal newspaper. The store owners, and the outside beer producers, feared that headquarters would be angry, and they were, despite prior verbal assurances to the contrary. The advisor explained, "So we had four or five things that really tested, explored or challenged the headquarters people. They were working still in the same way, reacting the same way, and that is our answer to the question" about whether or not a lack of courage had prevented the store owners from implementing the new policy.

Norm challenging was even clearer in a project with three participants who were "all the third generation of people employed by the Power Board." They were working on an internal project, which made it difficult for them to get an outside perspective, especially since they "never had the idea that there could exist anything whatsoever outside this company." After many unsuccessful efforts to spur this group to action, the advisor suggested they take him on a trip to the power plants: "I sort of switched the situation, so they were going to teach me about electricity and power distribution." He was surprised by the "ascetic" quality of the experience, "no liquor, the cheapest hotel rooms to be found in 200 miles surrounding, driving like hell through the woods just to reach a cheap hotel room." He had imagined late nights, drinking, and a more convivial atmosphere. So he asked them about his surprise, and they explained that in this kind of work, as passed down by their "forefathers, they could not drink heavily; being out in the middle of nowhere, they had to [be alert so they could] concentrate on what they were going to do."

This journey opened everyone to different points of view and turned the project around. They reframed the problem to "what the power company should do for the communities in which they built their power plants." When the time came to talk to the head of the company, who had only been in his job for about six months, they wrote him a very brief letter, and asked him to meet them at a power plant where they "did the same thing we did in the journey. We walked him around, in the woods, for a whole day, discussing."

The advisor found that these participants took great risks in the way in which they presented this information to the head of the company, who was quite a few levels above them hierarchically. He challenged them to explain their actions, asking dramatically if they thought the head of the company would "bite them.... And I don't think it was actually only symbolic, but it was also meant, in a way, quite literally. 'Bite!'" he said, voice rising. He continued to raise questions to help "in making a picture for them, a map about this authority thing" to draw out the lessons from the experience. He explained how difficult it was for them to see this because of the organization's culture: "it is based on a type of army organization, a millennia of organizational experience inherited from times immemorial. And you don't change that overnight."

Process consultation

The project advisor plays a key role, as illustrated in the above vignettes, even though the managers themselves ultimately make decisions about how to proceed. One woman manager, for example, noted that her group had more difficulty because their advisor, who came from inside the company, could not guide them sufficiently in terms of the process. Internal advisors are too caught up in the web of expectations and taken-for-granted understandings of "how things work around here" to be able to step back and ask the right questions.

Sometimes groups focus more on the product than the process. The individual manager can still feel he or she has learned much from the experience; however, MiL staff think that the real learning has not taken place, as in the following example. One manager worked on the feasibility of fish farming as a new activity for one company. He felt that his group's understanding of the problem "changed 180 degrees," but their definition and reframing was based on a rational analysis of the facts. Fish farming seemed on the surface to be a natural extension for this company, but an analysis of the technical difficulties, economic factors, competition, and risks led the group to recommend against it. This group, unlike many others in MiL programs, did not interview people in the company or look at the problem from its people-side. This manager described their approach as engineer-like, avoiding involvement in "internal decision-making habits or routines," and noted "a very negative reception." It seems that a wealth of learning was missed by this "technocrat" focus.

The technical, or more expert-oriented approach to projects, was not advocated by most staff members who felt that, when used, the emphasis was on consulting more than on learning. One staff member noted that, in the beginning, he does not give his opinions about the project because "if you can just keep your bloody mouth shut, then many things will happen." "Of course," he noted, "they will ask for help and, if you have information that will help provide a conceptual framework, you can and should share it." He continued, "the more I know about how we could actually solve it, the less I would like to say, and the less or more I can judge if we are at least in some kind of direction that could be possible. Because if it is not, then I have to step in" and help the group get back on track. Facilitators thus play a low-key role deliberately, even though they are not passive. They may wait for other members of the group to give the needed feedback, and then support it. The above staff member noted, "I prefer two minutes of an hour, than two hours every third time." To do this, he must step outside the consultant role, where one might be looked upon as an expert, and "try to sit on my hands and shut my mouth. That's very difficult if you actually have some idea that you want to promote."

One staff member, however, pointed out that this process-oriented "MiL way" of running projects leaves one "extremely dependent on the capacities of those in the project group, their specialized knowledge, and the understanding of the people in the company where the project is being held." He believes the project advisor must at times take a more active, content-oriented stance toward the problem, especially when the consequences for the host company could be severe. "Setting the stage would be having my team develop their own understanding, a very good picture with the help of some strong concepts" so they do not just discuss blindly. "By contrast, another staff member, who stepped in because there were only three months left and the team had not gotten started," found that the group learned little even though they wrote a good report. At times, the project might be considered a failure, but the degree of process learning that took place makes it a success in other terms. For example, one staff member described a situation where his group ran into, and learned from, power politics. A company asked for help in "recreating connections" between an R&D and a marketing group. The project host, from R&D, wanted a certain answer from the group and tried to prevent them from seeing the top boss. "So we went to the top man without him knowing it, and we got another kind of request [from him]. The host found out, was angry, and was cold to them during the rest of the project period, but the group learned a great deal from the experience.

Part of process consultation is learning about the dynamics of the group. One woman, for example, described the way in which her group learned from difficulties when a chief buyer of the organization in the project did not understand "why I was there and what I was talking about." It helped to have the reflection of another team-mate who observed and listened as she did the interviewing, and could help her think about it afterwards.

In another example, one advisor noticed that, when the group was interviewing people in the host company, one man kept looking at him. The man was unaware he was doing this. The advisor asked if anyone else noticed it, some did, and they decided to change this in the next meeting. It is not unusual for staff members to use group dynamics instruments at various points to help members observe the way they work and give feedback to one another. Through the dynamics of the project groups, tensions surface which, if brought to awareness and challenged, can lead to significant personal change since project experiences are often typical of other work experiences.

Multiple perspectives

In every phase of the project, and through other features of the program, a central concern is bringing multiple perspectives to bear on the problem. As Hofstede (1980) notes in his description of values in different societies, Swedes may lean toward a collectivist orientation. On the whole, they do not like to stand out in the group, an orientation that pushes them toward conformity and similarity in expressed viewpoints. Two dimensions of this orientation showed up in my findings: MiL's valuing of multiple perspectives, and a shift from seeing differences as conflict-laden to cooperation-enhancing.

First, as one staff member noted, "managers in Sweden who are 35 to 40 years old, they have the same kind of schools, they have read the same books, so they think very much in the same way." An explicit goal is to help managers value differences. One manager, for example, who participated in the senior executive program, worked with a group that built in multiple viewpoints wherever possible. They "visited our different firms, and walked around to get the feel of the other person's enterprise situations." Without outside ideas, "you are so close, you're not so wide in your sight," whereas these discussions help people see things "in different ways and different angles."

Related to the valuing of differences was high support for sessions on cross-cultural team building. The consultants who run this workshop treat culture broadly as any set of differences, whether they derive from personality (as identified through the use of the Myers-Briggs type indicator), family, profession, organization (or its subgroups), or national boundaries. One manager noted how these sessions helped him manage a problem between two different divisions in the organization, each of which had its own culture. He put these people into mixed groups, and helped each side see the other's point of view, a goal that took about a year to accomplish.

Questions, especially those that may seem "silly," are central to bringing different perspectives to bear on a problem. This may be less of a difficulty in the multi-company programs where "everyone is an outsider" than in internal programs. One manager described these questions, which he found valuable: "why people reacted in funny ways to the questions that were asked, why people were more or less amateurs trying to investigate something that we definitely didn't know much about, why they acted [in a certain way] if they were criticized." Another advisor described the way in which questions linked the creation of multiple perspectives with problem reformulation. "In the beginning, you have a kind of situation where [they have to] learn that they can think about the problem in different ways.... They very seldom try to challenge their problem definitions." Then the advisor can ask "nasty" or "naughty" questions and help the group think through how to test their perceptions.

One staff member described the way in which he used reflection to help managers see a situation in new ways. "You should stimulate them to go into themselves and ask the question 'what the heck does this matter for you, dear friend'" The advisor can draw out and con-trapose differences: "You don't reflect on things until you get the type of position where you have some sort of contrast." Contrasts "could be from many things, between both sides, between managers and the host company, or it could be between different areas of beliefs within the host company, it could even be between me and them, or whatever."

Project advisors also design activities on-the-spot to elicit different points of view. One advisor, for example, talked about a discussion with three members of his project group and top executives of the insurance company with which they were working. He saw that, "after an hour of asking questions, the group was just bewildered. They didn't know what the problem was so just at the time when these [executives were] going to leave, ... I asked them not to leave but just sit for a half hour and listen to the group." He asked the group to reflect on the conversation thus far while the executives listened to them, in a kind of fish bowl, where they could not interrupt until the advisor let them. After a half hour, he opened discussion up to everyone and found that both sides could see things very differently than before.

A rather basic design feature of the entire program, cited by several managers, that opened people up to different viewpoints was dialogue. As one woman noted, "They didn't leave you just to listen and forget." Discussion led to sharing opinions, which helped her learn more than any of the resource persons. Supplementary activities outside the project also foster divergent thinking, such as trips in or outside Sweden. In another example, a facilitator had managers interview people with different lifestyles and then dramatize what they had learned for those just interviewed. Staff also draw on artists, either by asking them to talk about their view of leadership or by involving managers in a creative activity around the topic of leadership. For example, one staff member brought in a puppeteer dressed in blue jeans. Managers did not warm up to the puppeteer until he "played a scene about a management leader." Managers were invited "to write a scene about management problems" that they could play themselves or have the puppeteer do. Most chose to enact it themselves.

Conflict and cooperation

One would assume from Hofstede's theory that, in Sweden, consensus is valued and conflict rejected. It is interesting to note, then, that the theme of conflict and cooperation in groups holds great interest to managers and is usually the title given to the personal development week. To use a term introduced by Argyris and Schön (1974, 1978), the notion of conflict may be somewhat "undiscussible" because it is not supposed to exist. At the same time, it is hardly feasible for consensus to occur without some divergent viewpoints, many of which might be suppressed. Many managers played down the role of conflict in their groups even though they valued the points of view of people from different disciplines or backgrounds. As one manager put it, for example, he felt his group "didn't have any tension." Other managers also talked about the way in which their groups brought out differences without conflict. For example, one manager noted that the group member with least seniority disagreed one time and "went home and thought very much and came back and said, well you are wrong, and we said OK."

Humor was used to diffuse potential tensions, perhaps when other avenues were not available. This might especially hold true for managers in internal programs where they had permanent relationships with other team members. One manager, for example, commented, "We made jokes about it, how engineers worked and administrators and so on. No one was offended really." In another internal program, building "bridges between the cultures" of a shipping company was a targeted outcome of the program, and an apparent success. A manager in personnel, who also went through a MiL program, noted that before the program, "I heard words like, 'marketing people – well, they're some kind of Gypsies'.... Engineering people said that. And marketing people said about the engineering people, 'only tools, tools, that's everything in their head, tools.'" But after the programs, engineers agreed that marketers were "not just Gypsies, they're really doing something to get people on board ships."

Several managers pointed out that they did learn to handle conflict more effectively. One manager, for example, previously regarded conflict as "a negative thing." Both in his work and family relationships, "I think before I rushed more into the conflicts which then often became destructive. Now I often think of my relationship to people in the company and in my private life too." He linked the management of conflict with being open, listening more than before, and teamwork. He said he learned this in the project, and also through feedback from others during the personal development week.

One's own theory of management as style

A central stated purpose for MiL's programs is developing one's own theory of management. Many interviewees had difficulty in describing these theories. One manager's comment was typical: "I am not very conscious about the differences in acting now than before, but when I think about it, I know I do things differently." There may be a connection here with the "tacit" nature of informal learning discussed in Chapter One of this book, that is, that lessons are often absorbed without thinking much about them. However, one purpose of action learning is to help people make this tacit learning more explicit so managers can examine it for potential error and improve on the way in which they act. One manager indicated, in support of this hypothesis, that he "now knows in a practical way" some of the theories of which he had only been aware conceptually prior to the program. For others, a common reflection was that the program did not radically change the way in which they managed, but it made them "more aware of how I do those things than I used to do before" and gave them confidence and courage to act as they believe.

Managers also learned new lessons, even if it was difficult to describe them. Lessons learned fell into the following categories: (1) understanding oneself as a person and manager; (2) working more effectively as a team leader and building better relationships; (3) enhancing generic skills, in particular, thinking strategically, working systematically, listening, observing, and interviewing.

Self-understanding

Interviewees made it clear that understanding oneself played a key role in their management theories. Unlike many programs in the United States and Sweden that focus primarily on "objective knowledge and skills," the MiL program is based on personal development. MiL staff believe that people who are in touch with themselves make the best managers because they can respond to ambiguous, unclear situations from "their gut," a "gut" that has been tempered by a strategic, systematic approach in which thinking is tested incrementally and experimentally through action. For one manager, for example, a personal theory of management centers around being "a whole human being. You have to find some sympathetic balance between work, job, family and friends. I think that's my principle for being a good manager."

In the MiL program, feedback was the most essential ingredient for personal and professional development. Feedback was mentioned as the hallmark of both the personal development week and the project work. In projects, thinking and acting were subjected to feedback from the group. Self-acceptance resulted from the self-analysis and feedback from others. Many managers used the jargon of popular psychology, "I'm OK and you're OK," which may reflect a concern, discussed earlier, that everyone be accepted without undue conflict in a consensus-oriented society. One woman described the way in which feedback and validation led to acceptance: "you can observe things and [see that] yes I am like that, that's good and that's bad. In that way to learn more because it is more visible to me." On the other hand, feedback was not oriented simply to doing what comes naturally, if that is not good leadership. There seems to be a balance between knowing and accepting who one is, while pushing oneself to challenge comfortable ways of being that are counter-productive. One manager, for example, described valuable feedback from the Program Director who talked about the need for leaders to balance a "social" orientation with the need to "tell people the absolute truth and give 100% of yourself in an opinion" rather than equivocating. This advice might have influenced the manager's own theory of management, which seemed to strike a balance between being open, listening, providing people with opportunities to take responsibility while at the same time not allowing "anarchy" to reign.

Leadership, team work, and relationships

Project work in the MiL program emphasizes team work and shared decision making. It is not surprising, then, that a number of managers learned to work more in this way when back on the job. One manager, for example, said that his "view turned more from a management specialist toward a leadership model [where you develop] goals together with the involved parties and see to it they are motivated enough to go along with your plans. It's more like a team leader really working on the personal motivation of every individual – that is the key to success." Another manager gave some examples of things he handled differently by trying "to get it done by other people" instead of just acting on his own "very strong feeling for what I believe is right and wrong." In one situation, where his company was establishing a new market for a product in another country, for example, he got "the cost analysis ... done by the one who's going to have to deal with this business later on." Before the program, he felt he "would have demanded to have the cost analysis detailed and on my desk, and then I would have phoned down and told him that this is the price you are going to pay." Another example is a product planning department which he has set up as a leaderless team: "And they're all working together, they are helping each other." That would have been "impossible two years ago."

A component of team work that was strongly reinforced was the development and enhancement of relationships. For example, a sea captain who moved into a managerial position said, "I have been working in the company for 14 years and some of the people in the group I haven't *met* before and in that way it's easier for me now when I'm working in the house because I know a lot more people." He felt that relationships were key to his effectiveness in his new job as project manager: "in the beginning I spent at least 50% of my time because I have to go very slowly forward with the organization because they didn't know what [kind of person] I was, and everybody was a little bit afraid." When asked how he dealt with people, he said, "I just talked to people, not pushing them, not trying to get things from them before I saw that they were ready." A personnel manager in the same company also hosted a project in one internal program. He became very close to the team helping him, with whom he felt he "made friends." He was struck that people with very different kinds of work experience looked at his problem and "very soon took it as *theirs*."

Generic skills

Managers learned a variety of skills that are generic to leadership and management. Several managers indicated that one of their key learnings was that there *are* generic management skills. One manager, for example, said that, no matter how many people a manager supervised, he or she had the same job as a leader. No matter what the context, he learned "we had the same problems. I wasn't unique." Most frequently mentioned were thinking strategically, working systematically, listening, observing, and interviewing, all of which were direct outcomes of the way in which teams went about their project work.

Thinking strategically involved visioning and goal-setting, tapping into the ideas of others, seeing the company as a system of interacting parts in which the decisions made by one affected many others, understanding factors that affect a company's plans and strategies, strategic planning for the future, and using one's time more strategically. A woman described how she learned to think strategically: "Every time we met we were going out to interview people; we always met a few hours before and exactly analyzed what are we going to get out of this visit." She described how differently she now handles things: "If you want to have something done in your way, you have to analyze [it] in another way ... [that is closer to the point of view of the] person you are going to change." Several managers linked thinking strategically to the development of a systematic approach, encouraged in problem formulation and problem testing in the projects.

Skills in listening, observing, and interviewing were learned or polished by many managers in the program. The learning strategies contributing most to these understandings included the project work itself, because of the differences within the groups and the way these were managed to contribute to a better product; the cross-cultural seminar; and the personal development week. A manager who was a lawyer by training, for example, emphasized how well he learned to listen to others, which is interesting in that another manager who worked in the same project noted he had learned questioning and interviewing skills from this lawyer. In the past, while this man may have listened, he noted he "decided my opinion earlier before and tried to make others have the same opinion as I had."

One manager indicated he is "more observant [of] how people behave and the organization works." A second talked about discrepancies he was able to observe in his project between what the President of the project company said he believed and what he did. For example, he talked about open communications and participatory decision making but seemed to enjoy his own position of power and amenities. Another manager said listening and observing body language were key lessons learned, particularly through the cross-cultural team building sessions. Observation tied in to the way in which managers said they learned from advisors and other staff, through role modeling. One woman felt she learned most about leadership by watching it in action, by observing people model it in the program: "it is knowledge, of course, but also personality and all that; and that you cannot learn from one person; you can learn it from a group of persons by [their] being there [and] showing that. They can't tell you."

Implications for informal learning

What can we conclude from the above discussion about informal learning for managers? This section is divided into two parts: lessons about how managers learn from experience and a discussion of the characteristics of informal learning.

How managers learn from experience in MiL

The findings from this research reflect on a small scale, with several exceptions, the findings of a wider-scale study done by the Center for

Creative Leadership (McCall, Jr. *et al.*, 1988). This study focused on learning through job assignments, through relationships with other people, and through hardships. The study looked at a wide range of job assignments, cited by their study population as critical to their development: early work experiences, the first supervisory job, developmental projects, line-to-staff switches, and leading on line. By contrast, the MiL experiences fell primarily in the category of developmental projects, with the additional difference that these projects were deliberately set up for learning and often not within the same company in which the manager worked. Managers also experienced the frustration of line-to-staff switches because their primary role in these projects was as consultants to other managers, not as the decision makers themselves. They thus had to build an entirely different repertoire of skills in supporting the learning of others. The Creative Leadership study focused on relationships with bosses, because these were the primary relationships cited as significant, whereas relationships in the MiL projects were primarily with peers in project teams or with a wide range of staff at all levels within host organizations. Finally, this study did not include information on hardships, which included personal trauma, career setbacks, job changes, and business mistakes.

The Creative Leadership study drew on managers who learned on their own, whereas the MiL study was a program that provides a forum in which managers can draw out these lessons. The MiL program thus counteracts one of the key weaknesses of learning from experience pointed out by the Creative Leadership study:

> Caught up in the action, immersed in the demands and challenges, the manager may have no time for reflection. It is easy to presume that if everything comes out all right it was because of what you did (and that all you did was correct). It is in the fast-action, high-pressure situations that people are most prone to rely on their already "proven" skills and approaches and put most of their energy into the demands and problems they have seen before. Thus, pulling off a tough assignment may "teach" the manager that he or she can, after all, manage anything.
>
> [McCall, Jr. *et al.*, 1988, p. 133]

Managers thus can rely on preconceived conceptual frameworks that may be erroneous but never examined, or accurate but inappropriate for a new situation. Managers are also rewarded for action by their companies, an incentive that leads them to tackle a problem as they see it without even questioning whether or not it is the right problem. The MiL study suggests that managers learn best from experience when they are able to think through these impulses with a small group of critical thinkers who bring different perspectives to the problem.

How can one describe the learning that takes place in the MiL program? Reflection is key to this learning, but it must be combined with action, else it becomes speculative. Through action, managers test out insights, but they also invite public examination of the premises on which they have formulated their perception of the problem, which leads to dialogue among themselves and the stakeholders of the problem. Action and reflection are not separate phases although, at times, managers may be doing more of one or the other. Action and reflection take place simultaneously or concurrently and, as such, are more like the parallel tracks along which a train rides. Managers do not learn without both tracks in place. Facilitators establish a climate of trust, guide the project's management (e.g., logistics, scheduling, liaison), help analyze group dynamics, and advise on the process as well as, at times, the problem. However, their most important role is as creator of new ways of seeing things. They do this by asking questions, drawing contrasts, trying out experiments, creating surprises, using "play" and humor, suggesting alternatives, using unfamiliar modes of thinking borrowed from the arts or other disciplines, taking people on journeys (literally and figuratively), challenging and then "holding up a mirror" for people to examine their behavior. The facilitator is the proverbial Socratic gadfly who is always one step ahead of the group. This involves a depth of knowledge about organizations and people, fresh insight, courage of convictions, and a willingness to challenge norms, be "naughty," and ask "dumb" questions. It involves modeling one's own personal theory of management without imposing it on others, so that learners can develop and act on *their* own theories.

Both managers and staff indicated that it takes time to learn from experience. In the first part of the program, managers are frustrated, disappointed, and sometimes angered by the ambiguity of what takes place. They are used to creating order from chaos, to efficiency, and to clear instructions, and are faced in MiL programs with what seems often to be anarchy. Somewhere in the program, usually about halfway through and often during the personal development week, managers begin to understand the reasoning behind their experiences. As one manager described it, "before that it was very hard to find out what it was all about because we couldn't put the pieces together and get something, all those loose pieces everywhere, but after that we saw a system in the whole program." Managers said they were ready to quit the program, to write an angry letter to MiL's president, or otherwise rebel before reaching this turning point. It is not clear what minimum amount of time is needed to maximize learning from experience. It is clear that many managers do not understand the value of this time framework until they have been through a program.

This reflective process fits with Schön's (1983, 1987) emphasis on finding the right problem, discussed below.

Schön's cycle of problem reformulation

Schön describes an iterative process that moves through assessment of the situation, testing of one's preliminary sense of the problem through experiments, examination of results, and reassessment leading to another cycle of reformulation until the best "fit" is achieved between one's definition of the situation and the perceptions of other stakeholders *vis-à-vis* the problem.

Schön suggests that the ladder of inference, discussed in Chapter One, can be used to build a ladder of reflection in learning, particularly when one person coaches another, a learning situation that is common between a project advisor and participants. In the ladder of reflection, the lower rung represents the directly observable data of a learning episode. People learn from a coach by listening to feedback on their actions, and watching the coach model an alternative approach. Sometimes communication appears to be clear among all parties; gaps in understanding are not examined unless a signal arises that indicates a misperception. Many signals are hard to read because people become adept at hiding their real thoughts and feelings and at controlling the situation to get the results they want. When people believe that learning is being sacrificed for these or other reasons, and are committed to full and informed dialogue, Schön suggests that the coach and learner return to an examination of the directly observable data.

Typically, the coach is in a better position to suggest this because he or she is often perceived as the leader or person in authority. In consonance with other components of action science theory, the people involved look at both what they think is taking place as well as the thoughts or feelings they hold private in the situation. These hidden reflections often are a key to misperceptions, discrepancies, perceived double binds and paradoxes that prevent both learning and action. Some of these private thoughts and feelings are based on internalized norms from the past about what a person thinks he or she should be or do in their interactions. Others are based on perceptions and expectations, that are usually untested, about what the other person thinks, means or intends by their actions.

Project advisors may not be aware of Schön's approach, nor do they uniformly follow these steps in helping managers learn from experience. It does seem, however, that the heart of their practice is an effort to look at the directly observable data of a situation from as many viewpoints as possible with a view to asking questions about what may not be directly apparent. Results depend on the artistry of the advisor, however, and may not be made explicit and further examined by the managers to see what they could learn from the technique itself.

Schön's approach seems particularly applicable to management development. The next and final section looks at the more general characteristics of informal learning in this program.

Characteristics of informal learning

The learning that takes place in MiL's programs is experience-based, centered around non-routine situations that have been highlighted as problematic, intentional but with likely incidental spin-offs, and both tacit and explicit. Learning is delimited by the nature of the program, in that the project itself is but a slice of life that is used as a kind of mini-laboratory for learning; and it is enhanced by the effort to foster critical reflection, creativity, and proactivity. In addition, while learning takes place primarily at the individual level, it is enhanced through the development of relationships within the programs, and when it is embraced by a company as a strategy to support change, it can also foster organizational learning. The experience-based nature of this learning has been described above, leaving the remaining characteristics for discussion in this concluding section.

The very nature of the projects makes them non-routine. When learning informally outside of a program, by contrast, a person would first have to experience surprise when a procedure does not produce its usual results. Informal learning thus demands that a person pay attention to the results of actions, and that he or she use judgment to compare these results mentally to a schema or model of what is expected based on past results. When it is clear that a situation does not fall within that schema, the learner realizes that he or she cannot rely on prescriptions from the past, or Revans's "P" knowledge.

Because the MiL program is designed, it could be said that people learn from their experience intentionally. However, staff can only control the placement of project experience at the core of the program and the arrangement of project teams. Managers are also intentional in their learning in that they agree to participate in a series of activities. In learning from experience, however, much is left to chance. No one can predict how people will respond to the initiatives of the project team, nor is it clear in advance what managers will learn from one another in this process. No doubt some incidental learning also takes place which may have little to do with the interests of MiL or the company sponsoring the manager.

As reported, managers learn much that remains tacit. Several people suggested that MiL staff could do a better job in helping managers spell out more clearly their own beliefs about leadership. Often, segments of the program are set aside for this purpose. However, since the program is designed around experience, it would be more effective if advisors helped managers put their theories into words as they discovered them, and then used the resources of the group to examine and test these theories. Every manager is given a blank book at the beginning of the program entitled "Management" to develop the habit of writing these ideas down. Little is done, however, to draw this learning more explicitly into the seminars.

Informal learning is delimited in this context by the artificial boundaries separating the project experience from real life. While managers come to see these problems as their own, the projects are defined as learning activities, not something for which a manager will be held accountable within his or her own organization. Hence, some of the risk is eliminated. Moreover, it is ideal to learn in a team, with time out for reflection and a coach to help the group understand its experience. Managers seldom have this luxury in the "real world."

Finally, informal learning in the MiL program is enhanced by three actively encouraged characteristics: critical reflection, creativity, and proactivity. Critical reflection is necessary in MiL programs because problems do not get reformulated without this kind of deep questioning. MiL programs also provide a forum for creativity. The arts are often drawn upon as an alternative world view. Many of the activities in MiL bring managers in touch with a creative side they did not know they had. Most importantly, staff show managers they can approach "serious" subjects in a creative manner. Finally, MiL programs also require that managers approach their learning proactively. It is not easy for a manager to remain passive in a program; the active experimentation and enthusiasm of colleagues stimulates a proactive learning stance.

Notes

1.   Research Notes for chapters 3–8 are located at the back of this book. The research on which this chapter is based was conducted in 1987 and 1988 with financial assistance from the Kellogg Foundation and from the Management Institute, Lund (Sweden). Thanks go to Lennart Rohlin, President of MiL, and his staff, especially Camilla Sternberg who helped conduct and transcribe interviews.

Chapter four

How community educators learn: Nepal and the Philippines

This chapter describes the way in which paraprofessional educational workers in Nepal and the Philippines learn about informal learning in order to become change agents who then help communities learn informally about health, family planning, and similar concerns.[1] These programs shed light on informal learning in several ways.

In programs such as these, communities of people are encouraged to change habits, practices, and beliefs that have prevailed for centuries. Adults in the developing world are often illiterate. While children receive more education than their parents, many of them are forced to drop out to help support their families before they have completed primary school. Poverty ensures that schools are often ill-equipped and teachers minimally trained. Many countries have adopted nonformal education programs, described in Chapter One, as an alternate route to a basic education or as a means to promote "development" considered beneficial to the community. This combination of formal and nonformal education is never enough to reach the widely dispersed, underserved populations considered most in need of development services. Informal learning thus plays a key role because it is expected that people will learn and change more easily by observing and following the lead of influential people who adopt new practices.

The programs discussed in this chapter illustrate the need for reflection and critical reflection on assumptions and norms in informal learning that is linked to development. People at all levels – from the policy level on down through the workers to the clients themselves – must change the way they think and work for change to occur.

In one way, these case studies are removed from the workplace. They take place in areas of the world remote from the United States and deal with development. However, they are also about people in organizations, primarily in the public sector, whose standards have to be met in job performance. Because the people work at the periphery in "selling" health services to a clientele highly resistant to change, these workers share some of the challenges faced by organizations with a service orientation whose front-line workers, many of whom are not highly paid, none the less represent "the organization" to the public. Finally, the turbulence in the environments in which these organizations function is not unlike the turbulence faced by today's organizations in some respects (Marsick, 1987a, 1988d). Whether at home or abroad, in the public or private sector, these organizations must invent, almost overnight, non-routine responses to newly perceived problems. Little can be taken for granted, and solutions involve the response of an entire system to change.

This chapter concerns learning at many levels, but the emphasis in this chapter is on group learning because the focus is on how communities learn to adopt change. In the Western world, it is assumed that individuals have autonomy in learning and decision making. In Nepal and the Philippines, change of the nature and scale addressed in these programs is more of a group and community affair, in part because people's lives are intricately bound together. Individuals make choices based on strong, influential social norms and community rules; their choices often have communal consequences.

Informal learning: workers and clients

Before describing the informal learning of these educational workers, a word is needed about their background and experience, as well as the learning task facing them and their clients. The Nepal and Philippines examples are typical of many programs of planned change. Educational workers interact directly with clients. These workers are not highly trained professionals, but are selected because of their above-average education, experience, and background, when compared to their clients. The job of these workers is primarily educational. They serve as links between clients, who typically reside in rural villages or urban slums, and other service professionals. They also provide some basic services and refer more complicated problems to higher levels. Prior to being recruited, many of these workers are unfamiliar with the changes being advocated, with informal learning, with the communities in which they work, and with the requirements of the new organizations to which they are affiliated. They themselves must learn informally much of what they are to teach to others. The heart of their task is informal learning. They establish and maintain dialogue with people in order to introduce planned change. This dialogue typically takes place in people's homes, community centers and gatherings, or in the fields where people work. These workers, then, had to learn about informal learn-

Table 4.1 Learning needs of educational workers and clients

For Client to Learn	For Worker to Learn
1. Recognize and define situation as needing change	1. Develop trust relationship and see through eyes of clients
2. Decide change is possible, providing options are there	2. Raise awareness of ability to act
3. Decide he or she wants to change	3. Analyze situation with clients and help them see it as intolerable or the alternative as desirable

If Program is Directive	
4a. See solution offered as desirable	4a. Persuade client to accept program's definition of solution and legitimate this choice

If Program is Nondirective	
4b. See what alternatives exist, help analyze them and choose from among them	4b. Explore variety of solutions, facilitate and legitimate client choice
5. Plan action	5. Help client plan
6. Acquire information and skills to implement change	6. Provide information, help client gain access to needed resources
7. Try out plan	7. Support client in implementing plan and working through fears
8. Assess impact	8. Help client identify and analyze advantages and disadvantages
9. Make change a habit and change lifestyle to support it	9. Develop linkages within community and to outside resources

ing. They did so, at least in part, through training that emphasized their own informal learning since trainers decided that field workers could not do something well that they themselves had not experienced.

Programs such as those discussed in this chapter attempt, at some level, to empower workers and clients to "let go" of dependence on others, of fatalism, of unquestioning reliance on the way things have traditionally taken place, and to "take over" in deciding what they want in life and how they are going to get it. As discussed in Chapter One, empowerment enables people to be proactive in learning and change. However, all workers do not consciously espouse the values of empowerment. Many live in fatalistic, traditional communities. With limited resources and opportunities, they have little experience in deciding what they want in life and pursuing these goals.

Table 4.1 illustrates the complexity of the learning task: what clients had to learn to do, and what workers had to learn to help clients. Ideally, dialogue for change is nondirective; clients make free choices based on analysis of their alternatives. However, both workers and clients alike often come from traditional societies where choices are dictated by custom or a ruling authority. The official message of a program based on free choice, then, may be contradicted by incidental learning about what is actually desired, that is, that people should adopt the promoted new behavior, regardless of their beliefs.

Nepal

Nepal is a small, landlocked country situated between India and China. It is a country of great beauty, but little modern industry, illiteracy, high mortality and morbidity, and an over-reliance on agriculture despite the fact that only 15% of its land is cultivatable. Nepal's high rate of population growth has prompted, in part, the deforestation of its countryside as people seek wood as fuel, thus contributing to the floods that have ravaged other countries in the region.

Many of the Health Aides were not familiar with villagers and village life since they were young males recruited from towns and urban centers.[2] Cultural barriers and low literacy levels made it impossible to hire women and members of many minority groups despite the fact that Health Aides served women and cultural minorities. Each village-based Health Aide covered approximately 2000 people living in several villages within five hours walking distance in a unit of local government called a *panchayat*.[3]

Bringing informal learning into the training design

As illustrated in Figure 4.1, the heart of their efforts was dialogue, most of which took place informally in people's homes. Since many of the Health Aides had not experienced this kind of dialogue, the training was designed to simulate real-life conditions by making the village the site for learning. Workers learned to see what health meant to villagers, through the eyes of their clients, by living in villages periodically throughout the training. They went back and forth between villages and the classroom as they experienced a phase of the work that was expected of them, and then stepped back and analyzed

Phase I: *Introductory Stage (1/2 day)*
Trainees meet one another and trainers, and begin to interact.

Phase II: *Course Introduction (2 days)*
Trainees are introduced to course content and methodology, and to the job description of *Panchayat*-Based Health Aides.

Phase III: *Introduction to Village Life (5 days)*
Trainees are briefed for overnight visit in which they will map the village's social and natural geography and meet with host families. Following the visit they prepare and analyze reports.

Phase IV: *Intensive Village Experience (8–9 days)*
Trainees are prepared for a three-day visit with host families in which they identify socio-cultural leadership and village life patterns and perceptions of health. Emphasis is placed on participant observation, methods of gathering information, and the dynamics of change.

Phase V: *Village Health Analysis (10 days)*
Trainees spend 5–7 days in the village conducting a study in one self-selected health area. In the post-visit analysis, trainers emphasize a broad definition of village needs and opportunities for change.

Phase VI: *Health Knowledge and Skills (10 – 12 days)*
Trainers help trainees delve more deeply into health knowledge and skills. They further develop skills in problem solving, communication, analysis, report writing, and record keeping.

Phase VII: *Village Education Practice (8 days)*
Trainees apply knowledge in family planning and one other self- selected area for 4–5 days. In the post-analysis, trainers emphasize overall understanding of entire behavioral change process.

Phase VIII: *Final Review and Examination (1–2 days)*

Figure 4.1 Nepal training model

their experience, using the resources of skilled facilitators and peers in order to develop a conceptual framework for understanding, action, and the building of new knowledge and skills to carry out these tasks better. Figure 4.2, extracted from Carlaw (1978), describes the original training design, which was modified subsequently as the program was piloted and revised. It called for an intensive period of training for master trainers who would then fan out and train field workers through decentralized regional training centers. The strategy emphasized empowerment of trainees increasingly to direct their own learning since, once on the job, they would be working in isolated places.

The workers had to solve problems for which there seldom was a right answer. Moreover, yesterday's answer might not work for today's problem, even though many of the conditions seemed the same. Learning activities were thus designed to wean trainees away from dependence on trainers or other experts, except as resource persons.

The Nepal training design was developed by consultants Raymond Carlaw and Jack Nelson. Carlaw (1970) based the model on an "interaction approach" which he developed in his own practice that:

> emphasizes that the subjective perception of the situation forms the active influence not only on learning but also on subsequent behavior relative to the tasks discussed. Facts become important to the trainee only as they are experienced or discerned as having meaning and application within the world of the trainee. Information presented outside of the matrix of subjective meaning or emotional experience has little reality and, unless reinforced externally, may soon be forgotten.
>
> [Carlaw, 1970, p. 754]

Carlaw based his thinking on George Herbert Mead and John Dewey, early thinkers on experience-based learning discussed in Chapter One.

Carlaw also drew on the laboratory method developed by National Training Laboratories (NTL) or T-Groups (Sensitivity Training Groups). T-Groups foster equality between the learner and facilitator. Facilitators increase awareness of reactions, personal values, feelings, and behaviors and then help people determine whether or not they want to modify them. Carlaw drew heavily on the nondirective style of T-group facilitators in designing training and used several sensitivity exercises. However, he had to modify this approach because of the Nepalese culture which was much more closed, status-conscious, and oriented to a model of education that prized knowledge transmission from people who were deemed experts.

Challenging Norms

Carlaw's model was designed around experience and reflection in a group. The aim was to understand oneself better as a change agent and to examine resistance to the adoption of new practices. Possibly the most significant dimension of informal learning was the way in which workers learned to challenge norms and the culture that interfered with success on the job. At the time of this study, Nepalese relationships were influenced by social position as determined by family, caste and subculture. People came from ten major ethnic groups and many more minor ones. Subcultural barriers were often intensified by caste lines within Hindu groups which comprised 90% of the population. At least 13 local languages were spoken. A few families traditionally held economic, social and political power over a large majority unused to questioning the élites. This was reinforced by the political system, limited facilities for education and communications, as well as an extended family system that kept decision making in the hands of a few elders and kept women in domestic roles except in a few tribal groups.

The foreign consultants to this project were introducing a system, for both the job itself and the training design, that diametrically opposed many existing socio-cultural norms. People often sought government jobs, for security, status, and comfort. People did not seek out jobs in rural areas like this one where one had to travel long distances by foot to try to persuade people to adopt practices that were in conflict with traditional beliefs about health and family size. Western medicine might be acceptable when accompanied by immunizations and disease-curing drugs, but these workers were to focus on *preventive* health practices, which are by far the harder to encourage, even in sophisticated audiences. Workers were not recognized as professionals, well-supported, or rewarded for hours of dialogue if that dialogue did not result in family planning acceptors.

Social barriers were strong: among workers from different social groups, between men and women despite a bias against female workers, between superiors and subordinates, and between workers and their clients. People from different groups were reluctant to speak openly in front of others, let alone be critical of another's viewpoint, especially that of a superior, because of a need to "save face." Despite this, training was designed to break down barriers and encourage values of democracy, openness, trust, and critique. This was reflected, for example, in a controversial series of ten carefully sequenced sensitivity training exercises designed to help "trainees know each other and know yourself," most of which were subsequently modified or eliminated.

The first step in learning to challenge norms was living in the villages with host families. This anthropological method was relatively new at the time and somewhat controversial. The training designers believed that the health workers had to "see through the eyes of the villager" in order to assess people's perceptions of their present health habits as a basis for change. Health workers might themselves consider villagers "ignorant" because they held these beliefs, founded in traditional medicine or folklore, since the health workers were often more highly educated and receptive to Western medicine. Through this step, trainees became aware of village norms and began to recognize that they themselves held views that were different from, but not necessarily "better" than, those of villagers. This experience, which for many was drastically different from anything in their lives, created empathy, trust, and new friendships. Some interviewees referred to this as the "family approach" because trainees were looked upon as brothers and sisters, sons and daughters. This had a powerful emotional impact for those not comfortable with meeting strangers from other social groups and especially for trainees who originally felt the village living experience to be unnecessary. Trainees were surprised by unexpected insights, as, for example, seeing that "they can't teach about giving eggs and meat for good nutrition if the families are Hindu and this is forbidden by religion."

Health workers learned how to interact with villagers informally by doing this, and by then analyzing their experience. Health Aides also learned from one another through a peer resource network developed during training. Trainees and trainers formed a live-in learning community in a remote area close to the villages. As in some European variations of T-Groups, the smallest detail of everyday life became a subject for discussion, from food preparation to evening entertainment. Trainers role modeled round-the-clock the behaviors and attitudes they expected of trainees. They created a family-like climate where, as one Nepalese trainer put it, "participants can be involved in discussion, in analyzing, in thinking. You must give them the right to make mistakes so they can learn from them. You must help them open their weaknesses, not hide them, so they can change." The physical environment helped set the tone for what one trainee called a "free feeling." Most trainers arranged seating in a circle, often on cushions on the floor. Trainers joined the circle and insisted that trainees not stand in deference to them when they asked questions.

The peer resource network built up in this way included other members of the health team, particularly supervisors and district managers, who were often team-trained with the field workers. Peer learning, engendered in training, was to be maintained through supportive supervision and coaching. The model being developed was not unlike that of a well-functioning decentralized work team, as typified in sales, where the manager coaches his or her field workers on-the-spot as it is relevant. However, in Nepal, supervisors were typically evaluators and judges whose primary role was enforcement, not assistance. Some supervisors caught on to the new strategy; most, however, were not rewarded for this new role or trained in it. Supervisors did not see this supportive role modeled at the top of their hierarchy, even though the consultants guiding this project attempted to change attitudes and behaviors at the top of the hierarchy to support the changes being introduced at the lower levels.

Norm challenging took place through analysis of informal experiences workers had in villages. One major tool for analysis was nondirective discussion – itself a departure from educational norms in which the "teacher" is expected to lecture. Workers learned to ask questions even though they were more comfortable when told what to do. The kinds of questions asked were important because they pushed workers to think more deeply than they normally would, and were not simply a repeat-back of what had been said or read. Trainers reported that they often had to exhort, "motivate," or "anger" trainees into a reaction when asking open-ended questions. It helped to begin in smaller groups, often without a trainer present, to encourage them to first "talk with their friends." Trainees learned to think deeply and critically, which they were not accustomed to in a fatalistic, passive society. They were asked to separate their experiences from individual biases and prejudices based on caste or culture. They compared conclusions with other facts and opinions, critiqued one another, and sought information that would verify or contradict findings.

Just getting workers to think in terms of problem identification was a major breakthrough because of the expectation of many in Nepalese society that one could not do anything to change circumstances. Hence, workers did not even look at the world in terms of things that were not going as planned, since many did not believe they could plan, control, or correct events. As one trainer reported, "Most of the time, the worker will just walk away when they have difficulties." Often, "at first they say they have no problems [while], on probing, all kinds of them come out." The type of problems often listed, when they did "come out," confirmed a sense of passivity since workers often felt they could not change these things.

The Philippines

The Philippines is, geographically and culturally, very different from Nepal. It consists of some 7,100 islands along the south-eastern rim of Asia. It is not isolated, as is Nepal, and it is industrialized and diversified economically, despite a continued reliance on agriculture and forestry. Literacy rates are high, with over 95% attendance at elementary schools. None the less, health problems abound and the press of population on natural resources is high. Politically, despite periods of autocratic rule, the Philippines has encouraged greater participation in government than has Nepal which may, in part, account for an abundance of private, non-profit civic and development groups. One of these groups, the Philippines Rural Reconstruction Movement (PRRM)[4] is the focus of this chapter.

PRRM's workers helped set up Community Education Councils that were to organize educational programs and select volunteer neighborhood workers from *barangays*, units of local government consisting of some 1800 people each. PRRM provided training to both the community leaders and these workers, paraprofessionals called Barangay Technicians. Like the Nepalese Health Aides, the Barangay Technicians were to handle simple problems and refer more complicated situations to professionals in other agencies. Their role was, first and foremost, also educational. By contrast, however, they were selected for the competence they already possessed in the skill area they promoted, they provided services that were requested by the community, and they were already respected by the communities, where they typically resided. Barangay Technicians maintained informal contact with neighbors, demonstrating the skill taught and providing service in areas such as veterinary care or tailoring/dressmaking. They also typically organized nonformal education classes in their skill areas every year.

Bringing informal learning into the training design

PRRM recognized that short-term solutions had not empowered the people with whom it worked. The training designers, primarily Tony Santiago and Connie Madayag, decided that informal learning should be a central feature of a systems approach that considered the long-terms needs of the entire community. Training inputs were alternated with community initiatives. Each input in column one triggered a community response, which then triggered the next PRRM input.

PRRM began an informal consultation workshop called "investment training," organized to help leaders in the community identify problems and decide whether or not to take action. After the workshop, leaders were asked to share their plans with others and decide whether or not they wanted further assistance. If they did, PRRM advised them to form a Community Education Council (CEC) to direct local programs since, without this infrastructure in place, programs were often one-shot efforts. If they did not want to do this, PRRM took no further action. If they formed a CEC, the Council sent several representatives to a workshop held at PRRM for a group from several barangays. These representatives then "echoed" (a locally used term meaning "repeated") this training in their own communities, and selected Barangay Technicians for training based on the criteria they had evolved through the workshop.

Once a sufficient number of Barangay Technicians were selected, PRRM held training in a specific discipline. If PRRM did not have the needed expertise, staff arranged for training with various partner organizations. PRRM used local facilities when available, as, for example, a course held by a local college to certify tailors. Pre-service training, usually held at PRRM, lasted at least ten days and concentrated on the educational skills. Following pre-service training, Barangay Technicians would organize classes and visit families. Technicians would gather for at least three to five days of in-service training every quarter for a period of a year to reflect on their experience and get coaching on how they could do things differently.

Training was thus arranged only in response to specific community initiatives. Villagers lived at PRRM during training and often arranged for some of their own logistics: bringing their own bedding, or fixing some of their own meals even though a central cafeteria was available. But unlike the Nepal model, villagers did not take primary responsibility for making these arrangements. Learning was continued through an indigenous "professional" organization which PRRM helped set up called the Nueva Ecija Barangay Technicians Association (NEBTA). NEBTA established a "professional" identity, held conferences, and developed standards for the selection and training of understudies who would eventually become the next Technicians.

The designers wanted to empower villagers to assume responsibility for their own changes. They did this through learning-by-doing, problem-solving workshops "sandwiched" in between action. The action taken in between sessions might form the basis for the next session and/or be built on decisions taken in a previous session, but it always carried the project a step further. Action was not a simulation, nor was it real-but-not-my-own. Action was a series of on-line realities for which the villagers assumed full responsibility.

PRRM's design was influenced by its own history and philosophy, as well as the thinking of adult education advisors from the United States. PRRM's philosophy was one of local participation toward evolutionary change. A staff member contrasted this to the "expert approach," where experts tell people what to do, or a "social action approach" in which people are prodded into taking political action for change. PRRM also took a common sense "is it do-able" stance in introducing change. Finally, PRRM was influenced by its international partner, World Education, a nonprofit organization that provided technical assistance. One of its consultants, Lyra Srinivasan, worked with PRRM on a project in which they co-developed and tested participatory learning materials.

Srinivasan (1977) developed a self-actualizing method which emphasizes learner-centered generation of ideas, peer interaction, a positive self-concept, and creative imagination. She draws on the work of Rogers (1961, 1965), Maslow (1971), and Bruner (1962). Srinivasan states, "The aim of this strategy is to transform learners from passive recipients of messages from the outside to active communicators and decision-makers" (p. 57). She attempts to free up each person's creative abilities so they can identify and actualize their dreams. In a personal interview she described the self-actualizing method as "strengthening the cloth," not just "mending weak cloth with strong thread."

The PRRM model, like the Nepal model, did help villagers challenge norms because its ultimate goal was to help villagers "own their own programs." As in many countries, villagers had been socialized into passivity by years of tradition which discouraged departure from the norm, by religion which encouraged dependence on the will of God, and by élites who had a vested interest in the status quo. PRRM wanted to turn this around by helping villagers realize they could change their lives, drawing on resources already available to them, and could change the way in which they thought and acted.

Creating an ongoing conversation

In terms of informal learning, however, challenging norms was less striking to the observer than the essentially "conversational" nature of the PRRM approach. Trainers challenged learners but they did so within a framework of ongoing hospitality and friendly conversation.

Staff at PRRM based their approach on the natural proclivity of villagers to gather and discuss concerns informally. The founders of several programs in Asia used the interest of villagers in discussion outside the classroom to launch nonformal education. For example, Dr. Kowit, the founder of a Thai functional literacy program, used discussion methods to create "khit-phen" men (translated literally as "to think – to be"), a Buddhist-inspired concept (Vorapipatana, 1975). Dr. Kowit did not judge success in terms of numbers of people who blindly adopted practices advocated by his program, but in terms of the capacity of people to think through a situation and make a reasoned decision as to what was best for them, even if that meant they did not accept the advice of the Government. The Bangladesh Women's Rehabilitation and Welfare Foundation designed a vocational training project on "the gossip approach", that is, the interest of women in discussing matters of concern to them, be that community affairs or the learning of vocational skills from people identified as specialists to whom they were apprenticed.

Discussion is different outside the classroom from in it, even when that classroom is a nonformal education classroom. The educator is often perceived as an authority figure because of his/her control and expertise, be it in subject matter or the learning process or some combination thereof, whether that person is formal or informal in style, or identified as expert or facilitator. Outside the classroom, individuals talk to fewer persons at a time and are not being watched by other peers or authority figures. People typically have more control over some factors that affect discussion in informal learning. They can choose the persons with whom they talk or, if they do not, they can choose the degree to which they are open in their conversation. They are not on stage, and thus may be more willing to expose their vulnerabilities, mistakes and deficiencies, especially if the person with whom they are speaking is considered trustworthy. For the same reasons, they might be more willing to try out new thinking or behavior and are more likely to get useful feedback not considered harmful to their self-esteem.

Staff designed workshops to be as informal as they could. Sessions were often held in circles, around tables, or under the trees. When villagers seemed inhibited by their presence, staff might find a reason to leave the room for a while to allow more freedom of conversation. However, staff also decided that there were times when they would have to be more directive if they were to change the way people thought about themselves and the change process. PRRM's Training Director called this "pump priming," that is, feeding ideas to villagers to prime the pump which was rusty from disuse. This metaphor suggests that villagers were not used to thinking independently. Trainers increasingly weaned Community Education Council members and Barangay Technicians away from dependence on them, forcing trainees to analyze problems and alternative solutions for themselves, and building their confidence in their own ability – as they expected them to do with the villagers with whom they worked. Barangay Technicians were encouraged to go to Council members for help when they had problems. When Council members turned to staff for answers, staff handed the decision back to them. It was not always easy for staff to divest themselves of the authority that Councils wanted to give them because, as one staff member put it, they also grew up "waiting to be told what to do."

This balance between dependence and independence as an ideal shifted in reality according to the beliefs and skills of the trainer, who at some point had to "let go" of his/her control, a concept diametrically opposed to traditional expectations of teachers and learners in the Philippines. Staff realized that, instead of just teaching other people what "they *should* be, we try to learn from them." Srinivasan (1977) reinforced this change in beliefs through what she identified as "a 'taking over' principle": "By this is meant that each level of staff, traditionally viewed as representing authority and expertise, divested themselves of their authority role and encouraged the learners assigned to them to 'take over'" (p. 58).

As in Nepal, trainers created an environment where status differences were reduced, where interaction among staff and trainers was free, and where learners could "express their feelings without fears" and be "accepted as adults," in the words of the Training Director. PRRM, however, had the advantage of an ongoing relationship with villagers over time, a relationship that was recreated between the Community Education Councils and Barangay Technicians and between Barangay Technicians and other villagers. The trust relationship was already established. Since the program was requested by the community and its pay off was immediately apparent, field workers did not anticipate the same kind of resistance from the villagers as did the Nepalese Health Aides. The Filipino workers were not being prepared for as difficult a task and, thus, could relax more and enjoy the process.

The Filipino people love to have fun. Training at PRRM was also fun. Unlike Nepal, participants came from the same communities. Both programs incorporated singing, dance, and other social activities, but people in the Philippines did not encounter as many social barriers and were willing to enter into a spirit of play while learning. Thus, sessions might begin with games similar to those played at parties, such as recalling names of others in the group, singing, or doing stunts. If training lasted more than a few days, trainees also put together a social evening, both for its entertainment value and as a means of encouraging cooperation. Games were also used as training exercises. For example, in the matching game, people lined up in two columns. One side thought of a problem his or her partner might have; the other of a possible solution for a problem. Problems were then listed on the board or newsprint, and learners analyzed them to get to the root of the problem. This game had the additional advantage of illustrating how differently people perceived the same situation. It also led into creative thinking exercises and brainstorming, which PRRM staff called "thinking wild," an important new skill for people not used to options. Games, however, were not used without making sure that learners saw their relevance to a specific topic or else they were confused with children's games and considered inappropriate. Srinivasan (1977, p. 62) points out, when talking of games and exercises, that "it is extremely important to design the sequence of exercises in such a way that the connection between the two becomes clear to the trainees themselves as they go through a series of experiences."

Because of Srinivasan's influence, PRRM staff experimented with the use of materials designed to minimize the central role of the trainer and maximize the importance of starting with the learner's experience. These included serialized posters, flexiflans (flannelgraph figures with movable parts, designed by Srinivasan), and problem dramas. In the first, a set of pictures was designed by the staff to reflect situations that villagers would recognize. The villagers were then asked to tell stories about their lives using these posters in whichever sequence they wished. Only when staff experienced the method could they see how enjoyable it was to tell stories, many of which were quite different from the version originally envisioned by the trainer. In this way, staff learned to give up their proprietary rights to the flow of conversation in the classroom. Flexiflans went one step further toward putting control into the hands of the learners. The flexiflans provide "simple 'props' which the learners can use in any way they wish to come up with any experience, incident, idea, story problem or aspiration they wish to share with the group" (ibid., p. 66). Through the third method, problem dramas, pre-recorded stories were played that described a typical dramatic situation villagers face. Care was taken not to embarrass anyone in the group, nor share a personal story that might be recognized by others. In addition to these three approaches, staff reported they also had trainees create real-life dramas to illustrate their viewpoints. One staff member said that these methods "usually take longer, but people usually get more out of it" because they have a chance to tell their stories about meaningful life situations.

In drawing on life experience, staff crossed the line between the impersonal and the personal, a line which was not strictly drawn anyway because staff and villagers usually knew one another through their interaction in other situations. However, in crossing this line, staff had to be careful not to cause someone to "lose face." A number of the games, discussions and activities were aimed at new insights into oneself and the way in which a person interacted with others. However, if these insights were discussed too openly or individuals challenged too directly, the effect could be potentially damaging. One staffer contrasted PRRM's approach to the NTL-type of sensitivity training described above. At PRRM, staff helped individuals arrive at self-insights indirectly, often by themselves, without overt group criticism. Staff felt this was particularly important because many villagers already suffered from a perception of themselves as inadequate.

Implications for informal learning

This final section is a look at the nature of informal learning in programs of planned change, in light of Jarvis's model (1987) discussed in Chapter One; a summary of how informal learning was incorporated into training programs; and an exploration of the tacit nature of informal learning illustrated in these programs.

The nature of informal learning in programs of planned change

As Jarvis (1987) points out, people do not always learn when they interact with others. Learning takes place when there is a disjuncture between one's biography and either a felt need or an idealized "want." At times people are too caught up in the habitual way in which they have viewed their worlds, and thus cannot see or act upon these disjunctures. Jarvis develops a hierarchy of nine learning responses to a social situation, and then describes what this learning would look like if the social situation were informal, nonformal or formal. The first three levels represent non-learning (presumption, non-consideration, and rejection); the second three are non-reflective learning (pre-conscious learning, practice, and memorization); and the final three are what he believes to be a higher form of reflective learning (contemplation, reflective practice, and experimental learning).

This section looks at informal learning in the Nepal and Philippines programs in light of these three levels. Informal social interaction did not always result in learning in these communities, perhaps because rural people are often socialized into rather rigid roles and beliefs. However, the programs did seem to move some people from non-learning to a mix of non-reflective and reflective learning.

Jarvis further describes non-reflective learning. He suggests that learning of this type might be pre-conscious, a kind of habitual response where meanings are taken-for-granted; oriented toward acquiring skills and practice by observing and imitating others; or a kind of uncritical acceptance and memorization of information gained from trusted informants. This type of learning is often encouraged in change programs because the designers of the programs have a hidden or overt agenda to which they would like clients to subscribe. The Nepal program, for example, was set up to change people's health and family planning behaviors even though the interventions that were advocated were sound and the workers were trained to respect current health habits when they were not harmful or based on inaccurate information. The Philippines program was

93

based on people's choices, but the program was structured around PRRM's initiatives, which were in turn governed by the agency's founding philosophy, beliefs and the services it offered. Programs with agendas do not typically encourage reflection that conflicts with goals.

Many programs of planned change, including the two studied here, are built on Lewin's stages of unfreezing, changing and refreezing, described in Schein (1969). The unfreezing stage involves an ability to see a situation from a point of view other than one's own as well as some disorientation so that what is taken-for-granted can be questioned, enabling people to move from pre-conscious reactions to conscious learning. However, the Nepal and Philippines programs were also designed to develop trust established between change agents and their clients so that people would adopt new behaviors. Community members could identify with the change agent, believe the information provided through informal interactions, and emulate the example set. Thus, the learning desired, while not pre-conscious, is typically aimed at acquiring skills by observing and imitating others, or making decisions based on the advice of trusted change agents.

Change programs are often primarily persuasive in their orientation (Marsick, 1987b). There is a paradox in such educational efforts. If the programs value learning above all else, then people in communities may decide not to adopt the behaviors desired by the program directors. On the other hand, if the programs value the adoption of specific behaviors, then the type of learning advocated may not be fully empowering. Program designers may be sincere in their hope that change will help people gain more control over many aspects of their lives. However, their programs are often still judged by their success in reaching specific programmatic goals, not in terms of the way people think. This creates dilemmas for educators in communities who feel they must talk about practices desired by the program even though these might not represent the best interests of their learners.

The persuasive nature of learning for health is not confined to the developing worlds. A co-author and I have looked at trends that suggest that the health care delivery system in the United States relies on a top-down educational approach that has not caught up to the demands of consumer activist groups for more control of decisions related to their health. (Marsick and Smedley, 1989). The problem of AIDS has brought attention to the need for change, because victims of this disease have had to organize to take care of themselves. Feminists have also rallied against blind faith in doctors, and have worked toward claiming more control of health-related decisions for themselves and their families.

Development programs that are truly empowering require informal learning focused at the higher three rungs of Jarvis's learning hierarchy. Jarvis describes three types of reflective learning: contemplation, reflective practice and experimental learning. Jarvis (1987) defines contemplation as "pure thought," a response to a situation in which a person decides "merely to consider it and make an intellectual decision about it" (p. 34). Jarvis relates reflective practice to Schön's model, but he confines the process to advanced skill development, whereas experimental learning is "knowledge that has been shown to relate to reality through experimentation" (p. 35), that is, a kind of scientific experimentation with one's environment. This separation may be warranted if Jarvis is distinguishing theory built through practice, or what Argyris and Schön (1974) call a theory of action, from formal academic theories. However, action science leads toward experimentation that builds new knowledge and theory, as discussed in Chapter One.

The Nepal and Philippines programs were trying to develop reflection-in-action in the workers being trained by focusing primarily on skilled practice, but without excluding experimentation aimed at enhanced scientific knowledge. Jarvis suggests that reflective learning can produce either conformity or innovation. The Nepal and Philippines programs sought innovation, not conformity, although this innovation was limited by a framework of pre-defined goals. The Nepal and Philippines programs aimed at reflective learning to the extent that they attempted to help village workers and community members think differently, question the way in which they have traditionally done things, and act outside of habitual patterns.

To use concepts discussed by Schön (1983, 1987), however, field workers and community members did not learn to frame or set problems differently. Schön's concept of problem setting or framing is similar to what Freire (1970, 1973) calls problem posing or problematizing. Problem framing, problem setting, problem posing, and problematizing are all very different from the focus of the Nepal and Philippines programs on problem solving. Goulet describes the difference in an introduction to Freire's (1973) book on education for critical consciousness:

> Problematizing is the antithesis of the technocrat's "problem-solving" stance. In the latter approach an expert takes some distance from reality, analyzes it into component parts, devises means for resolving differences in the most efficient way, and then dictates a strategy or policy.... But to "problematize" in his

[Freire's] sense is to associate an entire populace to the task of codifying total reality into symbols which can generate critical consciousness and empower them to alter their relations with nature and social forces.

[Goulet in Freire, 1973, p. ix]

People do not always problematize when they learn informally, particularly in countries like Nepal and the Philippines where much of their decision making has been guided by tradition. Problem solving, which was not as radical as problematizing, was the focus of the Nepal and Philippines programs. None the less, problem solving was also quite alien to many of these workers because they grew up in cultures where people feel they have little control over what takes place. Their role is to cope as best they can, not change the circumstances of their lives. Hence, it is more likely that they will have the attitudes identified by Jarvis of presumption, non-consideration and rejection. Learning may take place through informal interaction but, for that to happen, a person must become aware of a need for doing things differently and be willing to look at ordinary events from a perspective that deviates from what is expected of him/her.

Informal learning in training programs

Informal learning is central to the models described in this chapter. Dialogue was at the heart of programs in which trainees were to work. Dialogue was also central to the training designed to prepare people for this work. The following features were built into the training in the expectation that this way of thinking and acting would be used by trainees in their communities: involving learners in choices in the design and implementation of learning in order to develop proactivity; learning from experience through a combination of action and reflection; developing a collaborative resource network on which workers could draw to solve problems; and using methods and materials oriented to reflectivity. Training was also used as a forum to make explicit the frequently tacit nature of learning in this program.

Training features

First, learners were involved in making key choices during training, just as field workers and community people were to do. In Nepal, involvement began at the highest possible levels with policy makers and administrators. The program began with a lengthy training of trainers. People selected to train health workers experimented with the curriculum by being trained in it themselves. As they were trained, master trainers (consultants from the United States) would periodically stop and explain what they were doing and why they were doing it. Trainees, who were the program's future trainers, would then reflect on their collective experiences in order to redesign the training program.

Srinivasan followed a strategy similar to that used in Nepal in designing learner-centered participatory materials with staff in PRRM. In initial planning sessions, a team of field staff pretested the proposed activities both to experience them and to consider ways in which they should be adapted to the local situation. The same procedure was then used when these materials and methods were used with village women.

Second, learning was centered around experiences. Trainees took action, which was then analyzed so they could develop new understandings that spurred them to seek further experience. Many training models incorporate experience through practice sessions in which people follow strict guidelines as they try out new skills and get feedback from trainers. By contrast, in these models, the experience was a situation the worker would actually encounter on the job. The reason for this approach is that the jobs in which these people worked were ambiguous, complex, and not solvable by a single right answer. There were no clear guidelines or rule books; workers had to make judgments on-the-spot based on their best understanding of the situation, although they might later consult with others to enhance their understanding or get additional information. The key to reaping the benefits of this approach is to spend sufficient time in analyzing the experience and to be sufficiently reflective so that people can draw implications and conclusions from the experience. Theory was not excluded; when it existed, it was introduced after participants had first derived for themselves a basic understanding of the situation.

Third, both models encouraged the development of a collaborative resource network from which people could draw in order to identify and solve problems. Traditional hierarchical relationships were replaced, at least in part, by peer learning that was to be continued on the job. Neither trainers nor trainees were completely ready for this major reversal of role expectations. In both Nepal and the Philippines, teachers have been considered experts while learners resemble passive receptacles of knowledge. Status and authority barriers resulted from such a relationship, and were reinforced by it. Despite initial frustrations, however, these models showed that traditional roles could be reversed, given time, skill, and the willingness of individual trainers to "let go" of this expert position.

Trainers became facilitators, catalysts, guides, and creators of learning environments. Sometimes – particularly in Nepal, where personal and professional development was a goal of training – trainers were counselors, working in a one-to-one relationship with specific trainees over time to assist in developing self-insights as change agents. In PRRM, trainers were also friends and consultants before, during and after training. They acted as a sounding board, constantly asking the "whys" which set the stage for exploring difficulties.

Finally, methods and materials in each model were consistent with the level of reflectivity desired in each program. In Nepal, learners were guided as nondirectively as possible. The emphasis was initially on observation, active listening, discussion, role play, sensitizing exercises, and field practice. Materials were supplementary: newsprint and blackboard used in preparing for and analyzing experiences, notebooks which trainees used on the job to note down their observations, and simple information handouts. In PRRM, semi-directive methods were selected to "prime the pump." There was a continual mix of nondirective and directive discussion, games and exercises to stimulate thinking, and skill practice. Materials were sometimes core to involvement, particularly in games and exercises, and sometimes supplementary, such as handouts to round out lectures on technical knowledge or practice of skills. As PRRM incorporated more of Srinivasan's methods, materials became more important as tools which learners could use to compose stories, describe situations in their lives, and put forth their own views for further discussion.

In her work in the Philippines, Srinivasan also paid attention to timing and sequencing of subjective or objective materials. Trainees first were helped to look at new concepts or ideas in their own lives before extending their view outward to their external worlds. Trainers in Nepal likewise recommended that trainees first analyze their own subjective perceptions, then become aware of the subjective perceptions clients had of themselves, and finally analyze both the subjective role they took as change agents and the objective needs of the health situation. Trainers in Nepal recommended that learners keep journals which could be analyzed in class, an excellent resource to encourage introspection that is also recommended by Cell (1984). Both the Nepal and Philippines models used sensitivity exercises to help trainees gain self-insights. In Nepal, these exercises were eventually modified or eliminated because the challenge to social norms was too great. In the Philippines, they were also modified to heighten self-awareness without deliberate, intensive analysis. The group examined the objective reality but, while references might be made to the subjective reality, trainees were left to draw their own conclusions.

A forum for examining tacit learning

Learning for development can be intentional and explicit when people set out to gain knowledge and skills they know they do not have. On the other hand, in the process of interacting with skilled resource persons whom they might seek out, people can also learn tacitly. Learning often seems tacit in programs such as these because people learn new behaviors almost unconsciously by observing others and modeling what they say or do. Tacit learning is a goal of many development programs. Programs are designed on the assumption that villagers will follow the example of opinion leaders because the villagers look up to and trust these leaders even if they do not understand why they are adopting a new behavior. Field workers are selected, in part, because they are expected to be local opinion leaders or are trained for this role.

People thus learn tacitly by following the example of role models. One theory that could be used to describe this kind of learning is known variously as observational learning, vicarious learning, or social learning theory. Bandura (1977), who developed this theory, suggests that people begin learning when they attend to certain stimuli in their environment. As they observe others, they take in and symbolically code information which they can then store, reorganize cognitively, and retrieve. Learners can then symbolically rehearse the action mentally although they may not always do so before acting. People then reproduce the behavior; if they pay attention to the feedback they receive from others when they act, they will then cycle their future action through another round of learning. Bandura's model is used in many training programs to influence behavioral change.

Bandura's theory could explain learning when it falls into Jarvis's non-reflective category. In such cases, people are not asked to reflect critically on the principles behind their learning or the assumptions on which a particular response is based. When reflective learning is involved, however, the tacit nature of the learning must be made explicit, at least for a while. It is very difficult to make one's implicit, tacit reasoning explicit without the help of others and, hence, informal learning would be inadequate to the task unless the person drew on the help of colleagues who were willing to assist in this process. Moreover, many times people seek the opinions of others to validate their beliefs, not to question them. For informal learning to be effective, the person would have to approach the situation with an open mind and the willingness to test his or her hypotheses.

The Nepal and Philippines training models provided a forum in which tacit knowledge could be made explicit and examined with the help of others. The work involved was primarily action-centered, but rudimentary levels of abstract thinking were also required. In Nepal, workers had to diagnose health problems; in the Philippines, some Barangay Technicians were introducing agricultural innovations that involved simple scientific principles. Trainers tried to develop some skill in making what is tacit explicit so that workers could continue to use these skills on the job, preferably with the help of colleagues.

Notes

1. This chapter is based on dissertation research undertaken from 1977 through 1979 on three experience-based training programs for village-level educational field workers – in Nepal, Taiwan, and the Philippines (Marsick, 1979). Only two of these case studies are revisited here, that of Nepal and the Philippines. The dissertation was a study of how people were empowered, through education, to "take over" responsibility for their lives. "Taking over" is a way of looking at the world, a perspective, a general approach to life. It might be best described in its colloquial connotation of doing things for oneself.
2. Most Health Aides were young males since the Government required they be at least 18 years old and have at least eight years of education.
3. By contrast, clinic-based Health Aides covered an area within one and a half hour's walking distance.
4. Founded in 1952 by Taiwanese Jimmy Yen, PRRM was modeled on Yen's parent organization called the International Institute for Rural Reconstruction. Jimmy Yen's philosophy of "release, not relief" was adopted and operationalized through a four-fold program of health, livelihood, education, and civic responsibility.

Chapter five

How professionals learn: life experience and workplace educators

One lens through which to examine informal learning is unstructured, meaningful life experience that individuals, on reflection, identify as influential to their professional development. This chapter sheds light on professional learning by looking at the lives of workplace adult educators: how they learned as they grew up and how these patterns influenced subsequent workplace learning undertaken by themselves and with others.[1] The chapter thus touches as well on individual learning, and in some cases group learning.

These adult educators have a sense of professionalism but they do not necessarily identify with the profession, which most entered by chance, not by conscious choice. Many still do not identify with the profession. This finding echoes conclusions drawn by Watkins in this book and elsewhere (1989) about a lack of professional identity in the field of Human Resource Development. Despite their often serendipitous entry into the adult education field, the group as a whole reflected what seems to be a value bias in the profession: helping the marginal and less powerful to join the mainstream or otherwise to develop more fully their potential.

The first part of the chapter addresses what people learned in early life experiences that shaped their professional careers and choices. The second part of the chapter is a series of minicases that link these early life experiences to the informal learning of four professionals in the group. The conclusion is a look at relevance for informal learning.

Change agents

This group saw themselves as change agents, a role they seemed to learn early in life because of perceived marginality, which in turn led to an interest in empowering themselves and others to move beyond perceived limitations. However, this group did not always use the term "change agent" to mean "agents of social action," a definition frequently found in the literature. The gist of the term seemed to be a kind of intentional proactivity directed at change. Change was perceived frequently as a personal achievement – for example, self-esteem, self-direction, self-insight, credentials, new skills, jobs, or changes in educational practices – rather than as being inextricably entwined with transformation of social or organizational structures. Early family experiences, positive and negative, and the historical events of the times in which many of these people matured – primarily the turbulent social activism of the sixties – influenced their definition of change.

Several trainers spoke of empowering learners and of trying to change or work around systems to make them more conducive to growth for individuals, as well as benefits to the enterprise. Patrick, for example, was asked to customize a telephone sales training program for customer service representatives, who were primarily females "telephone selling to a predominantly male, small business owner group." Patrick realized that "all of the selling skills in the world will not serve an individual faced with sexual bias, in a chauvinistic environment." He addressed gender bias through role plays "in which I instructed customers to address the salesperson as 'honey,' to ask them for a date as part of the conversation, and included such responses to the initial phone call as, 'Will your boss call me later?'" Patrick was influenced in his thinking, in part, by his father who, "trained as an accountant and, dissatisfied with materialism and corporate aspects of that profession," left a lucrative job to work at half the salary with a government agency when Patrick was five. His father's ideals encouraged him to make choices based on his own values.

People were often motivated to change social structures because they perceived themselves as marginal to society and wanted to help others overcome barriers. Perceived marginality derived from a variety of family circumstances: being raised in families of lower socio-economic levels that sought to climb up the class ladder, growing up as a minority because of race or religion, or otherwise dealing with dysfunctional families where the negative aspects of divorce, substance abuse, and physical or mental illness created a sense of abandonment, isolation, self-reliance, and a search for what was considered normal.

One woman summarized what many noted: "The pattern of 'marginality' as it relates to adult educators seems the first to make sense as a *predictor*. I see its meaning for me as being on the margin of every group I have had contact with" (original italics). Edwin, a trainer currently working in the public sector, found "being on the edge of things is the most comfortable place for me to be." He illustrated the way in which marginality helped him push for change, despite resistance. He moved into a job as a supervisor of a unit that "used lecture almost exclusively." Edwin "seemed to be in constant battle with the staff. I clearly threatened them. I wanted to take the courses out of their exclusive control and help local people become trainers."

A number of adult educators valued their marginal roles in organizations for their "perspective" and "vantage point." They saw marginality as "a perception of oneself in the larger scheme as the keeper of mission and as innovative front runner." They also concluded that institutions, while "generally cautious about their marginal players, ... in most cases, prized [them] for their contribution to the organization." Marginality thus had positive meanings for many adult educators in this group and played a central role in their "praxis," that is, "informed, committed action where theory and practice are mutually interactive" (Usher, 1988).

Challenging beliefs, values, and norms

We noted that informal learning is enhanced by critical reflection. Yet many educators were surprised to find how strongly influenced they were by unchallenged beliefs, values, and norms, learned through families, communities, religion, and education. However, some situations, described in this section, that catalyzed critical reflection included: (1) a struggle with the school system; (2) awareness of differences (culture, race, socio-economic class, gender); (3) challenges to authority.

Struggle with the school system

The message passed on by many families was that education meant opportunity for improvement, through economic benefits, opportunities for "better" jobs, and social acceptance. However, education – through school systems – also created new norms, many of which were not positive. While a certain proportion of the sample did well in school and liked it, another large group internalized feelings of failure from their academic experiences. Paul, an urban, white male with a business background, noted, "Having attended nine schools in seven years meant that I rarely developed a predictable group of people in my life. I compounded this difficulty by accepting the role of class clown and believing a message that I had been given that I was not very bright." This pattern continued throughout high school and led to going through community college with "sixty units and barely a C average," dropping out of University, and ultimately completing college through non-traditional routes.

Several broke out of the strangle-hold imposed by messages that they were "not very bright." Edwin, for example, found success in high school through sports, not academic achievement. When in college, he "began to realize I wasn't as dumb as I thought." Edwin combined a rigorous class load with a part-time job that helped him "overcome two major obstacles: lack of faith in my intelligence and value, and the lack of money to go to college." However, when Edwin went to graduate school, he "felt isolated and unimportant. I didn't blame it on the school or the system.... Only later did I realize that I was only part of the problem." In a later paper Edwin commented on the "exclusive mentality" of graduate school, which he did not question then, but later recognized as something alien to the workplace: "The only thing that seemed to count in the world was how much one knew, and status was determined by how well one could display that knowledge in various forums." Edwin contrasted this with workplace settings where "hardly anyone ever talked about content from any course from the school in the context of work." Perhaps it was his disappointment with traditional education that led, in part, to this trainer's willingness to experiment with collaborative learning processes, despite resistance from the organizations in which he worked, because he found them more effective.

Awareness of differences

People in this group questioned norms when they could contrast them with those of another group. Sometimes this came through travel or cross-cultural experiences; in other cases, they became aware of differences because of their race or socio-economic level.[2] Edwin, for example, joined the Peace Corps and taught in an "alien culture" where "values and norms were radically different." The strange culture catalyzed an examination of fundamental beliefs, but Edwin was also "pushed and challenged by other volunteers to read, think, and discuss major issues like the war, politics, racism, poverty." He "developed a strong internal commitment to having my life make a difference. That commitment has never left me."

Phillip grew up in one of three different cultural minority families. "Small towns tend in many cases to be narrow-minded and we suffered for that as minorities. The only saving grace was that there was a 'bigger minority' of Catholics who were also not well treated." Phillip now sees himself as a change agent, willing to confront key people in the organization in which he works. But it appears that, early in his career, he also learned how to follow norms set by others, not question them. For example, in an early job in which he had to train people, some of whom were former high school classmates, he adopted the "very authoritarian, confrontive style" of his boss. While seeing "now that he was not a good role model ... I became just like him – strict, dictatorial, concerned with grades, tests, punishment, and power." This trainer was encouraged by the administration who provided "strong support and encouragement to 'keep cracking the whip,'" which he did not, at that time, question further.

Joyce, a black woman who has worked with both colleges and business, experienced differences in norms in the United States through participation in a live-in youth activity in another city. She remembers being taken home by her room-mate's family: "As we traveled through a neighborhood similar to mine, my room-mate laughed and told her mother that 'she would be embarrassed to live in a neighborhood like this.'" Joyce remembers "the silence descending over the car as we drove into my neighborhood and up to my house." She later challenged many of her beliefs, and those of others in society, both in school and in a variety of jobs, not only with respect to poverty but also with respect to race. Her willingness to examine and go beyond her beliefs has also led her to train from a "group process oriented perspective" which she finds much more demanding, but more effective for learners.

Being a minority did not always mean experiencing oneself as different while growing up. For example, one black male (not a trainer) grew up "in a community of free blacks ... who did not talk about racial issues as such. There were people who were worthy and those who were unworthy, good and bad, and there were members of all races in both groups." Another black male born in the South in the 1930s, who works in the school system, also did not experience discrimination as a child. He was born into "an unusual enclave of black farmers who saw themselves as businessmen. They hired their field hands, provided for their sharecroppers, and managed the sale of their harvest to white merchants in the small towns nearby." But when he was aged six, the family moved to a "profoundly mean" North where "I learned my lesson about tyranny which would so affect my political perspective."

Most women, even if they bought into a stereotypical role at some time, decided eventually to move beyond these limitations. For many, gender was intertwined with other concerns. For example, in the process of examining beliefs about "the Christian tradition that has so shaped who I was," one woman whom I will call Bridgit took a course based on Jungian thinking with a "brilliant, female professor" who helped her get "in touch with my feelings, values and attitudes around being female in a male-dominated world."

Challenges to authority

Bridgit, raised Catholic in a family with an authoritarian father, found that she challenged norms when she had to stand up to her parents and other authority figures. Bridgit went to secretarial school instead of college because her father would pay for nothing but a small Catholic women's college. She got a job at a college and experienced the riots of 1968 and 1969: "It was an incredibly powerful experience for me to witness people my age demanding to be heard. It was during this time that I began to consciously question the power I'd invested in authority – the church, my father, teachers." Bridgit decided to return to college, where she encountered several teachers who allowed her to test her beliefs without the kind of repercussions she might have encountered in her family. Bridgit grew through "relationships that felt safe for me." For example, in a philosophy course, she "realized that no one had all the answers; that there was no absolute authority on earth; that I could question whatever I wanted and nothing terrible would happen to me." Then there was a chaplain who "listened to my tirade" about a requirement to attend chapel, "and very calmly suggested that I could fly home, or I could think about why I was so angry and come back the next day to discuss it." Bridgit points to the strength of these people who "were examples to me of male authority figures who invited me to challenge everything about myself, rather than the male authority figures in my past who never invited me to question anything."

Some challenges to authority, directly related to work, had to do with standing up for principles or leaving situations where people felt they could not change the system. Phillip, for example, left a job managing a clinic over questionable business practices. Joyce stood up to her minority staff at a day care center who "described my expectations that they (a) come to work on time, (b) stay throughout the day, and (c) plan activities for the children, as the 'middle-class values' of a woman from [the suburbs]." Another example, a woman whom I call Miriam, left work in retailing because "I found that the climate in retailing supported the idea that the people that worked or shopped in the store were unimportant – profit was all that mattered." As a sales trainer, Miriam tried to experiment with programmed instruction, role play, and simulation and "was ordered to return to the original format." So Miriam left this job and went into distributive education where she used experiential methods and organized an employer advisory council to make learning more relevant. Later, after relocating with her husband, Miriam found a job designing, marketing, and teaching supervisory training courses for retail store owners at an all-white, two-year college. However, having experienced religious discrimination as a child, Miriam left when "there was a lot of angry discussion about 'niggers' and I was invited to come to a meeting to discuss how we were going to keep 'them' out of the school."

Informal learning: minicases

This next section is an in-depth look at the informal learning of four workplace educators which they linked to their life histories.[1]

Susan

Susan, a white female who has some training responsibility as part of her managerial work in the non-profit sector, noted that she has been driven all her life by a desire to "make deliberate choices about the direction that my life might take." She notes, "This philosophy has clear roots in the way that I was raised and, hopefully, is a chosen re-action to these roots." Susan remembers "limited economic resources" and a parent's severe illness: "My memory of these early years is that life didn't offer many choices to me or to the people in my life." Susan responded by creating choices for herself and others.

Choices for Susan are etched very clearly in her mind. For example, in an early encounter with racism, her parents objected to her sister's work in the Civil Rights Movement and her friendship with someone who married a black person. Susan recalls being "shocked ... not only from the point of view of the racism, but also that people's choices in life couldn't be respected." None the less, Susan entered into a fairly conventional marital contract during a period which she characterized as one of "reaction, survival, and getting by." Susan's husband was drafted during the Vietnam War, enabling her to become more independent and eventually leading to a divorce. A precipitating factor was her decision to support her brothers in their decision to join the army, even though she disagreed with their point of view, a decision her husband opposed. Susan felt this decision helped her "to see the world in a larger way and to reflect critically on how that larger world can and should be a part of one's life." After a period of what she calls "survival training", moving from job to job in Europe with a backpack, Susan settled into a series of jobs.

Susan described a rather independent style of informal, self-directed learning that she feels is "very consistent throughout my life history." She used this approach in pursuing a non-traditional undergraduate degree program. The flexible, experience-oriented curriculum allowed Susan to complete her degree in record time, so much so that her "work there is still being utilized as a model for in-coming students." Susan's later experience with a traditional graduate program showed her how different formal class work can be: "the outcomes were significantly different in the affective pro-cesses of education." She was determined, as a result, "to have influence over the educational process for other adult learners," a determination that is reflected in her work choices.

Susan illustrated her pattern of learning informally by discussing the way in which she learned how to become director of a program for people with disabilities. She likes "situations where I have to build 'things' with few resources and where the skills that are re-quired to be successful are independence, resourcefulness, and stick-to-it-iveness." With no guidance and few resources, Susan real-ized that she had to assess needs and find the resources to carry out programs, and "decided to research both items simultaneously." She sought out and talked with a wide range of people. "Armed with a smattering of information, I contacted everyone and every agency that had potential to assist me in meeting the needs of the students."

This preliminary search led to funding agencies and another learn-ing requirement, "to write in the style that was necessary to meet the funding agency guidelines." She drafted proposals and circulated them to colleagues with reputations for good writing skills. Susan also learned about how to move her proposals through "the cumber-some system" of her institution and "into the hands of funding agency staff." The next phase was trial-and-error, the submission of many proposals. Each time Susan received feedback on the adequacy of the proposal, and each time she incorporated suggestions into the next proposal. She visited funding agency staff, sought their advice, and used it. She realized that "this rapport" with agency staff was as important as her newly-developed writing skills because her visits helped staff "to know me, develop a confidence in my ability to con-ceptualize a program," and see that she "was responsible in following through on their requests." Susan cites as proof of her learning the growth in her program's budget from her salary alone to $2.5 million and a corresponding increase in staff resources.

Richard

Richard, an only child "born to a lower middle-class family with middle-class aspirations," is a white male who is now the president of his own consulting firm in training and development. Richard learned in college from "an inspiring, iconoclastic literature profes-sor" who "started me thinking critically about life through literature" and from a doctoral student in history who "imparted a reverence for scholarship and books." He entered the fields of personnel and human resource development after having tried out a variety of career paths, primarily to please his parents: medicine at which he did not do well, law school in which he "lost interest after the first semester," and finally teaching because it "seemed to offer a way to earn a living and pursue my interest in writing and literature." He left work as a high school teacher when it became limiting.

Richard talked about the role of reflection in his practice with an example taken from his third job as a personnel director. He saw himself doing the "same old job; new title" and observed that the new managers he "had hired to replace the old non-performing ones" were having as much difficulty as their predecessors. He decided that "organization development had to mean something more than recruitment and placement." This prompted experimentation with a new approach to management development which he subsequently used as the kernel of his consulting business.

As he moved from job to job, Richard developed a habit of writing about the field and published several books. He and his colleagues also strove for excellence, reflecting on each experience and using it to modify subsequent work. They continually examined their approach to instruction, "becoming more and more experientially oriented in our approach," and "revised our materials over and over again, determined to make every word, transparency and experience the best it could be. We wanted a feeling of mastery over our work."

Richard described his approach to reflective practice. His "learning pattern seemed to start with feelings of dissonance with what I was hearing, reading, and intuiting." This feeling that something was not quite right is similar to the sensitivity to subtle surprises that Schön (1987) talks about when describing reflection-in-action. Richard continued, "That led to thinking, talking with a colleague, more reading and thinking, testing out a hypothesis, confirming the hypothesis ... and finally feeling confident enough with its explanatory power that I incorporated it into my repertoire."

For example, in one case he was developing a negotiating skills program for retail buyers even though "I didn't consider myself a particularly good negotiator and privately wondered how I would teach others who did it for a living to do it better." Richard started the process with interviews with buyers, their managers, and their managers' managers. He then searched the popular literature on the topic, a pattern he often follows in program design, with disquieting results. He found that the literature spurred another "vague sort of discomfort" because it contradicted what he was hearing from buyers and from his own instincts. "Most of what I was reading advocated the use of trickery, grand strategies, and histrionics. Somehow that didn't fit with a collaborative, win-win approach to dealing with others."

Eventually Richard found a book on negotiating that separated content and process issues, which, upon reflection, "led me to create a new model of negotiating behavior that explained what happened when negotiators emphasized interpersonal relationship behavior and/or negotiating methods," each of which produced different negotiating styles that explained more accurately the process followed by his client group, the buyers. Richard tested his model with the buyers who "agreed that it seemed to represent what really occurred when they negotiated.... Subsequent presentations confirmed my hypothesis."

Richard described a similar process in instituting a new approach to performance appraisals in his own consulting firm. Again, the reflective process began with feelings of dissonance. Richard used performance appraisals because they were used at the large companies for which he had previously worked. "Habit, more than anything, caused me to continue the process." Richard "was never convinced that the company got full value for the effort put into the process." He "always insisted on incorporating a self-appraisal component in the process," which was sometimes accepted, sometimes resisted, sometimes ignored, but never made the centerpiece of the process.

One morning, while jogging, Richard was thinking about the upcoming performance appraisal process in his company and about a paper he had just finished on critical thinking: "The two ideas came together rather easily. How about a critical performance appraisal?" In talking about this idea with his staff, he decided to emphasize the self-appraisal portion of the process: "I asked them to think critically about what they had achieved during the past year, what they did not accomplish that they had hoped to accomplish, what obstacles got in their way (if any), and what plans they had for next year." So Richard consulted his colleagues, tried "out the approach in a low risk situation, and then refined the approach for later use on a larger scale."

Judith

Judith is a staff developer in a school system. As a child, her family moved frequently because her father changed jobs, which led to a pattern of isolation that she feels is still a strong influence in her professional life even though she has since discovered the value of collaborative learning, peer relationships, and team work. Judith's isolation was exaggerated because of limited social contacts at home: "Our family rarely had people over to our house because my father was always working." Judith compensated for this lack of social contact through a workaholic pattern similar to her father's which she feels continues today. She found herself trying to meet the expectations of parents, teachers, and eventually of peers.

Judith observed that she "fulfilled my role as any young married woman did in 1964, by becoming the dutiful wife who was responsible for all the duties 'assigned' to that role." In addition, "just as my parents had limited their social contact with the outside world, my husband and I had relatively few contacts outside of our professional life." Judith taught school, "which is an isolated career," and worked on the side in her husband's real estate investments. She eventually left teaching to work with her husband in a new home construction business. When she decided she did not want to stay at home, Judith "tried to get a job in a construction-related business." Her choices were limited in a male-dominated industry, so she eventually took a job as "a training coordinator for a large building supplies company." Subsequent events brought a child and a divorce, which led her back into the teaching profession. She eventually remarried and moved through a series of jobs with a staff development focus, beginning with participation in a leadership training program for which she eventually became a trainer. For a while she was appointed an assistant principal in a middle school and worked closely with teachers in a staff development capacity. She eventually "had to make a career decision whether to remain in a school-based career ladder that would lead to the principalship or take a risk and move to a district level position." Judith chose staff development.

Judith described her role in a recent three-year project in nine schools to develop team-based school improvement strategies. "The training program has involved training events over the three-year period, with coaching provided between the sessions. The participants have been principals and significant staff members from the schools." Judith reflected on the experience from the point of view of the isolation patterns she experienced in her life. When she began the project, Judith "involved a group of representatives from within our district" and sought the endorsement of top management, specifically the Superintendent, through various marketing strategies. However, while she received "the blessing" of top management through words, she never really received the Superintendent's commitment. She feels this hampered effectiveness. While "the project has benefited the district and the pay off will equal the efforts invested, in the future, I will not begin a major program without the full endorsement of the Superintendent." Judith noted that "my life history reflects a tendency to work in isolation and my devotion to the

111

project without top management support indicates a false sense of autonomy that may have hurt the effort."

Edwin

Edwin, introduced earlier in this chapter, grew up as the oldest of three children in the rural Midwest. "When I was eleven my mother divorced my dad and moved to the community where there were many of her relatives," relatives that Edwin admired. "I remember how liberating that divorce was for me." Edwin described several critical incidents that illustrated the way in which he went about learning informally. Edwin described his doubts about the effectiveness of training despite apparent success in his first job as a trainer: "The good feelings, meaning feeling productive and [having] people say nice things about my programs, lasted for less than a year. I began to have serious doubts that my programs made any real difference to people in their jobs."

Edwin changed jobs after several years, but did not lose these doubts until he encountered one situation in which action planning was successful. He split a one-day training session into "a mix of lecture, film and group work in the first half of the day" and action planning in the afternoon to resolve problems on the topic identified in the morning. "The problems were always real, but they were off-the-top-of-the-head variety. They were not the result of a careful assessment." None the less, for some reason this group took the work seriously and "completely forgot about me. I had never seen groups work that well before." Edwin "could literally 'feel'" the difference in the sessions and "thought about it constantly in the weeks that followed." He later learned that the changes proposed by the group that afternoon were used and had made a real difference in the way in which the agency worked.

Edwin pursued "experiments" to try to reproduce the same effect, experiments in which he acted as an organizational consultant. Using action research, he involved county departments in identifying and solving their own problems, rather than functioning as a trainer with expert solutions. He noted that he "was effectively ostracized for about 18 months": "There was a lot of resistance from my colleagues, but I saw this as survival for me as a professional."

Edwin's isolation ended, and a new phase in his learning began, when a colleague accompanied Edwin on a site visit and "watched as the director and I worked out what was going to happen, how, when, etc. It seemed that in a moment he knew what it meant" and "talked continuously about the project until midnight." The two began to work together and were invited to work on "a project in the New

York City area" that "was a variation on our earlier projects, but it was much more sophisticated." Through it, they met some consultants from the Boston area who invited them to join the Organization Development Network, a group of consultants who met regularly for intensive weekends in which they experimented with new learning strategies. Edwin did not join the group for a year but, when he did, he was in for an exciting several years of peer learning.

On a later project, Edwin learned how difficult it was to act in accordance with his espoused theory: "I was shaken a number of times to realize how I had prescribed and controlled so many of my projects with the counties. I began to learn about a thing this consultant called 'capacity building.'" Edwin saw how difficult it is to let go of old, established patterns. On the evening before the project ended, Edwin met with the project's chief outside consultant to plan for the next phase. When Edwin suggested the next phase be a repeat of the training program because he felt the program should be located in the training unit, the consultant responded, "'Edwin, you are going to have to realize that in the context of everything else, the training unit is a pisshole in a snow bank.' Now having grown up on a farm I knew what that looked like, but I was more than a little shocked at the thought of equating that with the training unit."

Edwin asked the consultant what he thought should be the next steps and the consultant described the action research process. Edwin noted, "I had seen this many times. I had explained it to others, but this time the limits of my thinking (viewing my work world as a trainer) were broken.... For the first time I saw that training should be secondary to the work of the organization" (Edwin's parentheses). For a while, Edwin "wanted to stop doing training altogether," but now he sees it as one of many useful tools "incidental to the larger issue of the organizational mission."

Lessons for informal learning

These minicases illustrate ways in which informal learning was influenced by factors in the life histories of these adult educators. Taken as a group, these minicases shed light on several dimensions of informal learning, which I discuss below in terms of the learning loop and characteristics of professionals as learners.

The learning loop

These minicases all represent non-routine learning for the individuals involved. Something in the situation was new, surprising, or perplexing. Susan described learning a new job for which there were no guide books. Richard talked about designing a new program. He always follows similar steps but, in this minicase, Richard described feelings of dissonance that told him he had to interrupt the process to explore new ideas that might be more relevant. Judith experimented with a pilot project that generated much enthusiasm, but which she felt did not achieve a primary objective. Edwin departed from standard operating procedures and worked alone in pursuit of experiments that would make learning more effective.

In Chapter One, we suggested that the process of informal experiential learning closely parallels the three stages of unprogrammed activity described by Simon (1965): intelligence, design, and choice activity. Figure 5.1 shows how we might combine Simon's stages with Schön's (1983) model of experience-based learning also described earlier. The circle represents steps in the process of setting and solving problems, steps that often lead to problem reformulation and another cycle of experimentation. Around the circle are superimposed Simon's stages: intelligence activity needed to assess the results of an intervention or the impact of non-intervention, which leads to setting and formulating the problem; design activity involved in investigating alternative solutions; and choice activity needed to select or pursue a solution. Added here is a fourth stage of experimentation once the choice is made, in which the person carries

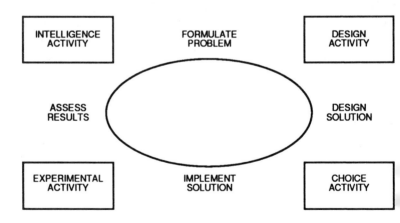

Figure 5.1 The learning loop

114

out, and perhaps modifies or plays with, the solution originally invented. Experimentation leads to intelligence activity although, in some cases, intelligence activity to monitor results takes place while people are experimenting.

Several of these minicases illustrate these stages. Susan's story incorporates all four phases: intelligence activity to identify first what she ought to do as program director (needs assessment and fund raising), design activity in which she researched further both priorities, choice activity where she decided to pursue proposal writing, and experimentation in which she tried out various strategies to become an effective fund raiser.

Richard's program development process included these stages as well, but his learning also illustrates the fact that learning is not always a linear process. First, Richard used intelligence activity to get a better grasp of the problem. He also wondered whether he had the skills to teach negotiation skills. Richard could have pursued what Argyris and Schön (1974, 1978) have described as double-loop learning at this point, but he did not. In other words, Richard could have questioned the expert model in which he was supposed to "win" by giving people answers, and the buyers were to "lose" by admitting they were doing things wrong all along. Instead, Richard proceeded to use design strategies to examine several possible negotiation models. At this point, Richard experienced dissonance which did lead to some double-loop learning. Richard questioned the win-lose strategies underlying popular negotiation models, which he did not think fitted with the more collaborative approach his buyers told him they used. Richard departed from routine program design processes, reformulated the problem, and asked what a model would look like that accurately described the negotiation strategies of his buyers. Further investigation led to new alternatives, a model of his own, which he then further tested with his buyers. Their response confirmed the direction in which he was moving, so he returned to more routine procedures to complete the design of his training program.

Edwin's learning loop illustrates movement back and forth among different stages of intelligence, design, choice, and experimentation activities. He also experienced dissonance, created by his feeling that training was not effectively meeting organizational needs and did not lead to change. Through intelligence activity, Edwin looked beyond the positive feedback received after training sessions through what are often known as "smile sheets." Edwin picked up signals of success when he conducted a one-day workshop in which people seemed to learn the principles he taught, used them to solve real problems, and instituted changes in their workplace. Puzzled by his success, Edwin tried to identify the conditions that made learning effective. This led

115

to design activity but, in order to make choices, Edwin experimented with different learning strategies. By assessing the results of his efforts, Edwin eventually reformulated the problem. Instead of seeking training methods that were individually and organizationally effective, Edwin decided to find organizational consulting methods that used training as one of several strategies for change. His reformulation of the problem led to another round of design activity in which Edwin sought out and chose projects in which he could practice and develop new skills, primarily by experimenting with action research methods in collaborative pursuit of solutions to real-life problems being experienced by agencies with which he was involved.

The dissonance Edwin experienced created an opportunity for double-loop learning in which he asked fundamental questions about his work role in the organization. He reformulated the problem so that he focused on his overall organizational effectiveness rather than his success as a trainer. Edwin's story also illustrates another dimension of action science, that is, the difference between espoused theories and theories-in-use. Edwin's highly personalized struggle for professional satisfaction and organizational effectiveness led him to espouse a collaborative model of organizational learning through action research. He firmly believed in this process, understood it conceptually, and taught it to others. Yet Edwin found he was not following his own advice; through interaction with another consultant, he could finally broaden his vision and role toward organizational effectiveness.

Proactivity, creativity, and critical reflectivity

These minicases illustrate the conditions that enhance informal learning which were described in Chapter One, that is, proactivity, creativity, and critical reflectivity. The four adult educators in these minicases were proactive in their learning. Jarvis (1987) might question whether proactivity was "pure" in all cases, since some of these educators responded to a situation that confronted them and thus began their learning reactively. However, in their responses, these educators took a proactive stance and actively sought out conditions and resources that helped them learn and carry out their visions.

Several of the minicases illustrate the role of creativity in the enhancement of informal learning. In Richard's second example, two ideas came together accidentally while he was out jogging. Richard could be creative because he kept his mind open to perspectives different from his own. He maintained an experimental attitude in which he felt free to take risks, try out new behaviors, and test out ideas that were not fully articulated with colleagues. Susan displayed creativity in her ability to function under highly ambiguous circumstances as she formulated the problem and sought out resources to implement her solution.

Finally, these educators illustrated a habit of reflection that led them to seek out the resources they needed to learn, to question traditional norms and practices when this seemed appropriate, and to experiment with alternative approaches to their work. Sometimes reflection was of a single-loop nature in which the educators reflected on obvious causes for their mistakes without reformulating the problem at hand. At other times, the educators were critically reflective, as discussed above using examples from Richard and Edwin's stories.

In addition, we might look at Judith's minicase because she looked at her own underlying values that might have influenced mistakes she made. Textbooks on organizational development all point out that wide scale interventions should not be undertaken without the commitment of top management. Judith could thus have explained her error without digging into her own values. However, Judith saw that her own patterns of isolation led her into "a false sense of autonomy that may have hurt the effort." While Judith had involved key stakeholders, a gap between her espoused theory and theory-in-use may have led her to downplay the lack of real support from the highest echelon. Judith's ability to be critically reflective has helped her learn about this blind spot and may prevent a repeat of this mistake.

Miriam, a workplace educator introduced earlier in this chapter, now directs an experiential cooperative education program at a college. She provided another example of reflection and critical reflection in discussing problems she faced in learning how to use a computer and word processing software. Using Schön's concept of a reflective conversation with the situation, Miriam described the mental conversation that accompanied her efforts to type and save a letter. Miriam explored fears: "I know that computers don't have their own mind ... yes they do ... see ... it keeps telling me what to do." When she lost the letter she had typed as she tried to save it, Miriam's fears of being directed by the computer resurfaced: "I knew that this was too hard for me to do alone.... The commands are confusing.... This machine is once again giving me orders and I hate to be given orders."

Miriam linked her fear of being given orders with stereotypes about women's difficulties with machines and with her earlier struggle to "become more than a secretary ... because being a secretary or someone's wife was the only 'career' for a woman in the 50s." When Miriam told her parents she wanted to go to college, they "suggested that I become a secretary or find someone to marry. I explored how I could finance my own expenses and ultimately went to ... a coop college." Hence, she rejected the secretarial role that the computer recalls. Miriam also noted how she struggled to control her own life by overcoming "obstacles that were real or imposed by my family, religion, times I grew up in, being a woman, circumstances that I had no control over [father dying], narrowness of the administrators that I worked with or conservative thinking in education." She also connects the experience with learning in grade school: "this is not the third grade ... remember ... an ink pen with those stupid pen points and ink that caused blots on the page and ... the rationing of paper during the war." Finally, Miriam reflects on a desire for perfection as an obstacle to learning: "forget your fear of writing and committing your ideas to paper and your unrealistic goal of perfection. There is no such thing as perfection. Just go ON."

Miriam's story illustrates the way in which informal learning can be enhanced by critical reflection. Miriam confronts her fears. Single-loop learning takes place as she learns how to execute the right commands to operate the machine. Double-loop learning occurs as she struggles to reframe the problems she faces in her learning, looks at the way in which her prior experiences have shaped her stance toward this kind of learning, and examines other tangential concerns such as her relationship to her secretary and her rejection of the skills her secretary has when she encounters these skills in herself.

Professionals as learners

The approach professionals take in informal learning may be different from non-professionals because of differences in training and perspective, such as those discussed in Chapter One. We saw that professionals are more likely to be driven by their commitment to a calling and a desire to update their knowledge base continually. Professionals seem to be more peer-oriented than supervisor-oriented; they want recognition from their peers and are likely to learn from them. They are autonomous, self-organizing, and self-directed. Several of these characteristics are apparent in these life stories. In this section, I will look more closely at three of these: (1) awareness and learning; (2) the difficulty of learning informally even when intentionally trying to learn; (3) the use of resources for learning.

Awareness and learning

Schön (1987) talks about the components of reflection-in-action, which begins when a routine procedure results in a surprising outcome. Surprise leads to reflection on the reasons for the unintended outcome and to a re-examination of the way in which we frame the problem. In this chapter, we see a heightened awareness in Richard's sense of dissonance in designing the negotiation training for his buyers or in his sense of unfinished business with the performance appraisals. Edwin likewise believes there is more to be gotten from a training program, which leads him to seek alternative solutions even though he must forge ahead without much support in his quest. Miriam did not shut off her feelings of unease with the computer; she used them to analyze why she did not like to be ordered around by the machine. In all of these cases, then, awareness is accompanied by sensitivity to feelings that cannot at first be put into words. There is a tacitness about the feelings that leads these people to further exploration and that ultimately results in an ability to put their implicit feelings of discomfort into an explicit explanation.

There may be several qualities of "being professional" – both in general terms and specifically in reference to the field of adult education – that influence the willingness of the people in these minicases to pursue their awareness even though it cannot easily be expressed. Professionals, for one thing, are trained to pursue ideas. Despite some limits to the scientific method, its strengths include both a willingness to seek out facts that might disconfirm a generally held belief and a willingness to explore all possible avenues. Moreover, as described earlier in this chapter, these professionals come to their craft from a wide variety of backgrounds. Most adult educators start to practice their profession before being formally trained for it, and many never seek a higher degree in the field. These adult educators learned from life to be flexible; it was their very flexibility that brought them into an occupation where there are few fixed rules. As Schön discusses, professionals may use judgment to determine which rule to apply to which situation, or they make sense of a situation and then use rules as one of many parts of their stock of knowledge, drawn from past experience, to determine the fit of the rule with the case and to decide how to play with the rule's limits in the situation.

Use of resources

Professionals are supposed to be proactive in their learning and able to seek out the means to reach their goals. I use the term "resources" in its broadest sense to include a mix of experiences to meet needs for general growth or direction-finding, as well as finding answers to specific problems. These professionals seemed willing to move from one situation to another in a quest for fulfillment. They sought a wide variety of experiences as resources: travel, new jobs, and education. Phillip, for example, had a psychology degree and worked as a staff developer in the mental health field but felt he did not have teaching skills. So he "took a year off and went back to school to get a bachelor's degree in elementary and special education." He repeated this pattern later in seeking a master's degree in management because, "as a manager, I felt lacking in supervisory and management skills." He also alternated between types of jobs to get the experience he wanted. After his staff development activities, for example, he took a job directing day programs at a small institution for the mentally retarded "to get more real-life experience 'doing' and not only teaching."

Professionals seem to be proactive in that they keep seeking something more without always knowing exactly what that might be. Richard, for example, wrote in his life history that an early encounter with programmed instruction triggered his thinking about how people learn, prompted him to write about the topic (a habit that Richard seemed to use to develop his own knowledge base), and sent him to college "to learn more about learning theory." Richard seems a natural lifelong learner; once, when taking a job in the insurance business, he "immersed" himself in it "although I had no particular interest in the content. Learning something new was simply a personal challenge."

Many of these adult educators illustrate a learning orientation that led them to resources they needed in their personal or organizational learning quests. Sometimes this information was specific, as in the case of Susan who was seeking answers to a specific question about program development. Susan sought out resources within and outside the organization to help her achieve her aims. In writing up her life history, Susan identified this as a pattern. In other cases, the person felt he or she needed to learn more even though it was not quite clear what was needed or how the information should be found. Edwin illustrated this kind of general quest when he felt that what he was doing in his job was inadequate even though he was not sure what would work more effectively or how to find people who could help him conceptualize this. In both specific and general learning quests, these professionals also seem open to accidental information, ideas, and resources that they originally did not conceive to be part of the package of answers.

Relationships with other people proved to be an important resource to these adult educators. Managers – according to a study (McCall, Jr. *et al.* 1988) – learn from bosses but they do not learn as much from subordinates or peers. By contrast, adult educators here talked about learning from a wide range of people in many different capacities. Miriam, for example, included in her list of important mentors "the business people on my Advisory council, the Vice President of Academic Affairs who has provided me with information and resources to remain current on emerging trends in higher education, and a management consultant who first introduced me to Management By Objectives." Judith noted how she has learned from "many talented adult educators who have been committed to providing quality management throughout the state." Richard noted that he tries out ideas with colleagues as he develops them. Edwin felt his learning increased when a colleague joined him in his experiments. Edwin also described the value that the Organization Development Network had for him. This group of peers met for a weekend every three months to share expertise. He noted, "Since all of us had been in the business for more than ten years, many longer, no one could get away with training gimmicks." Colleagues learned from one another and received valuable feedback on their ideas.

Many spoke in their life histories of learning from role models, people in their lives who modeled actions or life views they emulated. They also identified mentors as a key resource in learning. Teachers were often singled out, as were other older adults who played the role of a parent. Phillip described the important role that mentors continue to play for him in his learning. He defined a mentor as someone who: (1) "is supportive, compassionate, nurturing, and protective"; (2) "has relatively superior wisdom, skill, experience, and knowledge"; (3) "has my interests at stake"; (4) "has an interest in my personal, professional, and emotional growth and well-being"; (5) can be called upon "at any time"; (6) is "an advisor and a teacher"; (7) wants him to provide reciprocal "support, reassurance and dialogue"; (8) engages in frequent, critical dialogue. Phillip described a situation in which he needed help with "complications with some of the content and method of delivery required" in teaching a "packaged executive supervision program" in which he had been trained and certified by a well-known vendor. He could have called on product specialists in the vendor agency or "a network of fellow trainers who were certified with me and available to help." Instead, he called upon his predecessor "who is also an instructor because I wanted more than technical information, I wanted personal advice and reassurance that I felt only she could give."

Phillip noted that, throughout his life, he had "sought out mentors." In his early life mentors were teachers who often became a surrogate father because "my father worked long hours and was never at home" or because his father "died when I was only sixteen." Since Phillip was the eldest, he "became a parent to my brothers and sisters before I obtained all the benefits of being a child." When Phillip's father died, the family was "faced with a financial emergency. In order to survive we made the only choice available to us." He, his mother, and the next oldest boy took over the family business, a restaurant, which meant that Phillip could only attend school every

other day. Phillip found teachers filled the role of father; his emula-
tion of them carried over to unconscious imitation of their
"mannerisms, expressions, even in some cases the way they walked or
the food they ate." Mentors were important for their knowledge but,
even more so, because they provided protection, reassurance, and
confidence that enabled Phillip to learn and to be productive.

Difficulty of learning informally

Despite the apparent willingness of professionals to pursue their
learning, we know that they do not always learn as well as they would
like. As discussed in Chapter One, with respect to action science,
there is often a discrepancy between people's espoused theory (what
they say) and their theory-in-use (what they do). We believe that informal learning often goes awry despite people's best intentions and
that people often remain highly frustrated because they cannot see
why they do not produce the results they envision or, if they see it,
they cannot produce the results they want.

Judith, for example, could not produce the results she wanted.
Even though she was aware of the value of working collaboratively
with others, she may have discounted signals that she did not have
full support from the highest authority figure. She also recognized
that the culture inhibited access to top management, an obstacle she
might have perceived as more difficult to overcome than dealing with
peers. Judith has now become aware of her need to involve the top
level of the organization in projects, has probably accepted responsibility for that, and might be on the lookout for opportunities where
she can put her new insight into practice by building skills, compensating for her deficiency by enlisting the help of others, or continuing
to change this isolation pattern. None the less, Judith would probably not be too surprised if the pattern reemerged in other situations
because these deeply held values and practices, that she learned from
birth, may again catch her unawares. She might not naturally be surprised by early warning signals in a similar situation because, as a
child, these signals were "normal." Hence, she would have to develop
mechanisms to become attuned to these signals and might even draw
on the help of colleagues who could see the signals before she would.
In addition, there may be factors in the organization's culture that reinforce her unwillingness to examine these signals and that, in fact,
make it difficult to enlist top-level support for projects.

Finally, there is another dimension to the discrepancy between
what professionals should do and what they actually do. Many learning models suggest that people move logically through a plan
step-by-step. However, from what we have learned about informal
and incidental learning, we can see that professionals may plan to ex-

perience and learn certain things, but they will meet many unexpected events that could influence their thinking and change the way in which they frame the situation. If they are too linear in their thinking, they may miss rich opportunities. The unexpected may lead to reformulating a problem, experimenting with new products, trying out alternative ways of working, or uncovering a blind spot that affects one's skills in many areas of one's life.

Remember the discussion of field-independence and field-dependence (Witkin, 1949, 1950; Witkin and Goodenough, 1977) in Chapter One. It seems likely that the education of professionals would cultivate field independence because higher education fosters analytical thinking, independent (isolated) work, internal frames of reference, and a strong goal orientation. But we can see that effective informal and incidental learning depend on becoming aware of many events occurring simultaneously, seeing the context in which a problem is framed, collaborating with others who can help identify blind spots, seeing things from different viewpoints, and experimenting with ideas that were not in one's original plan.

Notes

1. This chapter is based on life history research conducted in 1988 with a cohort of adult educators in the Teachers College doctoral program. No attempt is made to generalize from this limited sample. Pseudonyms are used throughout this chapter to preserve anonymity.
2. Most of the examples here are taken from a subsample of trainers, but a few are also drawn from the lives of adult educators in other settings.
3. These data were collected within a year after the initial life history work by asking workplace educators for critical incidents.

Part three

Incidental learning

Each of the chapters in Part Three deals with the incidental learning of those who would bring about change in people, programs, and their professional practice. These beliefs about change and intervention are examined in terms of actual consequences and potential unintended consequences using a theory-of-action or action science perspective.

As we saw in Chapter One, incidental learning is a byproduct of some other activity. As such, it is typically tacit and unintentional. In the chapters which follow, Watkins examines the influence of these qualities on the nature of the learning which emerges. Learning under these conditions is largely in the form of assumptions, beliefs, and values which can be inferred from actions. Three different aspects of the role of the human resource developer are examined in order to explore the nature of incidental learning across each of these different roles: the roles of group facilitator, of change agent, and of trainer. In Chapter One, we suggested that informal and incidental learning bridge across all of the ten roles identified by the American Society for Training and Development for human resource developers. Human resource developers are increasingly involved in organizational development, which often involves group work, as, for example, through action research teams, quality circles, or other such group efforts. When organization developers build teams or help resolve interdepartmental conflict, they often intervene in a group learning process with psychodynamic overtones.

Pfeiffer and Jones (1969) developed a series of handbooks of structured experiences for human relations training, a series of exercises for group and organizational development. They designed the handbooks to move from simple, non-threatening activities to those intended for only highly skilled group facilitators. Over the years, more and more people have used instrumented, simulated exercises such as these, and increasingly these people have little or no back-

Incidental learning

ground in group facilitation. These group learning activities have sometimes led to conflicts and strong emotional reactions. A therapist recently remarked that whenever you bring people together in a group to learn, you unleash a group dynamic that has a life of its own that is largely out of your control. Recognizing as we do that group learning is a particularly effective means of learning for adults, we also acknowledge that it takes considerable skill to facilitate these open-ended learning situations. When we undertake even a task-oriented group learning project, a set of interpersonal and emotional dynamics are triggered that greatly influence the effectiveness of that learning.

In Chapter Six, Watkins and Rogers explore the learning of an interventionist who has brought together a group of adult children of alcoholics to reflect on their problems in interactions with others in the workplace. They examine the incidental learning of the interventionist and how this affected her ability to respond to the learning needs of the group. They also look at the way in which human resource developers deal with groups that include people who are affected by therapeutic issues. This case study looks at the interaction between these individuals and others in the group, and between them and the interventionist. Incidental learning is the tacit learning which is embedded in our actions. The beliefs about Adult Children of Alcoholics' therapy often led the interventionist to enact a control orientation which undermined the learning goals of the group. The case study illustrates how critical reflection on the incidental learning of the interventionist enabled her to move to a learning orientation.

Further, the issues which adult children of alcoholics bring to the learning experience also had unintended effects on the learning process. These issues are examined in light of the intervention strategies of action science. By proactively examining how these issues affected the learning process, human resource developers can see the possible impact of working with other individuals with therapeutic issues in learning situations. Adult children of alcoholics are an especially appropriate group in that they are often high performing, successful professionals. Although there has been growing interest in studying the impact of growing up in an alcoholic family, these individuals function quite "normally" and would not ordinarily have been identified as having therapeutic needs, even if a trainer were to prescreen individuals prior to a group learning activity.

Chapter Seven examines a frequent organizational development role, that of managing a change process. In this chapter, incidental learning is seen in the change managers' beliefs about the nature of the change and about leading the change process. The chapter describes cases in which colleges launched complex, large-scale innovations that began as little more than a concept. As a result, no one knew much about how to implement them. When the innovation itself is ambiguous and ill-defined, a learning process must occur in order to define the innovation sufficiently so that others may use it. When those who manage the change process are also new to managing change, they too are engaged in a learning process as they learn to lead others. In each of these cases, individuals made judgment calls regarding whether or not to emphasize defining and implementing the innovation, or to emphasize leading others toward larger organizational goals, which subsumed the change project goals but were more inclusive. The cases lead to some conclusions about leadership of change projects under non-routine conditions, about the nature of incidental learning for those involved in managing change, about the unintended consequences of beliefs, and about the impact of facilitating a learning process at the organizational level. The exponential increase in complexity and the diffusion of focus attendant on moving change to an organizational level leads to incidental learning which is more like an assessment of a culture or of leadership styles than a portrait of individual beliefs.

Chapter Eight focuses on the single most pervasive task of the human resource developer – that of delivering training. In this chapter, incidental learning is examined in the beliefs of professionals. Incidental learning at this level is quite heuristic, functioning more like implicit prescriptions for action. The chapter describes human resource developers in three different organizations: a research hospital, a government agency, and a high technology corporation. Included in the chapter is a discussion of the theory-of-action perspective that is illustrated in these data and that undergirds our concept of incidental learning. The theory is traced from its roots in sociology to the work of Argyris and Schön (1974, 1978). Using the mapping technique developed by Argyris (1983), the beliefs which inform the actions of these professionals are depicted. In this way, the incidental learning of a profession can be illustrated.

Finally, Chapter Eight includes an analysis of one case study of a difficult situation faced by a trainer. This example shows how the incidental learning of the trainer can be better understood using the action science framework and how this framework might assist the trainer in transforming her practice. Because professional learning is somewhat heuristic or even artistic, critical reflection on what professionals actually say or do is needed in order to identify the embedded beliefs which inform their action. The theory-of-action perspective enables professionals to analyze their practice for potential learning which has been acquired incidentally, through practice and assumptions about that practice. Through this analysis, they can surface that which is tacit and change beliefs that appear to lead to dysfunctional consequences.

Incidental learning, because it is outside of an individual's awareness, is particularly significant when it undermines goals. These chapters highlight instances when individuals' tacit beliefs interfered with their stated intentions. The chapters are not an indictment of human resource development practice. Rather, they critique current practice in terms of potential errors of which human resource developers would not normally be aware. Thus, they are intended to assist practitioners in reflecting on the tacit beliefs which guide their practice in an effort to uncover those which are unproductive in order to improve practice. Nevertheless, like the contradictions identified in these chapters between what people intended and what they produced, it seems likely that these chapters may also both indict and inspire.

Chapter six

Adult children of alcoholics in the workplace: incidental learning and intervention

One of the most important areas of incidental learning to explore is the beliefs of those who facilitate workplace learning. This chapter, like Chapter Eight, will examine this aspect of incidental learning.[1] While the latter chapter examines beliefs across a wide spectrum of the profession of human resource development, this chapter will take an in-depth look at the incidental learning of one individual, an interventionist as she reconciles two major intervention modalities – education and therapy. While the interventionist facilitates group learning, she also manages a change project. In this sense, Chapter Six shares some similarities with Chapter Seven.

The learners described in this chapter were self-identified adult children of alcoholics (ACOAs) who came together to explore problems in the way in which they functioned in the workplace. As a result, this chapter not only explores the facilitator's beliefs about learning-oriented interventions but also looks at her beliefs about therapeutic interventions. It is important to note that this was not a therapy group. However, the influence of this interventionist's beliefs about the nature of therapy continually surfaced in her practice as she sought to help this group of people solve interpersonal problems. They came together because they believed that their common family background would lead them to have similar present-day work issues. They were not "abnormal" but rather were effective, practicing professionals. At its most basic level, it was the attribution that they were "abnormal" or "sick" that led to the interventionist's therapeutic interventions, while her perception of the wellness of her group undergirded her educational or learning-oriented actions.

The chapter illustrates the interaction between the perceptions and attributions of those who facilitate learning with the perceptions and attributions of learners.[2] The chapter begins with an explanation of why ACOAs are an important group to study in the workplace.

Findings are presented in case study format with illustrative quotations from the transcripts of the sixteen group meetings and are then discussed using maps, a format developed by Argyris (1983) to show the relationships among reasoning, actions, and consequences, both intended and unintended, of actions.

The authors look first at the interventionist as she dealt with the therapeutic issues of these individuals. Participants were interested in a transformative learning process that enabled them to change their habitual responses when their therapeutic issues were triggered. This situation challenged the interventionist to move away from a therapeutic exploration of historical conditions and an emphasis on the disease of alcoholism. She encouraged experimentation with alternative ways of acting in their here-and-now practice. The process of understanding the differences between these two intervention modalities led to the discovery of interaction effects between action science interventions and individuals at different stages in recovery that illustrates incidental learning.

This chapter also examines the participants as they engaged in reflective experiences in a group setting. Incidental, vicarious learning occurred among group members with similar characteristics and backgrounds. Learning was particularly strong during unexpected "moments of surrender" when participants gave in to the process. Finally, this truly collaborative setting allowed participants not only to expect, but also demand, the right to learn the skills of intervention themselves.

Adult children of alcoholics

There are over 28 million children of alcoholics in the United States, 22 million of whom have now reached adulthood yet continue to experience emotional, mental,and physical effects of life in an alcoholic family (Russell *et al.*, 1985). As adults, children of alcoholics find themselves in families and organizations where the dynamics of their childhood recur with unsettling frequency. Children of alcoholics are four times more likely to become alcoholic than others (Cotton, 1979; Goodwin, 1978, 1985). Grandsons of alcoholics are at three times higher risk for alcoholism than other grandsons (Kaij and Dock, 1975); daughters of alcoholics are more likely to marry alcoholic men.

In the workplace, adult children of alcoholics (ACOAs) have recently been acknowledged as a group who face special challenges. The Kemper group reports that over one-third of those seen for family problems during a nine-year period by their Personnel Assistance Program were adults who grew up in alcoholic homes (Woodside,

1986). Similarly, the New England Telephone Company reports that 31% of its Employee Assistance Programs (EAP) general counseling cases in 1985 were children of alcoholics (Woodside, 1986). A 1985 study of top corporate alcoholic executives by the Alcoholism Council of Greater New York shows that 37 of the study's 62 alcoholic executives were also children of alcoholics (Woodside, 1986). Finally, a preliminary review for the Children of Alcoholics Foundation of 100 randomly selected case records from a variety of Employee Assistance Programs revealed at least 28% of the cases were employed children of alcoholics; the figures rose to 35% when other probable indicators of parental alcohol abuse were included (Woodside, 1986).

While many ACOAs in the workplace are referred to Employee Assistance Programs for substance abuse, many more seek help for other problems. They may feel something is lacking in their relationships, experience work dissatisfaction, have feelings of rejection, or maintain a low image of themselves. In addition, certain adaptive issues reported in the ACOA literature (Cermak and Brown, 1982; Gravitz and Bowden, 1984; Whitfield, 1980; Woititz, 1986) can be expected to cause difficulties in the workplace, particularly low self-esteem, problems with trust, excessive control needs, over-responsibility, a strong need for approval, and depression. Many ACOAs are at high risk for becoming workaholics, seeking self-esteem and a sense of successful coping from their job performance (Woititz, 1987). Like other workaholics, they may be unrealistic in the amount of work they take on, unable to balance personal needs with unrealistic workplace commitments. Clinicians (Gravitz and Bowden, 1985; Whitfield, 1987) observe that many ACOAs are addicted to crises, replicating in adult life the childhood role of taking responsibility in their crisis-oriented alcoholic family. The workplace provides a primary setting for re-enactments of family-of-origin dynamics.

Without help, ACOAs may not be able to resolve painful experiences from childhood. Even though they achieve many successes in the workplace, they may not be able to derive genuine fulfillment from their accomplishment. Over time they may become depressed or dissatisfied, realizing that nothing they "do" can address their feelings of emptiness. This condition can lead to ongoing stress and depression that seriously compromises workplace performance and makes them likely candidates for burn-out. This may be particularly true for many helping professionals, for example counselors or nurses or trainers, who have a high burnout rate and a high percentage of adult children of alcoholics in the profession (Kern, 1986; Woititz, 1986).

The impetus to understand and help individual ACOAs who experience difficulties in the workplace is growing. In addition, there is a need to address at a more macro level the dynamics of addiction which sustain dysfunctional, unhealthy organizational life. Schaef and Fassel (1988) describe four ways that the addictive system is enacted in organizations. First, there are organizations in which a key person is an addict and workers take on various roles of a dysfunctional family. Second, individuals who have grown up in dysfunctional, addictive families reenact family of origin dynamics in their organizations. Third, an organization can serve as an addictive substance in work addictions which are extremely destructive to families and personal relationships. Finally, Schaef and Fassel argue that the organization itself can be understood as an addict, functioning corporately the way an individual addict functions. Workers adapt in the same dysfunctional ways that members do in addictive family systems. These four interpretive metaphors for understanding organizational life make a case for the need to learn about and transform patterns of behavior learned incidentally in the workplace which are as destructive as those in addictive family systems.

Action science

The theoretical perspective used in this chapter is action science. Action science is concerned with interpersonal action that produces knowledge which is disconfirmable. Action science offers people who choose its values an alternative way to frame and solve problems (Argyris *et al.* 1985). Individuals report specific incidents of their practice – what was actually said, thought, and done. These incidents are then examined with almost scientific detachment for underlying themes or patterns. Action scientists search for clues regarding the dysfunctional behavior of the individual. Was it in the person's thoughts? Did they, in other words, make inferences and attributions without data to support them? Were they stuck in one way of framing the situation? Was it in what they said or did? Perhaps there is a discrepancy between what they thought and what they said? Is there a lack of skill in communicating difficult or complex information? Or is it a product of the individual's norms, such as a norm that it is not polite to share negative feedback?

Through a "scientific" analysis of questions such as these, new knowledge about the situation is developed. This knowledge can be stated in terms that permit individuals to try out alternate actions, to analyze them again, and then decide whether or not this knowledge was accurate and usable. The generation of alternatives is facilitated by the normative framework for interpersonal action, Model II, in action science. Double-loop learning or Model II is a normative model which suggests that human interpersonal action is more effective under conditions of reciprocity, openness to learning, and internal ownership or commitment to the alternative action or choice. Individuals present as problems situations in which they violate their own goals or values. By reflecting on what the individual did that contradicted those values, what competing pressures or reasoning may have led to the contradiction, and clarifying what actions would more consistently fit those values, individuals are encouraged to redesign their actions based on their own values. In Argyris and Schön's terms, this leads to action that fits two larger societal values, competence and justice.

In the following pages, the action science perspective and techniques for analyzing case incidents from an individual's practice will be used to examine the incidental learning of the learning facilitator or interventionist and of the learning group.

Interventionist's incidental learning

These learners were self-identified ACOAs, who had therapeutic issues, but nevertheless wanted to come together in an educational experience to explore problems in their present workplace functioning. The interventionist thus had to balance her beliefs about learning interventions with her beliefs about therapeutic interventions. She had to learn to distinguish between these two intervention modalities and to integrate a more evolved understanding of them in her practice.

Education and therapy

With the advent of sensitivity training (T-groups) and laboratory education, questions were raised as to whether these groups were really "therapy without a license." In responding to this issue, Chris Argyris (1968) differentiated between the conditions that lead to competence acquisition and those which lead to therapy. He began by defining interpersonal competence as the ability to cope with interpersonal relationships in such a way that individuals perceive the situation accurately, solve problems in such a way that they remain solved, and create conditions where the parties involved are able to continue working together as effectively as they did before they attempted to solve the present problem (p. 148). To do this, individuals need to learn to give feedback that is directly verifiable or observable, minimally contradictory or distorted, and minimally evaluative. Two preconditions are a constructive intent and a genuine desire or openness to learn.

In contrast, therapy groups are designed to meet the needs of individuals who primarily protect themselves to survive. Survival-oriented individuals are closed to learning and instead use defense mechanisms to withdraw, distort, or attack their environment. Of course, most people are neither wholly open nor closed:

> The important point, from a theory of learning, is that the educator and the client need to be able to differentiate between that learning which evolves around problems and issues about which the individual is more or less open or closed. Each state of affairs requires different interventions by which to encourage learning.
> [Argyris, 1968, p. 165]

In therapy, attributive inferences are often used to encourage a closed client to examine hidden reasoning: "I think you're denying your feelings here." This intervention is deliberately somewhat intrusive in order to break past a wall of defenses. By contrast, in a learning group this would be a high-level inference (thus a poor intervention), and the emphasis would instead be on sharing directly observable data. Yet, for a closed individual in denial, direct observations may either be fielded by his or her defenses or potentially too hot to handle as he or she may break down his or her denial in such a way that the individual would be left exposed and vulnerable, making educational interventions potentially even more intrusive. The survival-oriented person's behavior is "repetitive and compulsive" rather than "adaptive and functional" which means that this person may have considerable difficulty focusing on here-and-now behavior or his or her impact on others (ibid., p. 169). Moreover, he or she will cling to previous ways of acting despite evidence that they are dysfunctional.

Therapy means to cure or restore a person to a healthy condition. People need therapy when they have become inappropriately closed in their present circumstances or when they are unable to marshall the internal resources to solve their own problems. Under these closed conditions, techniques such as dream analysis or free association are needed to facilitate diagnoses of what lies behind the individual's defenses. The therapist offers interpretations to the client which may be based on a theory of the client's dysfunction (e.g., the typical responses of children in growing up with parental alcoholism). An exploration of personal history can help individuals see that they are capable of solving problems now and that their present state is a result of their "historical" situation. Yet this exploration is not enough to bring about competence acquisition.

According to Argyris, the interventionist needs to collect as much information as possible on the relative openness of the learner's responses to a growth-oriented learning situation. To do this, he or she needs to create the environment for competence acquisition and observe responses. If individuals seem to be increasingly frightened and withdrawn, they are probably more closed than open. If they are given feedback on a genuine dilemma they are facing or on gaps and inconsistencies in their practice, yet appear to have little or no motivation to change, they may be closed. Finally, if competence-oriented feedback is given and experienced as threatening while survival-oriented feedback (interpretive, inferential, and evaluative) is given and experienced as helpful, the individual may be more closed than open (Argyris, 1968, pp. 172–173).

To Argyris, then, the decision to pursue therapy or learning is quite complicated and interactive for any interventionist. While individuals usually enter therapy because they need help, educational settings often include individuals with unacknowledged therapeutic needs. Moreover, individuals in interpersonal learning situations may move in and out of a competence orientation, based on the topic and the nature of the feedback given. Groups also influence the capacity of the educator to enact a growth-oriented learning environment. If the group includes members with a survival-orientation, who need to explore the genesis of their present behavior more than to change that behavior, the group itself may resist a here-and-now orientation. Moreover, this survival-orientation may further inhibit the group's capacity because individuals in this frame of reference are less likely to give minimally evaluative and inferential feedback or to be helpful to others seeking to change their present behavior.

Judgment calls

This chapter illustrates the judgment calls that must be made by an interventionist who is trying to create the conditions for competence-acquisition rather than therapy. Within this group, individuals moved in and out of competence-acquisition and therapeutic orientations. This was complicated by the fact that all participants (including the interventionist) shared ACOA therapeutic issues, but had spent different amounts of time in therapy dealing with this family history. Those participants who had been in therapy were used to making survival-oriented interventions based on their understanding of ACOA family roles (hero, scapegoat, mascot, lost child) or common therapeutic issues (e.g., shame, perfectionism, or grieving early losses). For example, when an individual brought in a case with less than half of a page of actual dialogue, the group quickly assumed that the authority figure was the individual's father and the other person in the vignette was the individual's mother. The survival orientation of this client became evident when these attributive interpretations were immediately accepted and followed by lengthy poignant illustrations of painful incidents in the individual's family of origin.

Interestingly, it was the participant herself who had the strongest sense that her therapeutic needs might be different from the competence-acquisition intent of the learning group. When asked where she wanted the group to focus in working her case, she expressed concerns about creating a therapeutic situation.

> Participant: [I would like you] to give me an alternative to working with men who intimidate me...but a long time ago we talked about this not becoming a therapeutic setting.

This participant had a sense that in exploring with the group her experience as a child of an alcoholic, she would be moving it in a different direction. In fact, this participant's awareness of her own therapeutic need was greater than the interventionist's understanding. At this point in the discussion, the interventionist was struggling with the notion that she had somehow created a dichotomy between the group's interests and what the participant really wanted to talk about.

> Interventionist: I have some concerns, but...why in the world would I think I'd be working with a group of adult children of alcoholics who wouldn't be concerned about the structure I might be imposing. But I've really framed [this experience] as a mutual exploration that we're on, and if I restrict it...I feel like we're going to lose a lot.

The participant went on to explore, primarily by answering interpretive, attributive, and inferential questions, the meaning of the case from an ACOA perspective. After sharing a painful story about her alcoholic father's death, she poignantly described how unresolved family-of-origin experiences can haunt present-day interactions.

> What's interesting is that the minute I saw [another male participant], it was like, pardon the analogy, the other day I passed a fig tree and I immediately thought of my grandmother's house be-

cause she had this marvelous fig tree and I never see fig trees around here. But the first minute I saw you, you're the size of my father. It was kind of a feeling freeze and I didn't understand why. And I thought, thought, and thought about it and I thought, yeah, it's the size ... *and isn't that an unfair thing to do to another human being, just because you're the size of another human being I'm going to be wary of you.*

This exploration of family-of-origin dynamics was highly emotional and cathartic. When the group met again the next week, the interventionist pronounced the participant's case finished even though they usually spent two weeks on each person's case – the first week to discuss the case, the second to reflect on what was learned. When asked about her reasoning, the interventionist said she believed the client's case reflected unresolved grief issues that precluded focusing on her here-and-now action. When the interventionist went back to the group and shared that her co-researcher had questioned her actions, the client confirmed that the interventionist's actions bothered her.

The participant had disclosed intensely personal information and the interventionist wanted to go on to focus on something else. When the interventionist later attempted to go back to working on this participant's practice, using something she had said to another group member, the participant declined to redesign the incident and shortly thereafter left the group and did not return. Among the participants, she had the least experience of examining the influence of parental alcoholism on her life. Since she was also inexperienced with action science, she interpreted this type of learning from a therapeutic frame of reference and assumed that action science redesigns equalled "cures." Since she knew she could not "cure" the fact that she had been born into a family with alcoholism, and did not yet have the experience of transforming her current behavior, she was overwhelmed by the task. Later, she said the experience motivated her to seek ACOA therapy instead of the competence acquisition focus of this group.

Moving out of a therapeutic frame of reference to a competence-acquisition orientation was a challenge for both the interventionist and the group. Because therapeutic interventions were both familiar to and well-received by the participants, the tendency was to fall back on what was known. Gradually, the facilitator began to move out of a therapeutic orientation in her interventions with the group. However, the various action science strategies which she attempted to enact created different effects on individuals at different stages of ACOA awareness and recovery. Thus, one byproduct of using the technology of action science with this particular group of individuals was that certain strategies had unintended side-effects in terms of challenging specific ACOA issues. Table 6.1 illustrates these interactions.

As summarized in Table 6.1, action science strategies often interacted with specific ACOA issues in potent ways. In a session after the emotionally cathartic experience described earlier, the group worked on a transcript of the previous meeting, using action science strategies. They stayed grounded in the data, focusing on what was actually said and done. There was a great deal of tension throughout the group with individuals experiencing this session as much "hotter" than earlier sessions. A possible explanation for this is that dealing with verbatim dialogue in the here-and-now confronted learned

Table 6.1 The interaction of action science and ACOA issues

Action science strategies	that may threaten	these ACOA issues
Using directly observable data		Breaks down denial; induces feelings of shame
Confronting "fancy footwork" (saying two contradictory things in order to "be right")		Confronts learned patterns of coping with irrational angry parent by saying whatever contradictory things one must to deflect blame
Using feelings as data for learning		Requires high level of surfacing of feelings, yet ACOAs are often unaware of feelings or try to suppress or control them because they were not "safe" in their family-of-origin.
Using mistakes as learning		Confronts all-or-none, right/wrong thinking typical of many ACOAs
Redesigning problematic habituated role-bound behavior		Asks person to move beyond behavior which the person has developed to survive
Reframing theories-in-use, frames of reference about what works		Appears to require a "cure" of childhood view of the world yet current behaviors developed to provide coping mechanisms
Advocating one's view while inquiring into another's view		Confronts common ACOA family-of-origin behaviors of withdrawing, hiding, or saying nothing

ACOA behavior, particularly an unconscious process of denial and a strong sense of shame regarding one's perceived errors. In the early weeks of the group meetings, a number of individuals asked the researcher to "edit" their comments so that their grammar would be acceptable and there would not be any "uh's" or off-handed comments that might embarrass them. We describe the effects of action science strategies on ACOA therapeutic issues as incidental because the group was not attempting to use action science to intervene therapeutically on each other. Rather their intent was to move beyond therapy to create conditions for competence acquisition but, in doing this, learning occurred which turned out to be both therapeutic and educative.

The group's incidental learning

While much of the learning for individuals in this group was deliberate and purposive, there were also examples of unexpected, incidental learning. Moreover, through the intervention, tacit beliefs embedded in people's actions – in other words, incidental learning stored from the past – were surfaced and examined. Thus, incidental learning surfaced both as a byproduct of the group and from individuals' past histories.

Double hits: learning from one another's blind spots

Frequently, as one person worked on a case, it triggered learning in a second person of similar or greater intensity. These were described as "double hits" – two interventions packed into one. For example, Lynn's negative attributions about a person in her case reminded another participant, Scott, of a case he had brought to another action science group several months before.

> Scott: We were saying some things about X, but I couldn't laugh because I was sitting here going, my god this is my case, and I figured you [the interventionist] were going to say, well, why don't you reframe this. [Laughter] 'Cause it's the same; I didn't recognize it until you started talking about it.

Later, when the group began working with Scott's case, Lynn identified with Scott's resistance to changing his negative attributions about the person in his case.

141

> Lynn: I identify with Scott...there are just so many things in here that I identify with and it's real good for me...I'm not as anxious because I'm not the one doing it.

Lynn's identification with Scott was not exactly welcomed by him. During the discussion of his case, the interventionist described Scott as an "artful dodger," skillfully defending against the group's interventions rather than inquiring into their validity. When Scott rejected this characterization, Lynn indirectly advocated the diagnosis by expressing her strong identification with Scott's defensiveness.

> Lynn: But Scott, I felt exactly the same way. I came in here and I thought everybody was going to see it my way...even though I was uncomfortable about the whole transaction, I still felt I was right. And then I heard all this other stuff...and there were little holes pricked in my story too.... Every time anyone asked me a question, I could come up with another story.

This type of incidental learning from others occurred for the other group members as well as for the co-researchers who often saw their frameworks of understanding illustrated in participants' behavior. Of course, this may be one of the reasons for theme or single-problem therapy groups. When people share a common experience, the learning processes of one person can be recognized as relevant learning for others as well. Yet, because individuals owned these insights and often found that they came to them almost from their subconscious, they seemed to experience them as particularly potent.

Moments of surrender

Another type of incidental learning occurred at moments when an individual gave up striving to be understood or to be right and surrendered to the confusion of a process later recognized as learning. Lynn described this act of surrender:

> Lynn: I mean to me it comes down to just sheer letting go. And that's the thing I was real aware of...I see at some point that I have just to let go of my frame on X that she is incompetent or that she is all bad because of this one thing.

These "moments of surrender" when an individual yields a cherished belief or yields control appear to be fundamental in each of the theories depicted below. Table 6.2 compares the stages of development

142

Table 6.2 A comparison of three transformative learning theories

Model II skills	Stages of reflective learning	Stages of ACOA recovery
		Survival – do what was functional in family of origin but is now increasingly dysfunctional
Owning Unfreezing	A sense of inner discomfort, a sense that something does not fit, or of unfinished business	Emergent awareness – first glimpse that reality is not as previously imagined; requires a trigger
Recognizing dysfunctional control-oriented theories of action	Identification/clarification of the concern; the problem is conceptualized in relation to self and often includes a significant shift in perspective	Core issues – trust, feelings, all-or-none functioning, intimacy, neglect of personal needs, high tolerance for crises, and inappropriate behavior – become everyday problems
Openness Reframing for learning	Openness to new information, a variety of sources of information; suspension of need for closure; trust of self to discover information	Transformation – reframing or restructuring of a core issue
	Resolution – the "aha" stage, when people experience being changed, having learned or reached closure; a coming together or creative synthesis; contains surprise and is often preceded by psychological readiness	Integration – make a whole from the separate parts to create order; view learning in relation to the issue, taking one core issue at a time; is preceded by 3–5 years in a recovery program
	Establish continuity of self with past, present, and future self; changed perspective leads to seeing things differently	Genesis – spiritual development
Experimentation	Decide whether to take action, whether to "go public" with new behavior, to test against others' reactions	

in action science (Argyris, 1970), reflective learning (Boyd and Fales, 1983), and ACOA recovery (Gravitz and Bowden, 1985). This comparison illustrates the centrality of a kind of surrendering or yielding as a prerequisite to transformative learning. The power of surrender in learning processes is illustrated by the drastic change in the group dynamic which occurred when the interventionist yielded to a critical examination of her own action, rather than just advocating this norm. During Meetings 6 and 7, the interventionist and the participants vacillated between therapeutic kinds of interventions and those using action science strategies. In Meeting 8, the interventionist consistently used action science strategies in her interventions with the case writer, Scott. As noted earlier, these discussions were tense and Scott, who was on the "hot seat," was often defensive. After the eighth meeting, the interventionist and her co-researcher explored ways in which her interactions with Scott were ineffective. Together they developed the "Interventionist Map" (Figure 6.1) which depicts the unilateral way she and others had been advocating their often therapeutic interpretations.

In Meeting 7, the interventionist shared this map with the group, illustrating it with incidents in the group interaction. In this meeting, a dramatic shift in the group dynamic occurred. Scott, who had earlier been defensive, began to explore the ways in which others' observations about his behavior might be true. He acknowledged his "fancy footwork" (defensive routines to keep from understanding and integrating others' feedback) and later described this as the most significant learning for him in the sixteen weeks. In subsequent meetings, the group began to work together in a more functional way, experimenting and playing with exercises to facilitate reframing and redesigning their action. In effect, the "Interventionist Map" marked a moment of surrender for the interventionist and this became a model for others in the group.

The process of learning to transform core ACOA issues is emotionally charged. Emotional learning is an integral part of the reflective learning process. The interventionist and other group members exhibited a control orientation toward emotions throughout much of the early group experience. Later the interventionist led others in adopting a more reflective orientation regarding their emotional responses. With the control orientation, the interventionist assumed that, by controlling emotions, others could be helped to work through core ACOA issues and move into transformative learning. Informed by this assumption, she tended to minimize her own emotional reactions as well as those of others and then to minimize the impact of this minimizing. She also tended to interpret her own and others' emotional responses unilaterally, shift-

Conditions	Assumptions	Action Strategies	Consequences
When intervening with fellow ACOAs	Frame them as avoiding experience of specific feelings	Interpret what they say and do as evidence of this frame using data which are self-sealing and at a high level of inference (e.g. body language)	Leaving my understanding of ACOA dilemmas intact, including belief that emotional confrontation is unavoidable in addressing these dilemmas
	OR	Minimize inquiry into the interpretation or its impact; do inquire into family roles to find data to support interpretation	Low level of impact in terms of present day functioning
	Frame them as having a specific deep-seated need	When client reacts strongly to intervention minimize or obscure impact of intervention See client defensiveness as further evidence of original assumptions	Possible paralyzing frame if attributions of present problems are solely to family-of-origin experiences

Figure 6.1 Interventionist map

ing responsibility for others' reactions to what was happening to them. As another way of coping with the strong emotions, she often unilaterally interpreted what happened to group members in positive terms, describing events as leading to learning, growth or success. The unintended consequences of this orientation were that group members often had difficulty trusting their strong feelings. To some extent, the sense of shame around having strong feelings was heightened, which in effect recreated the ACOA childhood experience that feelings are inappropriate or dangerous. This in turn mitigated

145

against building the climate of trust necessary for working on core issues because participants experienced a lack of congruence between what they were experiencing and what was explicitly espoused. This replicated in many ways the familiar family-of-origin binds.

As the group process evolved, both the interventionist and participants began to develop a more reflective orientation toward the emotional learning. With this orientation, the interventionist assumed that, by accepting emotions, others could be helped to work through core ACOA issues and move into transformative learning. She began to identify and publicly acknowledge emotional reactions within the group and to inquire into the impact of these emotions. The interventionist thus shared her attributions about the emotional impact of her interventions and inquired into their validity. And finally she began to share her interpretations of the effects of interventions in terms of learning and growth, but also inquired with others into their interpretations. The consequences of this more reflective orientation were that a climate of trust was strengthened where the impact of emotions could be explored. Both the interventionist and participants began to learn about the impact of their emotional reactions on others. In doing this, they began to learn how to manage their strong emotions in a group which did not replicate dysfunctional family-of-origin dynamics.

This reflective orientation toward emotional learning was most explicitly enacted as the group worked through their final case. In Meeting 14, the group began to surface emotions and eventually reflected on how specific emotions played an integral role in the group dynamic. One of the group members, Matt, had a strong therapeutic background and tended to make attributions about ACOA characteristics in a unilateral, uninquiring way. Although he wanted and asked for feedback, the group increasingly avoided directly confronting him. In Meeting 14, the group began to reflect on their inability to give Matt direct feedback.

This led the co-researchers to develop two maps depicting the group's practice. Figure 6.2 illustrates "The non-feedback loop" which led to Matt not receiving direct feedback in the group. When he expressed his feelings, he made explicit ACOA fears and raised the emotional tenor in the group. This, in turn, raised core issues for other group members who began to enact action strategies to avoid precipitating or confronting Matt's feelings. The unintended consequence was that Matt did not get what he needed and wanted (i.e., clear feedback).

The second map (Figure 6.3) depicts the mutuality of the developmental journey that Matt and others in the group needed to make. In the family of origin, Matt learned to shut down feelings; in recovery

Matt's actions	Group's actions
Matt expresses his feelings; makes explicit his worst ACOA fears; ups the emotional ante	These explicit feelings raise core issues in others
Matt does not get what he needs and wants (i.e. clear feedback)	Others enact action strategies to avoid precipitating or confronting Matt's feelings

Figure 6.2 The non-feedback loop

Matt's stages of incidental learning	Group's stages of incidental learning
Both test the competence and justice of their interventions with others.	
Matt learns to express feelings and information about his internal state in terms of testable hypotheses and to inquire into the reality of the attributions he has made that led him to experience those childhood feelings.	Others learn to test their attribution that Matt will reject them when they honestly confront his action and examine the viability of a relationship where they cannot be honest.
Matt learns to feel his feelings and express them.	Others accept Matt's feelings and permit him to express them.
Matt learns to shut down feelings in family of origin.	Others learn to fear rejection/abandonment in family of origin

Figure 6.3 Developmental journey map

147

he began to feel his feelings and express them. In the next step, Matt needed to learn to express his feelings and information about his internal state in terms of testable hypotheses and inquire into the reality of the attributions he made that led him to experience these feelings. On the other side of the dialogue, participants learned to fear certain feelings (e.g. rejection/abandonment) in their families of origin. In their developmental journey, the participants needed to learn to accept Matt's strong feelings.

The next step for them was to learn to test their attributions that Matt would reject them when they honestly confronted his actions. Moreover, they needed to consider the viability of any relationship where they could not give honest feedback. Finally, at an even later stage in the mutual developmental journey, both Matt and the others needed to test the competence and justice of their interventions with others.

When the interventionist presented these two maps to the group, participants expressed their belief that the maps not only depicted what was happening in the group but also described the next stage of their learning. What was especially interesting was the way in which each person's new skills demanded greater and greater skills on the part of the group. It is the interaction between the incidental learning of the group members that was most significant here.

Group empowerment

An intriguing dynamic in this highly collaborative situation was the increasing tendency for participants not only to expect but to demand to learn the intervention skills themselves. At the beginning of the study, neither of the co-researchers expected participants to learn action science in one 16-week group experience. In our own experience, the learning process had taken well over two years. The expressed purpose of the group was for individuals to learn about one specific workplace interaction which was creating difficulties for them, rather than to acquire action science skills.

However, this created dilemmas for participants from the beginning. One group member was not sure how to talk about the cases since this was an action science group, not a therapy group: "I'm feeling a certain amount of awkwardness...is it okay for us to say what our gut feeling was or is there a format?" While the interventionist could acknowledge the dilemma, she could only advocate at this stage in the learning that the group embrace the dilemma and learn by doing.

Renee: I see that I have created that dilemma.... I'd like to advocate that...we just do it and learn it in the process.... What's necessary for the group to work is for people not to feel censored and...challenge the rules...but that sounds like I'm speaking out of both sides of my mouth because I tell you about the structure and then I tell you it's okay to break it. And I feel like saying a real Model I thing like, "just trust me."

Another participant remarked on the irony of asking them to do something (i.e. action science) but not explicitly teaching it.

Scott: I think it's interesting...because we're all adult children, we have a need to be perfect and do it right...that you [the interventionist] would think you could get away with being obscure about the technology [laughter]....

You've thrown a ball out here on the table but you're not going to tell us the rules or how points are scored and it's freaking everybody out.

As the group progressed, participants began to learn the intervention skills and increasingly took on this role in the group discussion. This incidental dynamic increased the learning capacity of the group significantly; especially when the group generated a map themselves to depict the learning dynamics in one member's case.

Implications for incidental learning

This chapter holds numerous implications for the facilitation of incidental learning. Perhaps the most important implication is the need for openness to the surprises that are characteristic of practice. Schön (1987) defines professional artistry as "the kind of competence that practitioners sometimes display in unique, uncertain, and conflicted situations in practice" (p. 22). He adds that this artistry is a highly advanced hybrid of ordinary competence and involves tacit knowing, knowing-in-action. A similar skill is reflection-in-action which involves reflecting on the "backtalk" from a situation, questioning the assumptions underlying knowing-in-action, and conducting on-the-spot experiments. The successful moments in the reflective learning experience involved just such an openness in "uncertain and conflicted situations." Because the insights and developing awarenesses which evolve "in action" are often unpredictable and unplanned, the learning process requires trial-and-error experimentation. This openness is illustrated in the unexpected learning from others and the "moments of surrender" experienced by the participants. The experimental attitude is illustrated by the risks participants took in trying on new roles and challenging the role definitions posed by the interventionists.

While openness and an experimental attitude seem essential in maximizing incidental learning, this type of learning is always delimited by the unexamined assumptions and "frameworks" of understanding that participants bring into any learning process. Participants had a useful framework for understanding their historical condition of having grown up with an alcoholic parent. However, as they sought to move beyond therapeutic understandings and interventions with each other in order to change their here-and-now action, a therapeutic framework became a delimiter of their new learning. These kinds of delimiters can be overcome by the skills of critical reflection. As participants moved toward a competence-acquisition orientation, they began to explore the ways in which therapeutic insights were helpful but further development involved a transcendence of any one particular framework.

The "double hits" of incidental learning described above seem to be potent for several reasons. In our deliberate learning processes, there is often a natural tendency to distance ourselves psychically from new, painful learning. In observing others "learning our lessons," the process can be less threatening or, conversely, deeper since our defenses are down and we do not expect suddenly to see ourselves differently.

In line with the potency of incidental learning is the fact that it is, by its nature, empowering. In the process of examining their experience, learners acquire those "learning how to learn" skills which go beyond content mastery. Since the learning is generated and owned by participants, it is not dependent on teachers or facilitators. Perhaps the most important task for teachers and facilitators is learning how not to impede the process while simultaneously creating enhanced opportunities and capacities for reflection. Surrendering control of the learning process leads to new discoveries about that process that enrich the learning of everyone involved.

What is most overwhelming is the architectural clarity with which we can see the interventionist's practice. As Schön (1983) depicts so well, the artistry in expert professional practice is in the quality and range of responses available in the myriad judgment calls these individuals must make in professional fields which lack a routine procedure for accomplishing tasks. These many judgment calls depend, in large measure, on the capacity of the individual to surface and critically examine incidental learning.

Notes

1. This chapter was co-authored by Karen Watkins and Renee Rogers.
2. These findings are drawn from a larger study funded by the Hogg
   Foundation for Mental Health, conducted by Karen Watkins and
   Renee Rogers. One purpose of the study was to deepen our understanding of issues faced by adult children of alcoholics in the workplace.
   Another purpose was to test the efficacy of action science as a method
   for facilitating reflection on incidental learning with this population. The
   study described the beliefs and actions of the action science facilitator
   which changed the understanding of group participants about problematic interpersonal incidents by surfacing the unintended consequences
   of their actions and the underlying assumptions or frames of reference
   which produced their actions.

Chapter seven

Higher education administrators: incidental learning of change managers

In Chapter One, we discussed the way in which tacit beliefs and feelings are embedded, but can be surfaced by examining what individuals actually do and their reasoning about the actions that they take. This incidental learning typically takes place in non-routine conditions. This chapter explores the leadership roles, concerns and beliefs of higher educational administrators about managing change under non-routine conditions.[1] Incidental learning is examined in these leaders' beliefs about leadership as well as possible unintended consequences of their beliefs.

Since incidental learning is tacit, we have first to make it visible in order to determine what has been learned. The following chapter illustrates some of the beliefs leaders have about managing change and about innovations, as well as the impact of these beliefs on change projects in higher education. The chapter includes a case description of the implementation process for three innovations, selected because they were particularly difficult to implement. These innovations were either very complex and/or not clearly specified so that project leaders had continually to work to define the innovation. This compounded their task. Through these case studies we can see the impact of the nature of the change on the tasks needed to manage the process. Of special significance is the implication that, when the change is highly non-routine and unspecified, the attributions and assumptions of those who manage the change project are a critical variable. It is through these assumptions that the innovation begins to take shape. Key to success was a willingness to work with those who must implement the change and encouragement of their assistance in "mutually adapting" (Berman and McLaughlin, 1976) the innovation. In each of the innovations described here, there has been a constricting of control by the project leadership which led to intense management effort and an uncertain future for the innovation.

Because these innovations were non-routine, they also represent learning projects at the organizational level. Many policies and procedures had to change in order to support them. Moreover, they had to be designed or adapted by these key people in the organization as they were implemented. The original innovation goals were more like a point of departure than a blueprint. Since several of the change leaders were new to change management, they were also engaged in a parallel learning project, learning to manage change in their organization. Their beliefs about the nature of leadership and their leadership roles constituted a form of incidental learning which also influenced the success of their implementation process. The case studies depict the impact and drama of this type of learning in the organization.

In the previous chapter, we looked at incidental learning at the individual and group level. At the organizational level, incidental learning is still tacit and largely observable in the actions of key players and the intended and unintended consequences of those actions. Yet, because there are so many more players and so many more antecedents to the actions to be observed, the values are more diffuse at this level. The displacement of goals over time, seen in the studies in this chapter, illustrates the difficulty of learning from experience in the organization over a long time period. Organizational memory includes the impressions and attributions of organizational members about the ease or disease of the implementation process. As experiences are transformed from a concrete event to an impression across many different people, the details disappear and only a colored outline remains. When an organization is attempting to implement an innovation over a period of ten years, decisions reached and progress made in the past erode and have to be remade or recaptured. Over time, the focal issues of the organization may change and prior experiences are reinterpreted in light of the new emphasis. As a result, goal displacement often occurs. With changes in project leadership, radical changes in the interpretation of the project may also occur. These case studies clearly show the impact on incidental learning when many individuals are involved in determining what is to be learned and when learning takes place over a long time period.

The chapter begins with an outline of the problem which guided the case studies and a brief review of relevant literature on the change process to determine the values and beliefs of the field about the process of managing change. Findings are then discussed in terms of their implications for incidental learning.

The problem of change

Few innovations persist beyond the initial period of federal support (Berman and McLaughlin, 1976). Yet the educational problems these innovations were developed to solve do persist and often become more intense (e.g. increasing the retention and achievement of high risk students). A number of studies have charged administrators with responsibility for the failure of innovations to persist (Ross *et al.*, 1951; Gross *et al,.* 1971; Emrick *et al.*, 1977). Yet, Berman and McLaughlin (1976) state the problem somewhat differently: they find that administrative support is a "necessary but not sufficient" condition for persistence. This chapter looks at the roles and concerns of managers of change projects in order to determine whether or not these suggest possible incidental learning that may affect the success of the change effort.

Research on innovation implementation has noted a distinction in the rate of persistence of different types of innovations. Perrow (1967) coupled the nature of the technology with the need for different types of managerial tasks. Knight and McDaniel (1979) hypothesized an ideal prescription for managers, based on the nature of the information one has about the innovation, in other words, the relative routineness of that information. Non-routine innovations, then, are innovations about which we have very little readily analyzable information. Instead, information is likely to be value-laden and the implementation will be less predictable. Another important factor is continuousness of an innovation, that is, the extent to which the procedures for implementation dovetail with existing practices and organizational norms. Using this classification, it seems that considerable incidental learning is required to implement a non-routine, discontinuous project. What it is and how it fits with the organization is not known at the time of adoption of the innovation; which means that its nature and structure will be defined out of the values of those who implement it. These values, acquired incidentally, are largely tacit and not visible.

Several studies (notably Emrick *et al.*, 1977; Reinhard *et al.*, 1980) found that administrators at different hierarchical levels must provide different degrees and types of support. Emrick *et al.* (1977) called for a "proximal gradient of support" (p. 113). Pincus and Williams (1979), who studied large urban school districts, proposed that district-level innovations may typically be an "irregular cycle of advance and retreat with some collective experience gained from each such cycle" (p. 733). This is one form of incidental learning. They further found that the district's innovativeness, however well-managed, is a very delicate condition that can change rapidly. Also pertinent to incidental learning is the fact that beliefs about hierarchy and authority often lead managers to act in instrumental ways (with an emphasis on procedures) rather than to act experimentally or in ways that might best fit the project's learning needs.

Managing change over time

Innovation implementation takes a long time, much longer than originally thought (Hall, 1974). DeGreene (1973) describes the impact this long time frame may have on the success of implementation. Systems behave differently over the short term than over the long term. Over the long range, they evolve toward a balance of forces; over the short range, they show frequent oscillations (pp. 83–84).

The fact that systems respond differently over the short term than over the long term is not likely to be obvious to the administrator caught up in what feels like resistance to change and frequent ups and downs in project progress. Under these conditions, it will be difficult to maintain a long-time perspective or even to forecast the direction in which one is going. Planning is difficult over a long period of time. Successful managers of change projects alluded to the fact that the original plan was only a point of departure. Terreberry (in Kast and Rosenzweig, 1973) suggests that the "rapidity and complexity of change may increasingly preclude long range planning" (p. 85).

Several important effects of implementing educational innovations over a long time period can be noted, as adapted from McDaniel and Morris (1978): the potential for means/ends reversal, a focus on the change process rather than the change goal; the difficulty in determining (or predicting) the long range effects/benefits of the change; the difficulty in planning flexibly enough to accommodate intervening organizational and environmental changes; the difficulty in providing support relevant to the users' time frame. Because change is a developmental process *with a certain amount of learning by doing*, the process cannot be hurried, which increases the cost without correspondingly increasing the likelihood of persistence.

For the project manager, then, the stage of implementation is a significant variable. Since the stages do not necessarily occur in a linear sequence, but may instead be more like cycles, key indicators of the different stages must be identified and the manager can then determine the stage of a given project. This process is made more difficult by the extended time that it takes to implement most educational innovations. Thus the most important skill for the administrator under these conditions is to be able to make incidental judgments in real time, which set in motion the long term pattern

155

that will lead to persistence, what Weick (1984) refers to as "small wins."

Small wins are controllable opportunities of modest size that produce visible results and that can be gathered together into synoptic solutions (Weick, 1984, p. 40). They are a concrete, complete, implemented outcome of moderate importance. One small win sets in motion the forces that favor another small win. Small wins do not line up in a linear progression but rather seem to cohere in a general direction. They also stir up settings in such a way that a linear progression is unlikely. Small wins provide information that facilitates learning and adaptation since they are like small experiments that test implicit theories. For example, Weick cites efforts at eliminating sex bias in language as an experiment that successfully proved that language is susceptible to change. Yet, it also stirred things up considerably since it revealed how deep-seated and entrenched sexism was and made more visible allies and opponents. By contrast, attempting to pass the Equal Rights Amendment is a large-scale change and, unlike small wins, one that can unravel at any time.

Small wins are the basic building blocks of change. Research by Hall and Hord (1987) found that incident-level interventions – for example, those small "one-legged conferences" held while walking together or notes on bulletin boards – were the most important determinants of successful implementation. The authors concluded that "little things mean a lot." It is the collective wisdom gained from each of these attempts to move forward that constitutes incidental learning.

Roles and concerns

If the above contingencies influenced administrators, how might their behavior be operationalized and measured to determine differences produced by the above contingencies? The theoretical model of administration developed by Getzels and Guba (1957) was used, which defined administration as a social process consisting of two distinct dimensions, a role dimension and a personality or needs dimension (concerns). Mintzberg (1973) conceived of the nature of managerial work as a *gestalt* of ten roles (Figurehead, Leader, Liaison, Monitor, Disseminator, Spokesperson, Entrepreneur, Disturbance Handler, Resource Allocator, and Negotiator). These roles and the innovation-specific tasks which logically follow from them described the role dimension of administrative functioning.

It was important to look at the concerns of administrators about their task of facilitating change. Hall (1974, 1978) and colleagues developed a model depicting the concerns of users, non-users, and facilitators of change as they moved in a logical progression over the course of a change project. This progression is mapped by asking individuals questions about their current feelings relative to the innovation or to their roles. The concerns dimension taps a provocative aspect of administrative functioning not often examined. The stages of concern move from (lack of) Awareness, to Information, Personal, Management, Consequence, Collaboration, and Refocusing Concerns.

The above conceptual frameworks, on roles and concerns, led to a central question: what are the managerial roles and stages of concern about facilitating change which characterize administrators of persisting projects for different types of innovations, at different stages of the change process and at different hierarchical levels?

Case reports

This section describes incidental learning in three non-routine, discontinuous, innovation projects.[2] The cases range from the most complex, early-stage projects to the most complex, later-stage projects.

Meeting American Indian learning needs

This small community college, located in the heart of an Indian reservation in the Northwest, serves approximately 175 students, 70% of whom are American Indian.[3] A unique feature of this college is its Upper Division Studies Program which provides the opportunity to receive a Bachelor's degree with an emphasis in management (e.g. natural resource management, human services, etc.) through an individualized program of studies. This program, offered in collaboration with the nearest state university, is important since travel from the reservation to the university is often difficult. A key feature of this program is the option of obtaining Credit for Prior Learning, a competency-based program featured in this discussion.

The innovation

The institutional context alone would qualify this innovation as non-routine. In addition, the project is highly complex and bundles several innovations in one. It fits the essential characteristic of a non-routine innovation, that is, its lack of definition or analyzable components. When receiving Credit for Prior Learning, a student identifies relevant learning outcomes and documents them. As such, this innovation is always open-ended and markedly different from traditional programs because of the implicit assumptions that stu-

157

dents can define their learning and that learning need not take place in a traditional college course.

The program also provided an Upper Division option within a hitherto undergraduate institution. New institutional procedures had to be established. In offering credit for prior learning, a totally new concept had to be defined and taught to faculty before installing new institutional procedures. The program was to be competency-based, reflecting competencies needed for reservation jobs. Staff needed training in writing competencies and working with local agencies, such as the Bureau of Indian Affairs, to identify co-operatively competencies in these new jobs. Finally, the program was originally to be governed using traditional tribal patterns, notably the extended kinship or *tios paye* model. This element of the innovation was never well-defined and fell by the wayside. The number of new procedures and faculty reorientation called for by this innovation disrupted the system and made it discontinuous with prevailing institutional procedures.

Project leadership

The Academic Vice-President – who was the organizational sponsor of the innovation – appeared to be a dynamic leader familiar with concepts and leaders in non-traditional education. His concern about his role relative to this project was that "I'm too interested in it." In his zeal to make the project work, he was concerned that he "may overstep [his] bounds." Earlier he had commented that the other Vice-President had a more intimate knowledge of day-to-day operations. He was primarily concerned with problems of articulation (that is, acceptance of these credits by other institutions), the survival of the innovation, and management concerns.

By contrast, because of the project director's brief tenure in this role, many of her responses to current task involvement were "I will be doing that." She had only begun to understand the program and its requirements of her. As she described her role, she saw much of it in terms of working directly with students. At one point she said she'd basically be doing "a little of everything." She summed up her work so far by saying that she had really "only touched on some tasks."

During our telephone interview, she responded that she had not yet written new goals. They had, she said, been written by the former project director but she "can't find them now." Though she had written an advertisement and made a trip to recruit students, she said "We have 26 students in the program now, which is enough for me to handle, but we can always handle more." In these comments she showed some ambivalence in terms of her new role and its demands on her. Her primary interpersonal involvement and leadership seemed to be in working directly with students. She was not too sure about the new method. As an Indian, she was concerned that this would be a high quality program. She suspected it of being too non-selective. "Many non-Indians think 'They're just Indians; I'll go ahead and give them an A or B.'" Her concern was that students who graduate from the program have the necessary knowledge, skills, and attitudes when they graduate. She said later that her main concerns were ensuring the quality of education students get in the program "even though it is non-traditional" and trying to develop a curriculum that will meet students' needs when she "doesn't know what meets their needs."

The project director's change concerns profile was that of a classic non-user. She had remarked that she would like to take a management course, since this was her first administrative role. She had coordinated the Teacher Training program for the college, a somewhat parallel experience. Of prime importance was the newness of her position. Not only was she new to this role but she was also new to the innovation and to management. For her, what was already an innovation bundle of great complexity had another very complex innovation added to it, management. That she would respond with some contradictions, ambiguity, and uncertainty seemed entirely appropriate to the universal experience of starting a new job.

Discussion

Both leaders were primarily concerned with developing new program options to ensure the continuance of the project. The sponsor's comment that many of his tasks were overlapping fits well with Mintzberg's (1973) original conception of the ten managerial roles as a *gestalt* of managerial activity. The focus on this one key problem gave a similar content to each of the tasks, making them converge as different aspects of a whole.

This case became more complex because of the role of an external advocate, an unusual phenomenon in itself. CAEL (the Council for the Advancement of Experiential Learning) has a long history of developing and disseminating information on experiential learning. The organizational sponsor called the Director of CAEL personally for advice on articulation. The project director had read CAEL materials and attended national CAEL meetings. The project staff also attended a workshop by a regional CAEL consultant (arranged by the sponsor), and the entire evaluation design of the project was based on a model originally developed and disseminated through CAEL. CAEL had defined the general components of the innovation and shaped its values. Their materials include routine procedures for developing credit for prior learning portfolios, forms for stating competencies, and guidelines for training assessors. While CAEL was not the only force shaping the innovation, its staff apparently helped accelerate both the implementation and acceptance of the innovation by the college.

Providing outreach to Eskimo villagers

Situated in a remote wilderness area in the far polar Northwest, this small public community college is part of the state university system. The college serves a native community of less than 1000 students. The entire staff consists of seven full-time faculty and 45 part-time faculty. The college is in a peninsular area. This discussion centers on an attempt to reach 15 outlying and relatively isolated Eskimo villages. These villages are characterized by a subsistence economy and little contact with the outside world.

Project history

This project was initially funded for three years to provide learning centers at each of 15 villages as a way of creating a college Outreach program. After two years, funding was discontinued. In those two years, the former president of the institution had been removed, the project director had resigned, and the incumbent interim president was given twelve months to get the college on track before it went completely under. The college experienced a 200% turnover in staff over that first year of the interim president's tenure in office.

In the midst of such dramatic turmoil, the interim president assumed control of the project, stating that its early history was somewhat obscured and that project reports were inaccurate. He cited as an example his talking to villagers, who were supposed to have earned credit through the new centers, who had never heard of the centers nor of the project. In fact he was quite reluctant to share any project documents at all because of his doubts about their authenticity. He did later send an "Interim Project Report" which details some of the project activities, though in language which is more public relations than documentation: "A euphoric aura in this first-time endeavor seemed to create boundless energy which made possible the early progress ..."

The learning centers were to be collaboratively staffed by the college and another Adult Basic Education agency. Materials would be purchased for the most part, with only a few being developed over the course of the project. However, subsequent assessment of the purchased material showed that it was inappropriate for college credit. Further, the locally developed material was adequate for college level, but staff turnover caused a lack of continuity in their use. The

Adult Basic Education teachers had "relation skills, not process or tutoring skills."

In short, from the president's perspective, there were significant flaws in the original plan. The project was altered to reduce the number of materials; all of the materials were evaluated for appropriateness for college level and for use by the existing staff, given their skills. The facilitators were trained. Originally there was a project supervisor, but they found that the cost of traveling so far was too great. Student performance was also unsatisfactory, with many students receiving "incomplete" grades or attaining only a low level of mastery.

The college decided to take what worked, as is, and deliver it for the remainder of the project year. Since they were no longer externally funded, they phased the project down to four villages, with one full-time faculty member responsible for coordinating each village and teaching in his or her discipline. Additionally, there was a local facilitator in each village. They asked for state funding for an Outreach learning coordinator and a materials specialist. They started a telecommunications program with one-way video and two-way audio for delivery of courses to these centers. They refocused the program where the demand seemed to be, offered fewer options, and re-engineered most of the materials.

The innovation

One might not initially consider this program a non-routine innovation. It offered teacher education, business and clerical training, health programs, and building construction and maintenance programs on an Outreach basis. The delivery of the programs was non-routine, but the content was traditional. In fact, this project was originally selected for study as an example of a routine innovation based on the description of the project in *Resources for Change* (FIPSE, 1979). Yet, place these fairly routine programs in remote villages, with unskilled faculty, poor materials, and offer them to a subsistence-oriented villager and you have a thoroughly non-routine innovation. Further, make travel difficult and sporadic, and turn staffing and administration for the project and the college upside down, and the situation is discontinuous as well.

These were routine programs offered in a printed medium. However, they became value-laden and non-routine when offered to clients from a predominantly oral culture which has not often seen (let alone adopted) some of the roles these programs would prepare villagers to assume. Even the selection of these particular career programs for this setting involved new values and ways of thinking.

161

Project leadership

In this project, the organizational sponsor also functioned as project director. An image of the quintessential entrepreneur emerged. Not surprisingly, this was his highest role from the Tasks to Support Innovation Questionnaire (really his only high role). Three of his highest priority tasks also came from this role category. He stated that his critical task was defining leadership rather than implementation: you "emphasize the nature of the vision and what it propels or motivates." He also noted that he basically twisted the project to fit his own vision, then molded his resources to fit the vision as well. As he saw it, the nature of the project was really to define the nature of the college's interaction with a rural population – a goal that was the overall mission of the whole college, a "rural developmental institution." Once you have so shaped a vision, your role is to develop a shared vision among your constituencies. Thus, the project had to be bent to the apparent needs of the community too.

Because of the exigencies of getting the college back in order he said that he had spent a year having to "diagnose rapidly, intervene as rapidly as possible, all with surgical precision." When asked whether he had had to negotiate with others about the project he quipped, "You negotiate with administrators over your head; you negotiate with village people regarding their needs. But you seduce, whip, or fire faculty. Some of all three were done." He characterized his role for the past six to nine months in one word, "Rescue." He had spent the last ten years in the Third World (Eastern Europe, Cuba, and Tanzania) without contact with the "main 48." He thus cast his vision for the college from a socio-cultural perspective. Telecommunications were essential to his college because they are the "road that links the dominant culture with the non-dominant, a tool for rapid social change for Third World countries."

From his perspective, then, he launched two major reconceptualizations of the project. The first, partly fired by lack of external funding and partly by his conviction that the State must show its priority for aiding villages, was to petition the State legislature and the university to underwrite the Outreach program. The second redirection was part of the first – he proposed offering the Outreach program at least partially through telecommunications. To do this, he mobilized native groups, health and industrial commissions, and villagers to "storm the legislature." He was able to convince people that such a vital link would bring not only increased educational opportunities but other tangible improvements. Over time, he proposed increasing the number of villages with receiving and sending capabilities, eventually adding computer terminals to the system.

He commented that his major concern was that he could have been "180 degrees wrong" in the direction he had taken. For the most part, he saw himself as not concerned with his role. Yet there was a concern for managing the details of implementation and perhaps even a question as to whether there was a better approach.

Discussion

A feeling of fiction or incredulity at the saga of this project is further fueled by some of the inconsistencies of the sponsor's remarks. He did trouble-shooting "all of the time," yet rated it at the fortieth percentile (his second highest ranking with three roles at this level: Figurehead, Disturbance Handler, and Resource Allocator). He "mobilized" groups yet ranked the Liaison role at 0. He portrayed himself as a rescuer yet seduced, whipped, or fired faculty.

The sponsor was first a man of vision. Perhaps his underplaying of the interpersonal roles was appropriate. The potential cost of his overriding concern for task and for its expedient accomplishment is evident in his doubts, his reflection that he may be wrong, that he should refocus. In his dissolution of project leadership and personal trips to the villages to monitor the program, we see his preference for direct control. Perhaps this style is one that he adopted as necessary, given the need to make many changes in a very brief period of time with a changing staff. It seemed a style, however, that would prove difficult to maintain over time.

Competence in liberal arts

Like many small (less than 2,000 students), private liberal arts institutions, this church-related university has achieved a reputation for its learner-centered reform. Located in a large urban area in the Southwest, this traditional institution with its older, almost medieval structure has seen the entire surrounding area become a very poor, predominantly Latin community. Embracing as its mission the service of this population, a number of curricular reforms have been instituted. Of these, the most comprehensive was the competency-based learning project, the subject of this discussion.

Project history

The project began in October 1967 with a presidential steering committee to recommend a long-range plan. Three years later, the steering committee recommended a more individualized curriculum that would nevertheless guarantee a common base of competence among graduates. After several college-wide meetings, the faculty accepted these recommendations and began designing programs to

163

implement the general framework. But the faculty groups found the task too large to handle. By obtaining outside funding, a team was created that assumed major responsibility for this innovation, while providing frequent reports to all faculty.[4]

By the spring of 1975, competency statements had been developed and accepted by the Academic Affairs Committee. A mentor program and a personal development seminar had been started. A learning center and an assessment center were greatly expanded to support the program, and complementary funding was secured. This period was one of great change; it read almost like a renaissance period in the small college's history. One key member of the change agent team emerged at this time to become the project director's "implementer" and a major, recognized author of the first year report.

Over the next couple of years, competencies were refined and activities implemented. The two key innovators (the project director and her "implementer") became involved in the national competency-based education community. In fact, the university began a newsletter about competency-based education for that community. The fall 1978 issue featured an article on the problem of transfer students who face "double jeopardy" in competence-based programs. The newsletter fizzled out, but the problem did not.

In November 1978, the Academic Affairs Committee conducted an extensive 142-item survey of faculty and student opinions on the competency-based learning program. The study was the result of a request by the Faculty Assembly. The results were analyzed and shared with the faculty in January 1979. The program received very negative ratings; project leadership was criticized; and both students and faculty appeared confused about the nature of the program. The strongest concern was in the area of the impact of the program. Faculty not only did not think the program had brought the hoped-for improvement in the quality of undergraduate education, but they believed that it was turning students – especially transfer students – away. Advisors were described as "confused, demoralized and unconvincing" in presenting the program to students. However, the faculty continued to indicate strong concurrence with the underlying values and philosophy of competency-based education (CBE).

The university redirected the program in accord with the faculty's wishes. A new plan separated validation of skills from knowledge areas which meant that students' transfer courses could satisfy content requirements without further validation. External assessment was now limited to skill areas, with major reliance placed on the competence assessment battery developed by a national testing firm. The project director had been a very active participant in that test development effort. Project leadership changed during this period: the Academic Dean reassumed a leadership role, the faculty "implementer" left the college for a position elsewhere, and the project director resigned her administrative position to work in advisement of incoming students.

The innovation

The innovation was clearly discontinuous with normal procedures of the institution and required continual modification to fit prevailing practices. The decision to use the American College Testing competency test for external validation was an example of an attempt to streamline an otherwise difficult testing process. Nevertheless, the testing remained an additional practice outside of normal classroom testing procedures. That this validation process had been disruptive could readily be seen in the discussion of the "double jeopardy" of transfer students in the newsletter article and in the large numbers of faculty who indicated in the survey on CBE that they felt the testing process had deterred transfer students from attending the institution. Testing became the focal point of the innovation, even though implementation was in the hands of the faculty and testing tends not only to wrest control from the faculty, but also to serve as a means to monitor their efforts. An external test would exaggerate this potential, at least as compared to a test developed and administered by faculty.

Project leadership now

The Academic Dean, who was the organizational sponsor, had been a central figure throughout the history of this project, even helping to write the initial FIPSE proposal, though he had only recently reassumed leadership. He described his role in the project early on as one of helping people remember that this was their idea. During the transition to Plan II, he said that this project took almost all of his time. At the time of this study he saw himself in more of a caretaker role, with emphasis on the role of monitor. He mentioned, for example, that he would be checking very carefully to see how their students did against national norms on tests and that all faculty are required to use a new standardized format that he had developed for describing course outcomes and the means of assessment. Overall, he described his role as "general supervisory." In defining his current task involvement, he saw himself as in charge of both day-to-day management and oversight of the project. He commented that the project was now run within the current organizational structure, with him and the Curriculum Council in charge. The program is now "part of the regular operation of the college. I don't think of it as experimental at all." He also had some personal distance from the innovation: "CBE may be a thing of the past in five years but I know of nothing better for faculty development."

The project director was no longer officially in this role; she taught part-time and worked in advisement to orient new students to the competency learning program. She thus spent half time in teaching and half time in program development and implementation. She emphatically described herself as *not* a facilitator, but an implementer of the innovation. Most of her remarks centered on the innovation and its use. To a very large extent, she directed her energies either toward external involvement (with the national testing agency for whom she consults) or toward students. There was no small hint of burn-out in her former role as facilitator of change among her peers. When asked about her decision to work in advisement, she alluded to student confusion over the competency program, as reported in the survey, and remarked that "The problem with advisement is who advises." She remarked that purists would quibble with the direction the innovation had taken, but that the new plan was more practical for this college.

Because her role was modified greatly only two months previously, she had continuing commitments, yet very low task involvement in facilitating this innovation. Her only really high involvement as a facilitator of change was the Figurehead role. She was still identified with the project, perhaps even *as* the project to outsiders. Her next highest role was as a Spokesperson. She did a limited amount of consulting with others about the innovation. Her key role, as she expressed it, was "explaining the competence plan to students."

Her message seemed to be: "I'm removing myself from facilitating this innovation because the cost of implementing and managing the project is too high." Among the Awareness items, she ranked highest "Currently other priorities prevent me from facilitating this innovation." Significantly, she was not refocusing. She had redirected her energies, but not her concern for the innovation. What emerged was an image of a change facilitator who had been less of a process facilitator and more of an innovation advocate, who had become somewhat alienated by events. Faculty resistance may have temporarily stymied her, but it had in no way altered her goals. She selected a critical area of need (advisement) and decided to "do it herself."

Discussion

Perhaps the most important distinction about this project was the size of the undertaking. With the more than 75 faculty at the institution, the decision to make this change college-wide was indeed a

166

significant influence on what followed. Many changes did occur, and the faculty as a whole never lost the basic values that led them to this project. The innovation underwent considerable change – from fairly simple (a general framework prior to FIPSE) to complex (Competence Plan I) to less complex and more routine (Competence Plan II). CBE is a relatively low specificity, value-laden innovation and demands considerable effort in communicating and defining the nature of the innovation. One might speculate here about the role of FIPSE with its emphasis on CBE and the attendant national visibility that followed funding. Shifts in audience for the innovators are chronicled by the fact that initial documents were in-house planning tools, followed by national reports and even a national CBE newsletter, to a document largely intended to clarify the innovation to both students and faculty.

Implications for managerial learning about change

What follows are a series of hypotheses regarding the nature of management functioning during the change process which have evolved from close examination of the findings of this study.

The more non-routine and discontinuous the innovation, the more unpredictable and non-routine will be the nature of management functioning. With the emphasis in non-routine projects on Leader and Entrepreneur roles comes greater discretionary behavior on the part of organizational sponsors. At this stage management is as experimental as the innovation being implemented. With an elevated involvement in Disturbance Handling comes a tendency to be reactive rather than to design proactively alternative solutions because of the ambiguity created by non-routine discontinuous projects. Thus, there is a much greater demand on the manager to engage in critically reflective informal learning at the same time that the nature of managerial tasks may make reflection more difficult

The nature of the innovation may change over time. Indeed, if the basic principle that there is a press toward routineness (Thompson, 1967) is accepted, then the innovation should gradually evolve in this direction. Even in this movement, however, there are subtle differences that will affect the manager's ability to gain control over the innovation. It may be that some non-routine innovations have an intrinsic non-routine or analytic floor, below which no level of effort can make them move toward further routineness.

In such a situation, the task of the manager becomes even more complex. She must determine whether or not she can afford to maintain an innovation that requires a constant high level of additional effort. Full institutionalization of such an innovation is never possible without systemic change, since, even with a high level of expenditure of effort and resources, it remains unpredictable and non-routine. These innovations involve a high degree of learning by both the users of the innovation and the organization. Over time, they may lead to a changed or transformed organization. The manager must determine which innovations have this intrinsic quality. At the very least, a manager must be able to determine when an innovation is routine and/or becoming more routine. She must be alert to the evolution toward routineness and adapt her functioning accordingly. So different are the needs of projects that have evolved through institutionalization to routineness that some have suggested that different people should manage the change project at this stage. Indeed, in two of these projects, one can see a transition from a more development-oriented administrator to a maintenance-oriented administrator.

The Figurehead role is an important aspect of innovation leadership. The Figurehead role demands that the manager confer status on the project through her presence and through the messages conveyed to the organization of the importance of the project. Mintzberg (1973) found that this role is often overlooked by managers, yet it was rated first or second by nine of the thirteen respondents in this study. Perhaps because an innovation is an unusual phenomenon in the college, it needs representing to others. Moreover, the project director had to represent the project to the outside world since these projects were funded by a federal agency and were nationally visible. The Figurehead role may be an important managerial role generally, but it seemed more critical for these innovation leaders. In fact, several project leaders said, "I *am* the project." This signalling to others of the importance of the project is a form of incidental learning which encourages others in the organization to use the innovation.

Turnover in project leadership is not necessarily a critical factor for nonpersistence of an innovation. Turnover of project leadership has been cited as a contributing factor to the nonpersistence of educational innovations (Baldridge and Tierney, 1979; Pincus and Williams, 1979). Yet five of the seven projects studied had experienced turnover in one or both roles, and the other two colleges indicated that they too were considering a change in leadership. It may be that turnover is fairly common among both persisting and nonpersisting change projects. What a manager does may be more important than who does it. This role replaceability is a basic characteristic of socio-technical systems (DeGreene, 1973). More likely, when turnover does not lead to disruption of the implementation process, the organization may have learned. In other words, leadership needs of the innovation project may have become part of the organizational memory, encoded in policies, procedures, and budgets.

Certain extrinsic characteristics of a project's setting and history are inextricably tied to the intrinsic characteristics of innovations in determining the nature of an innovation. The nature of an innovation appears to be at least partly in the eye of the beholder. A priori classification of projects on the basis of intrinsic innovation characteristics proved inaccurate. A project originally selected for this study as routine emerged as the most non-routine, discontinuous project in the study because the setting was so unusual and formidable. Another project was originally selected as an early-stage routine project, but was almost improperly reclassified as non-routine based on the description of the project's organizational sponsor. After repeated probing, it was discovered that he found the characteristics of non-routineness to be desirable attributes (e.g. lack of precise definition, complexity) which he wanted to ascribe to "his" innovation. It was the attributions of non-routineness of project managers which most influenced how they functioned with respect to the innovation.

The role definition of project directors influences the intensity of their subsequent managerial functioning. When project directors perceived an element of their role to be managing the project, they were more likely to be more intensely involved in administrative roles supportive of innovation implementation. They were more likely, for example, to be using "lock in" strategies early on to lock the innovation in to traditional procedures. Three project directors were disseminating information to other colleges or departments almost from the first, meeting with other departments to build linkages and support for the program, and actively seeking a more stable institutional funding base. By contrast, two project directors who saw themselves exclusively as implementers were engaged in designing the program and its materials, and in recruiting students for their special parallel programs. Though necessary activities, without the other administrative tasks, these activities kept the project as an ad hoc part of college operations. The role perception of the director – in other words, how she has internalized her role or learned incidentally about it – will affect how she carries out the innovation leadership tasks.

Implications for incidental learning

Unintended consequences

In the case of the American Indian project, the sponsor and project director voiced many interesting contradictions. The project director

169

was an Indian recruiting Indians for a program designed for them; yet, as an Indian, she was not sure that the program had the best interests of Indians in mind. Moreover, "she doesn't know what meets their needs."

The sponsor was concerned that he may have been too interested in the project and would thus "overstep his bounds," and his highest concern was Management. Moreover, he had written the grant. The grant called for developing competencies with the Bureau of Indian Affairs for reservation jobs, but was to be tribally governed according to the Indian kinship pattern called *tios paye*, a governance process that was never defined and never came off. One can sense some ways in which Indians might question whether this project was designed for or with them. Certainly they knew the meaning of *tios paye*.

Another interesting phenomenon was the role of CAEL. One possible unintended consequence of their assistance was that, as an organization devoted to making more routine ways of using experiential learning methods available to colleges, they "solved" the sponsor's problems of clarifying his own innovation in ways that accelerated his ability to use the experiential learning portion of the grant. This may have inadvertently led him to abandon the search for a means of routinizing or clarifying the *tios paye* portion of the grant. Through CAEL he had access to a national network of resources, national visibility, and consulting invitations. The "value-added" he may have gained by implementing this governance pattern was not visible since it existed more as an idea than an operational image.

On the other hand, to the extent that this pattern called for Indian participation in the design and governance of the project, one can sense that the project's articulation problems might be one example where this program might have made a difference. The problem of articulation has been encountered nationally by credit-for-prior-learning programs. Upper Division institutions have a long history of not accepting every course that community colleges want to transfer, and courses earned through portfolio assessment were often viewed as especially questionable. The project director's concern that this was a non-selective approach that "put down" Indians – in essence intimating that they cannot learn through traditional courses – might have led to more open dialogue about this issue. Of course, her concern that this might be a put-down is the opposite of CAEL's message that we need to validate the worth of the learning that adults have acquired through life and work experiences, but neither view can be shared while the issue of latent or tacit racism is undiscussible. Ironically, the inclusion of the *tios paye* concept in the grant was also intended to further Indian empowerment. What each has "learned" incidentally in the implementation of this project is that innovations with good intentions do not necessarily "work."

The second case is a colorful story of a similar potential ethnic blunder. The original project, well-intentioned as it was, asked a largely illiterate, subsistence-oriented Eskimo population in remote locations to come to learning centers to use print materials to learn to teach, to type, and to work in hospitals or in construction. Even if they could read, how could they picture these occupations when they had not really seen people who are in them?

The Third World vision of the new president to bring a rural institution into the twentieth century might have been equally problematic. He saw his role as having a vision, then shaping resources and people to fit that vision. By converting the project to a telecommunications project, he was able to deliver not only these educational programs but also emergency relief and health care information. But, without the willing interest of the villagers, this project could exponentially escalate costs, without changing the educational circumstances of the villagers. Most of all, without the cooperation of the faculty, the project would not receive any continuing care and feeding. The direct control exercised by the president enabled him to do it his way, but it also left him the only person able to deliver the services, a role he could hardly maintain. Doing trouble shooting "all of the time" is to move from crisis to crisis.

Nowhere was the need for some threshold of routinization more evident than in this case. What the organization learned is that radical innovations or changes did not necessarily solve the problems either. In both phases of the project, what the Eskimos may have learned was that they could not participate in deciding on changes to meet their educational needs. Once again, this is a dramatic contradiction of the intentions of the project and its directors.

The third case, for all practical purposes, should have been a routine innovation after 12 years. Yet the complexity of the innovation (competency-based education) and its college-wide nature led to a fairly rocky implementation history. What is perhaps most striking is the contrast between the sponsor's and the project director's view of the project. To the sponsor, it is no longer really experimental and is most definitely regarded as a great tool for faculty development. Yet, he has had "to keep reminding faculty that this was their idea" and has *required* them to use a common format to institutionalize the innovation. By contrast, the project director was almost totally focused on the innovation and did it herself to get it done right. Hall and Hord (1987) say that interventions must be aimed at the people first, the innovation second. If you cannot demonstrate that the innovation will meet people's needs and that it will fit with their value

171

system, they are likely to reject the innovation. To the sponsor, that is alright because they have learned a lot along the way.

What these two administrators may have in common is a control orientation. Even as the sponsor reminds faculty that CBE is their idea, he requires faculty to use it and measures their effectiveness. The project director reads that students complain that the competency-based learning program is unclear. She attributes the fault to the faculty advisors, not the innovation, so the solution is to do it herself. Ironically, the approach of both individuals may have the unintended consequences of leaving faculty feeling manipulated and without recourse to the development they need in order to become skilled users of the innovation. If the project director does it herself rather than teaching others to do it, they will not learn. If the sponsor reminds faculty that it was their idea, then requires them to implement it "his" way, they neither learn his way nor develop their own unique adaptations. Since the Berman and McLaughlin (1976) study noted that mutual adaptation characterized successful persisting educational innovations, the lack of this mutual learning in this project may account for its tumultuous history.

These projects were selected for this analysis because they were the most non-routine innovations. As such, they placed the greatest learning demands on the users and change facilitators. Without a clear picture of what the changes would look like when implemented or a game plan for implementing these types of changes, facilitators were forced to engage in trial-and-error, incremental, incidental learning. Locked in their own tacit perceptual frames, they may have "learned" that others need to be "seduced, whipped, or fired" to get the job done, or that they could modify the original outcome to get a win (from an Indian-governed experiential learning program to a CAEL-developed credit-for-prior-learning program; from a print-oriented program to telecommunications for Eskimo villagers; from a totally competency-based institution to a competency-based assessment program). They may have learned that they could produce prejudicial results while intending equity and empowerment, or that external funders and innovation advocacy groups may produce *replicable* programs that do not meet the needs of the learners for whom they were developed.

The impact of a control orientation as developed by Argyris *et al.* (1985) is clearly apparent here. People were not able to learn alternative approaches when they were unaware of the gaps they had produced between their goals and their results. Their desire to control the change process led them to act in ways that may have suppressed information about their actual results.

The problem of differential short- and long-term results is also a critical aspect of our understanding of incidental learning. If people get positive results from control strategies over the short term, they may accumulate experience-based knowledge that these are effective interpersonal strategies. If, over time, things appear to disintegrate and people then change the nature of the innovation from one requiring learning and the advice and consent of users to one that is more routine and "controllable," they may have effectively engineered the situation to prevent their own learning as well as that of others about how to implement complex changes. If these changes are needed to solve complex problems, the problems will also remain.

Incidental learning about emotionally hot, interpersonal topics, such as prejudice, is especially difficult. How can programs designed to help and empower a group inadvertently appear to put down that same group? Yet, when one group offers help unilaterally, based on their assumptions about the needs of a people, and those people hold untested attributions about the motives of the helpers, little genuine learning can be expected. Instead, people may "learn" incidentally that the other group is intractable and impossible to change.

Incidental learning in programs and organizations

When implementing an innovative program, learning is a necessary byproduct. When that innovation is itself ill-defined and counter to prevailing practices, learning what the innovation is and how to do it will be essential. Concurrently, by definition the facilitator must also be learning how to facilitate implementation of the innovation as it takes shape. This largely trial-and-error experience-based learning takes place in the interpersonal arena. Thus what is learned will be influenced not only by the complex, many-layered task but also by the individuals involved. The more individuals that are involved, the more complicated this becomes. Finally, learning is framed by the way in which the individual frames the change management task – as managing people, advocating an innovation, providing resources to enable others to use the innovation, or developing faculty. When more than one person is responsible for facilitating the change, this increases the learning available, but it may also exponentially increase the potential for error.

This concept was illustrated in the study of a social change project that failed: *Implementation*, by Pressman and Wildavsky (1973). These writers depict the failure of the Economic Development Administration's Oakland project, a project that was initially supported by all constituents, to reduce poverty by employing the hardcore unemployed. They found an "inability of the machinery of implementation to move fast enough to capture the agreements while they lasted" (p. 92), and concluded, "Least of all do we appreciate the geometric growth of interdependencies over time where each negotiation involves a number of participants with decisions to make whose implications ramify over time" (p. 93). In this example, as in the research reported here, the sheer complexity of dealing with many people increases the need not only for shared goals but also for shared meaning about how to enact those goals. With precious little information available about how to implement these innovations, a process of mutual inquiry was essential, yet rarely present.

At the programmatic level, the strategic purview required is one focused on long-term change goals. Yet, the framing of those goals interacts with individuals' framing of their role. If I see myself using an innovation to develop faculty pedagogical skills, I am likely to seek many opportunities to do this, with less emphasis on the innovation overall since it represents only one way to reach the desired goal. The long-term perspective of the innovation-focused interventionist appeared to influence the national movement which spawned his or her innovation by improving on the current form of the innovation. As such, theirs were more like research and development projects than implementation projects.

It is clear from these examples that institutionalizing an innovation that produces desired learning effects is only one goal, one that may, more often than not, have been a secondary or even a short-term goal for the program or institution. As a result, it seems possible that one reason for the failure of so many educational innovations to persist is that their persistence was not a long-term goal.

Peter Senge (1988) notes that complex systems share classic, interrelated characteristics. They tend to delay, dilute, or defeat well-intentioned policy interventions, and to shift the burden to the intervenor who sought to offer temporary aid and found instead chronic dependency. They illustrate addiction, or an atrophy of internal regulatory processes along with harmful side effects in which intervention produces the need for additional interventions. The system lowers its sights as the gap between actual and desired performance persists. Finally, things that are beneficial in the short run are often harmful in the long run. These characteristics can also be seen in these attempts to install complex changes. They help explain the diverse goal emphases and goal displacement of project directors and sponsors, as well as the difficulty implementers face in attempting to maintain a project over a long time.

Conclusion

A significant factor in the outcome of these projects was the way in which individuals framed the nature of the innovation and their role in managing the change and one another's motives. This framing was a byproduct of the task of implementing these changes and was largely tacit. It is perhaps this tacit quality that had the largest effect on the project. Through it, the intentions of the project designers to meet the needs of Indians, Eskimos, and faculty were inadvertently undermined. Having framed their role as the persons responsible for the project ("I am the project"), they were unable to reframe their task as the facilitators of a process of mutual inquiry with the intended beneficiaries of the changes, even when the innovation itself was not clearly specified in the first place.

Similarly, the non-routineness of these innovations created conditions of complexity and ambiguity which seemed to trigger not learning but rather efforts to manage or control that complexity. In these efforts, an inability to conceptualize the whole program led to part–whole dichotomies as in the third case, where one component of CBE, competency testing, became the sole focus of the innovation, which then threatened the continuance of the whole innovation.

Notes

1. This chapter is based on the unpublished dissertation of Watkins (1981).
2. There were seven projects in the entire study. Each of these projects represents a unique attempt to bring to life a new approach to teaching and learning. Each project was federally funded by the Fund for the Improvement of Postsecondary Education (FIPSE).
3. The college began as an extension of a nearby junior college and developed under the advice and guidance of the Tribal Council. That affiliation has continued. The college received a charter from the Tribal Council in 1973. The enrollment immediately increased by 40%, and the course offerings doubled. College credit is still received through the parent institution, the nearby junior college.
4. FIPSE, which had concurrently announced an interest in competency-based learning, funded this project over a two-year period. With funding, the position of Project Director was created and given to the Assistant Academic Dean. In addition, five faculty were given released time to serve as a change agent team.

Chapter eight

Human resource developers: producing unintended consequences

Incidental learning, which may be readily apparent in individuals, is less apparent in programs and organizations. It should not be surprising, then, that incidental learning in a profession is even more subtle and difficult to discern. This chapter looks at the way in which the professional, incidental learning of human resource developers produces unintended consequences. The examination of this incidental learning should help those who develop these professionals.

The chapter begins with a case, a device commonly used in action science to help people learn from their experience, that illustrates the way in which human resource professionals can frustrate their own goals because of the unexamined incidental learning they have acquired through their practice. The case is used to illustrate several of the tools used in action science that shed light on incidental learning: language analysis, the ladder of inference, theory-in-use propositions, mapping, and puzzle interventions. This case, focused on one individual, sets the stage for a look at professional incidental learning through a study on human resource developers in several different settings. Both the case and the broader study point to the value of reflective learning, which helps people identify and transform the beliefs that have been part of their incidental learning.

The theory-of-action perspective, discussed next, elaborates the conceptual framework for this kind of reflective learning. In this chapter, the theory-of-action perspective is used to identify espoused theories and theories-in-use in the stories collected in interviews. A map of these beliefs is then developed to illuminate an alternative theory of action through which human resource developers can ultimately transform their professional practice. The chapter looks at both what human resource developers do when confronted with recurring problems and their reasoning about these problems.

Finally, implications are drawn out for the profession and for incidental learning.

Reflective learning: a trainer's dilemma

In the case that follows (Figure 8.1), an individual has shared a frustrating, difficult interaction in a training session. It is in some ways more dramatic than most learner–trainer conflicts, but it is quite typical. This case has been used in numerous training sessions with trainers and teachers of adults who invariably find that it is one that they "recognize." The trainer has written this case in her own words, with dialogue and events as she remembered them. This fosters a sense of personal responsibility for the case, its outcomes, and for implementing any alternative strategies or responses suggested by the analysis of the case.

A sense of personal responsibility is essential if "unfreezing" is to occur. "Unfreezing" is Kurt Lewin's term (in Argyris, 1952) which refers to a process in which an individual goes from a kind of equilibrium to a sense that things are out of balance. In unfreezing, people experience dissonance and anxiety that create readiness for learning. Without it, individuals are less likely to engage in the difficult and sometimes painful process of exploring their beliefs and working to develop alternative actions. Unfreezing may occur when individuals listen to others' cases, as noted in the discussion of double hits in Chapter Six, or even when discussing future or hypothetical cases. The critical ingredient is the individual's *belief* that the case accurately portrays a problem in his or her practice. Thus, an individual may also construct a case that will not lead to unfreezing if it is one that the person no longer feels needs resolution or if the person remains convinced that others are responsible for producing the outcomes of the case.

Most individuals retrospectively rationalize events in ways that favor them and tend to believe that situations and/or people are not changeable (Argyris *et al.*, 1985). They also vary in their sensitivity to using mistakes for learning (their "psychological brittleness"), particularly when this learning occurs in public. Yet, Argyris points out that our proclivities for retrospective rationalization and for holding ourselves blameless for our actions make it especially necessary that this learning occur in a group or in a public setting where others will help us deal with what really happened.

Learners will more easily take the risk needed for unfreezing when they have free and informed choice, mutual control of the learning process, and mutual responsibility for the learning outcomes. Learners are more effective when they see themselves as active agents responsible for their learning, and when they see mistakes and errors as raw material for learning rather than sources of embarrassment. In order to reflect on these experiences, learners must make their reasoning public so that the private understandings and meanings that they assigned to the events and statements can be critically examined by others from many viewpoints.

The Kingsley case

The left hand column of the case which follows (Figure 8.1) surfaces the thoughts and feelings which underlay the actions in the right hand column. The characters are: T, a professional, female trainer; Kingsley (K), a male, somewhat resentful medical doctor; and a co-trainer, seated in the back of the room, who is silent in this dialogue. It is the third day of a three-day training session, the purpose of which was to teach interpersonal communication skills and techniques for dealing with the public to a group of 40 medical professionals employed by a federal program. Many complaints had been received regarding the way in which these individuals interacted with their clients, their younger peers, and other federal employees in the building. Most complaints centered around the medical staff who were described as "rude, abrupt, condescending, unfeeling, and generally acting above everyone with whom they came in contact." All individuals in the class were required to be there by federal mandate. The four participants with the most seniority were the ones most resentful and vocal about "wasting their time in another useless training session." The ring leader of this gang of four was Kingsley. He had spent the first two days of the training session sitting in the back row with his briefcase open, working on paperwork. The only time he participated was to disagree with the trainer or to ridicule one of the newer staff member's contributions to the class. The trainer had done her best to minimize his negative impact on the class by ignoring his paperwork and by responding in the most positive way she could to whatever he said, using humor to engage his attention and to take the edge off his comments. The trainer had just given directions for completing a questionnaire on behavior styles and was passing out the questionnaire when the conversation in Figure 8.1 took place.

The action science strategies illustrated in the sections that follow are designed to help learners recognize the gap between what they intend (their espoused theories) and what they actually do (their theories-in-use). The specific strategies discussed are the use of language analysis to determine the meanings in the dialogue and the relative use of facts (directly observable data) over inferences and at-

What was thought or felt, but not said	What was said
	K. I refuse to participate in this stupid exercise (spoken, as usual, to no one in particular).
T. Don't mess with me you silly fool. I've already had to deal with a bad situation back home this morning and I am in no mood to put up with any more of your harassment. I just want to get this training session over with so I can go home where I'm really needed.	T. Come on K., lighten up. You might accidentally learn something.
T. I'm warning you K, I'm about to lose it. I just do not have the psychic energy or patience to deal with you anymore. You have been goading me for two days now. Enough is enough.	K. Unless you can give me, and I am certain you cannot, quantifiable data verifying the validity and reliability of this "instrument," then it's garbage pop psychology and a total waste of any sane person's time.
	T. Well actually, K, there is reliability and validity data available for this instrument. I don't have it with me; it's not something anyone has ever asked for before. If you participate in this exercise, I promise to mail it to you.
T. Oh no. I am going to cry. I should have taken some time to myself to calm down before coming into class.	K. It doesn't matter anyway. I doubt there is anything useful YOU can teach me that I didn't learn in medical school.
T. I will not let that so-and-so see me cry. Real trainers don't cry in class. . . . Dear God, somebody make me shut up. I should not be talking to him this way. What kind of example is this to set for the others in the class? What will they think of me? What will my co-trainer think of me? I have lost it completely. I am a horrible trainer. I hate being a trainer. I'll never get another job with these people. If I start crying now, I'll never stop.	T. (Placing both hands flat on the front row of tables and leaning forward as far as possible, fixing K. with a look that has been known to stop Mack trucks) Kingsley, let me tell you something. Let me explain the facts of life as far as responsibilities in this classroom go. You, and you alone, are responsible for your learning. You can learn or not, as you choose. I'm responsible for providing the environment and the opportunity for you to learn, should you choose to do so. So it's up to you. It's no skin off my nose if you don't learn anything. I get paid no matter what you do.

Figure 8.1 The Kingsley case

tributions, the ladder of inference, theory-in-use propositions, mapping, and puzzle interventions. Each of these strategies is described in Argyris *et al.* (1985).

Language analysis

One of the most pervasive problems in interpersonal interactions is the frequent discrepancy between what one intends to communicate and what others hear. This problem supports the view that meanings reside in people. Yet, some types of language convey more universally shared meanings than others. Facts in the form of illustrative details, observable events, what was actually said or done, are more objective than statements that offer our inferences about the facts. By illustrating for individuals the ways in which their communications with others are more inferential than objective, people begin to see the ways in which they contribute to poor communication and encourage others to bring *their* own interpretations to the events. An illustration from the above case in Figure 8.2 may illustrate the usefulness of this approach.

Similarly, we can examine the case for examples of the attributions that K. and the trainer make about each other. In this case, we observe the predilection of both people for making attributions without illustration and for advocating their position without inquiring into the other's responses or reasoning. For example, K. says "I refuse to participate," which is advocating a position, and "in this stupid exercise," which is an attribution about the exercise that is neither illustrated nor supported. On the other hand, the trainer says, "You might accidentally learn something," which attributes by implication that K. cannot or will not learn intentionally, but again does not include examples of this view. The trainer also states, "You and you alone are responsible for your learning." This statement advocates a

What the trainer said	Inferred meanings
"Come on Kingsley, lighten up. You might accidentally learn something."	The trainer is coaxing K. to relax, to let the trainer continue. The trainer believes that K. will not learn intentionally.
"Tell you what, if you participate in this exercise, I promise to send it to you when I get back to my office."	The trainer wants to strike a bargain with K. to regain control of his participation.

Figure 8.2 Language analysis of Kingsley case

position but does not inquire into K.'s view of the learning situation. Moreover, there has already been some evidence that K. has a different view: "I sincerely doubt there is anything useful *you can teach me* that I didn't learn in medical school." In fact, the context itself has also already been described by the trainer as one in which the doctors were *required* to attend this session by the federal program that is sponsoring it, which suggests that the learner may not be totally "responsible" or in control of his learning in this instance.

These techniques help to diagnose the nature of the interpersonal dilemmas faced by both the trainer and the learner. The highly inferential nature of their language and the lack of inquiry into each other's reasoning, in a manner that promotes shared meaning, leads to an escalation of both individuals' attempts at asserting control over the other person's behavior. Paradoxically, both espouse, albeit with some sarcasm, a goal of having a meaningful learning experience.

The ladder of inference

The "ladder of inference" provides further insight into the reasoning that produced opposite results from those intended by both parties. The ladder heuristic, adapted in Figures 8.3 from Argyris *et al.* (1985), consists of a hierarchy of inferences; each level becomes more abstract.

---

3. Theories about what produced these meanings

2. Cultural meanings imposed by us

1. Directly observable data

Figure 8.3 The action science ladder of inference

For example, Kingsley asked for validity and reliability information about the behavior styles questionnaire. Kingsley's reasoning, and that of the trainer, can be described using the ladder of inference, as illustrated in the top two diagrams in Figure 8.4.

The diagrams show the potential validity or invalidity in both people's reasoning. In addition, public scrutiny allows others to suggest alternative views, as seen in the third diagram in Figure 8.4. In fact, in the learning process, many alternative conceptions are typically offered. For the case writer, this reinforces the fundamental idea that meanings reside in people and that no one of us holds a patent on the one official "true meaning" in a situation. It is also clear that these two individuals acted in ways that prevented the sharing of

Kingsley's Ladder of Inference

3. Pop psychologists use invalid instruments which insult my intelligence and my medical training.

2. Without validation, the results of this instrument will be meaningless pop psychology.

1. "Is this instrument valid and reliable?"

The Trainer's Ladder of Inference

3. Participants who question my methods must be controlled or handled if I am to be credible and professional.

2. He's questioning my credibility and professionalism.

1. "Is this instrument valid and reliable?"

An Alternative Ladder of Inference

3. It is my professional responsibility to use only those reliable instruments I am trained to use and interpret; and participants have a right to be concerned about this issue.

2. The participant wants to be assured that I have chosen a "safe" instrument.

1. "Is this instrument valid and reliable?"

Figure 8.4 Possible ladders of inference in the Kingsley case

meaning (e.g. "Unless you can give me, *and I am certain that you can not*").

Theory-in-use propositions

Propositions in logic are if–then statements that offer cause-and-effect explanations of a phenomenon. Similarly, theory-in-use propositions are if–then statements that convey the "if-I-do-this, -then-this-will-happen" understandings of actors that are embedded in the logic of their actions. Unlike retrospective rationalizations that often explain actions as we would like to have constructed them, these propositions attempt to convey the logic that produced the gap between what the person intended and what they actually did in a given situation. A "formula" for identifying possible theory-in-use propositions was developed by Oscar Mink to aid new action scientists. A feature of this approach is that it attempts to capture the puzzling and often paradoxical nature of our reasoning processes. Figure 8.5 depicts the formula.

When _____ happens,	
triggering situation	
I am afraid that_____ will happen,	
what I don't want to happen	
So I_____	
what I do	
Which guarantees that_____	
what I don't want to happen	
will happen.	

Figure 8.5 Theory-in-use propositions
Source: O. Mink, University of Texas, Austin, Texas.

This format helps individuals see the self-reinforcing quality of their reasoning. For example, in the Kingsley Case, the following might be one of many theory-in-use propositions one could derive from the trainer's actions:

> Whenever a learner challenges my actions,
> I am afraid that I will lose control and my credibility,
> so I use humor or sarcasm, bargaining, and aggressive
> confrontation to control the learner, which guarantees
> that I will lose control and credibility.

Such propositions differ from logical propositions in that they are often blatantly illogical. Yet, they should also be testable. The trainer should be able to reflect on her practice to see to what extent she has responded to learner challenges in this fashion and with these results. She should also be able to experiment in future training situations with the same actions, to see if they produce these results, or alternative actions to see if they produce different results.

Maps

Like theory-in-use propositions, Argyris uses "maps" of individuals' reasoning both as a form of data display and as an intervention to spur reflection. Maps are a form of data display developed by Argyris (1983) that identify governing values or framing orientations, the action strategies that actors have described which fit these frames or values, and the predicted intended and unintended consequences from these strategies. Embedded in the maps may also be a suggestion of an alternative course of action.

A map illustrating single-loop learning in the Kingsley Case is depicted in Figure 8.6. The fourth column shows the unintended

Framing orientation	Values	Action strategies	Unintended consequences
P R O T E C T I V E	Remain in control of the training event to ensure learning.	Design Activities for learners with- out their input. Ignore challenges to the design Use interpersonal control strategies to manage partici- pants.	Little learning will occur. Participants may "learn" that they are expected to par- ticipate and "behave", but not learn.

Figure 8.6 The Kingsley case: single-loop learning map

consequences of framing the problem self-protectively, which unintentionally reduces opportunities for learning.

Maps portray the interdependence and self-reinforcing quality of the variables individuals identify as relevant. They illustrate a causal theory of learning in which learning proceeds from governing variables or values to action strategies which yield intended and unintended consequences. Maps describe repetitive patterns that recur over time, patterns that are also typically related to social systems and beliefs. The maps show a pattern that is highly unlikely to change unless individuals' theories of action, their reasoning about the pattern itself, is altered which in turn can alter the organizational norms supporting their current reasoning. Argyris further notes that the maps transcend individual demographics to describe a system so culturally reinforced that most individuals in the system will either act consistently with the map or describe themselves as "bucking the system." A map is a causal depiction of the underlying logic in actions taken by an individual, an organization, or a profession.

Maps are often fairly strong portrayals of the ways in which constructive values may lead to dysfunctional outcomes. They are also too inferential to use effectively without the detailed analysis of the actual data of the case given in the preceding sections. They can be used effectively to portray the reasoning of a large group of individuals in a sufficiently generic way, so that people in the same group can look at the map and think of examples in their own lives, or that of others, that would validate the map. Maps are most powerful when they are accompanied by an alternative map that suggests a double-loop or Model II reframing of the case. An alternative map for the Kingsley Case is depicted in Figure 8.7.

Framing orientation	Values	Action strategies	Consequences for learning
R E F L E C T I V E	Share control of the learning process.	Jointly design learning experiences. Explore challenges to the learning design as hypotheses to be tested, as potentially helpful alternatives.	Both trainers and learners are more likely to learn. Learners and trainers will feel equally responsible for the learning and non-learning outcomes.

Figure 8.7 The Kingsley case: double-loop learning map

Puzzle interventions

Puzzle interventions are used to convey the inconsistencies in a person's reasoning and behavior. They include directly observed behavioral data from the learner coupled with the cultural meaning the interventionist assigns to that data, a terse description of the learner's actions or strategy, followed by a description of the way in which this violates the learner's stated values or goals. Finally, the interventionist inquires about the learner's reactions to this intervention. The puzzle intervention is particularly useful as a part of the unfreezing process, but it can also be quite unsettling. Consider this intervention in the Kingsley Case:

> When you refuse to participate in this stupid exercise unless I can give you valid quantifiable data about the validity of this instrument, and at the same time you say you are certain that I cannot give it to you, I infer that you have already decided that there is either no reliability or validity data or that I do not have it. Am I making a correct assumption?

In effect, the trainer asks the client to be accountable for his or her logic. But this can only by accomplished by modeling this action. The trainer must make explicit the data (i.e. what the other said and did), then share his or her inferences about that data. The trainer must then inquire into the correctness of these inferences and be open to the possibility that Kingsley has a valid perspective. In effect, the trainer is open to the possibility that the training design will not work, while at the same time sharing her reasoning with Kingsley regarding why she thought the instrument would contribute to learning about communication. Such an exercise in sharing meaning is itself a demonstration of effective communication. An important injunction for individuals engaged in this type of reflection is to go slow.

Taking the dialogue further, the action science interventionist might look at the impact of Kingsley's actions on the system that the trainer was supposed to affect. This workshop was designed to address communication problems between doctors and those with whom they work in this clinic. Kingsley has just illustrated the kind of behavior that led the federal program personnel to call for this workshop in the first place. At a more macro level, however, if the federal staff and the patients and other staff did not communicate their concerns directly to the doctors, but rather let them come to this workshop to find out what they were doing wrong, then the larger system is replicating the dysfunction that others perceived in the doctors. The administrators are treating the doctors in a rude and condescending way by not dealing with them directly and honestly. At yet another level, the trainers might be replicating similar communication problems. Since the co-trainer for the workshop stood in the back of the room and let T. handle K.'s concerns alone, we might suspect that the co-trainer, like the patients and the clinic staff, is letting T. find out what she's doing wrong from someone else.

Puzzle interventions help individuals reframe a situation from the perspective of the other actors in that situation. An alternative intervention might be to ask the trainer to reflect on the dilemmas and double binds she may have created for Kingsley:

> T., when you say, "I get paid no matter what you do", I infer you to mean that you are doing this training session in order to get paid and that whether or not Kingsley learns is unimportant. This statement could be interpreted as rude and condescending, which are the qualities attributed to the doctors which you were paid to address in this workshop. How do you respond?

In the hall of mirrors of human action (Schön, 1987), we often replicate one another's actions and find ourselves in a single-loop. The trainer and the doctor may actually share dysfunctional theories of communication, and thus will not be able to break out of this cycle until they recognize this aspect of their behavior. Another intervention might examine the similarity between the criticism of the doctors as "unfeeling" and the belief of the trainer that "Real trainers don't cry." Or, the interventionist might question the trainer's belief that she is "really needed at home." Does this mean that she does not believe that she is needed or helpful in this training session? Might this not inadvertently mirror K.'s belief?

The case technique offers learners a way to delve deeply into the tacit, taken-for-granted assumptions that guide their actions. It can be used as a form of guided practice in reflection that, when coupled with attempts by learners to reflect in action and to try new double-loop learning strategies, is an effective way to improve learners' ability to surface tacit incidental learnings and to learn from work experiences. When skills in facilitating reflective learning via action science are added to the training skills that human resource developers already possess, they will be better prepared to address informal and incidental learning situations in the organization.

Caught in a double bind

The above case, involving one trainer, sheds light on the incidental beliefs of the profession. Another study, discussed here, takes this analysis to a broader level by revealing three framing orientations of trainers toward their profession: training as magical or naïve, as political, and as learning.

According to Argyris (1983), individuals often get trapped in single-loop learning or patterns of recurring error because they have competing values or competing constraints that make it difficult for them to act in concert with either of their values. This chapter describes findings from a study that depicts the beliefs of trainers about their practice that might have prevented them from enhancing their learning and that of others. Double binds are identified in which individuals said two things that were inconsistent; when they said one thing and did another; when they described an event that was later described differently by other individuals; and when the group as a whole appeared to be in contradiction with either their own espoused theory or that of the profession. This led to a list of possible double binds – incompatible beliefs which could impede competent action (Figure 8.8).

From this list of double binds, themes were identified and depicted in theory-of-action maps. The map is itself an intervention and can be thought of as an hypothesis for later testing of the underlying theories reflected in the map. As a result, it is one form of data display in action research, but consistent with the iterative process of action research, it is also a potential impetus to new action.

Figure 8.9 is based on a mapping technique used by Argyris *et al.* (1985). The figure depicts recurring dilemmas about the nature of

1. Training is for others; trainers must get it on their own.
2. "Be a technical expert first, an educator second."
3. Learning on-the-job is preferred; yet most training is off-line.
4. The best way to tell if training is effective is to assess what students do in the field later; but if trainers collect data, others will know of their mistakes, and mistakes are high profile and costly especially in terms of trainers' jobs.
5. "People who are here have been here a long time. They don't need a lot of training." "If you're old, they throw you away, never teach you new skills so that you can be up-to-date."
6. "Industry as a whole puts training and development in an overhead position. Verbally they will support it. It's a matter of human resource development people having to justify their existence." "Yet I am at a loss as to how to defend that or to convince them that training is cost-effective."
7. The supervisor is the gatekeeper to training *and* recognition; so the supervisor uses training as recognition.
8. Trainers blame managers for lack of follow-up on training but do not train managers to do follow-up coaching.

Figure 8.8 Double binds and inconsistencies in trainers

training that were encountered in practice by human resource developers in all three sites. One site, the governmental agency, predictably had the most instances of references to the theme of training as political and the fewest references to training as magical. The map components used here include a framing orientation (column one) that identifies the cognitive set of the respondents or the filter through which they appear to have interpreted action, followed by a statement of an underlying belief or assumption about the nature of training that would follow from this framing orientation. The second column is an interpretive description of the actions identified in interviews or inferred from the actions not taken as a result of the stated beliefs. The third column documents the results these trainers experienced when implementing the action strategies noted.

The framing orientations in column one and the consequences for learning in column four are based on work by Freire (1970) as well as Shor and Freire (1987). The first two stages from Freire (magical and naïve) are similar to Argyris's ideas about a Model I control orientation, yet with the Freire-like distinction that the first stage is more like being out of control. Both of these orientations lead to single-loop learning, while the final stage (critical consciousness) is like Argyris's learning orientation that produces double-loop learning. Freire developed a series of stages to reflect the development of consciousness that is necessary for individuals to move out of their oppression. People may be oppressed without necessarily knowing it. Freire characterized those who are unaware of their oppression as *magical* thinkers. In their state of consciousness, luck or magic determine their fate. These individuals lack control of their lives. In the second stage of consciousness people begin to blame others or "the system" for their oppression. This, Freire says, is *naïve*. Only at the last stage of *critical consciousness* can people begin to transform their lives. In this stage, they begin to recognize that it is *their collusion* with the oppressors that oppresses them, and that they must band together to form new communities beyond oppression to empower one another. Only in this way will they find a state of consciousness in which they are neither the oppressed nor the oppressor.

Freire's subject was literacy and his argument political but the stages of reflection he developed appear to fit many other contexts. In this instance, these stages augment the Argyris and Schön conception of single and double-loop learning by making a critical distinction between two different types of single-loop learning.

Training is magical

Magical thinking about training, in Freire's terms, might be that it is something you are either born with or are lucky enough to be able to figure out on your own. This viewpoint is illustrated by the following:

— The person that amazes us is one who has learned how to work with people in his classes. He uses a creative approach.
— I considered going back to school (for training to do training), but I wasn't sure it would buy me that much.
— I figure out how long it takes me to learn something myself in a trial-and-error fashion and compare it to going to take a course. I usually can't justify taking the time off to go to a course.
— It seems like we are always in the position of learning to teach something that doesn't exist yet, that we can't do and for which we don't have the equipment or materials.

These statements are magical because the speakers see creative, skillful training as "amazing" and out of reach. It is not readily learned in school, and they do not think there is a technology anyway that will improve on their informal, learning-by-doing approach. Moreover, they can not control the context in which they train, which leaves

Figure 8.9 Three views of training

Framing orient-ation and beliefs	Action strategies	Consequences for the training function	Consequences for learning
Training is Magical	Support the idea that trainers who have "it" don't need training; those who don't couldn't learn. Hold excellent trainers in awe and discount personal capacity to emulate them. Discount technology of training by emphasizing technical expertise over training expertise when choosing own learning activities. Minimize clarification of outcomes, purposes, time needed for different outcomes and purposes, and cost justification of training. Avoid seeking valid data about performance.	Almost no one can do it "artfully," so few achieve a high level of professionalism. Trainers will not do professional work. Managers have little solid information about how to use training. Training will become expendable.	Culture of Silence
Training is Naïve or Political	Assume training is a negotiable benefit for self; blame others for holding the same assumption. Delegate determining training needs and modality to supervisors who will enact personal cultural norms about how best to learn. Remain unaware of implicit priority setting in bending rules, compromising educational goals, and setting budgets.	Training is part of reward and punishment system rather than task accomplishment system. Trainers are vulnerable and personally responsible. Training is expendable.	Culture of Sabotage

continues ...

Figure 8.9 Continued

Framing orientation and beliefs	Action strategies	Consequences for the training function	Consequences for learning
Training is Learning, or Critical consciousness: "We're colluding with our oppressors. We need to break out of the system that oppresses us."	Trainers actively learn about learning. Trainers encourage different views of training and design ways to test them. Trainers publicly share and test their understanding of human resource problems. Trainers jointly design and implement solutions with learners. Trainers and learners publicly reflect on results.	Learners and trainers will experience less defensiveness, more trust. Learners and trainers will feel mutually responsible for results. Learners and trainers will feel freer to experiment and to take risks	Culture of Empowerment

their constraints insurmountable. These individuals looked at trainers as experts and held them in awe in a way that appeared to relieve these individuals of the responsibility of achieving a similar level of expertise. In effect, this left them out of control of their level of skill.

The idea that training is magical can also be seen in the many instances when trainers were asked to develop courses within time frames they knew were not pedagogically sound. One individual reported to the training director that many more training programs had been requested by her department than she could possibly develop and schedule within the allotted period of time. In addition, influential members of the department had complained to the training director that this trainer did not listen or pay attention to their needs. The training director suggested that she listen attentively to their requests, nod empathetically, then continue as before. On the one hand, this strategy may convey that trainers are empathic. But by not clarifying the limits of training, this strategy may also inadvertently encourage people to believe that the training department can do anything they ask, which might increase the demands on training. It might encourage a lack of realism or magical thinking regarding what is feasible in terms of the purpose and outcomes of training. This could also lead to even more times when individuals would see that the trainer does not "listen to their needs," which would exacerbate the present problem. Ironically, this strategy would promote a view *in others* that training is magic, the very view the trainer had hoped to thwart in the first place.

Training is naïve or a political act

A naïve view of human resource development is that training cannot be done well because trainers are so oppressed. This can be seen in the following statements:

— We want to give HRD training to our [training] staff, to provide it as a benefit. We have to meet our group commitments or goals first. The priority becomes the technical learning and the HRD courses become secondary.

— Well, we want to pilot a class just before we start shipping the product. The product controls course development time. They're not going to wait to ship until you have the course ready.

— In the past, the training staff had been someone who's been a misfit, someone who is not competent in another role.

— People emulate their bosses and their managers don't practice what we teach in training. Managers say they have no time, that they already know it or that all they need is an overview. What we

need is for the managers to demonstrate their commitment.
— HRD is one of the first areas to go when the company tightens
its belt. It's an insecure place to be.
— It is really middle managers who don't value training. Higher
level managers take the long view and lower level managers see
the immediate impact. For middle managers, it's more cost effective to tell people to get it on their own.
— You get about three mistakes in a training session and then you
lose your credibility.

The recurring theme is that someone else controls training effectiveness. Whether it is managers who assign misfits to training, judge
training results too harshly, or fail to practice what trainers preach, it
is clear that trainers perceive that managers often undermine their
professionalism. Yet, this view may be based on untested attributions. In one organization, for example, trainers were asked to
prepare a training course within two weeks for about two thousand
people. The trainers said that this was the sort of unrealistic, ridicu-
lous request they always faced. Yet when asked what they had done
this time or previous times to explain why this could not be done,
they said that higher level managers would not listen or would imply
that they were trying to get out of work or were unable to "come
through." Thus, once again they would work 80-hour weeks and deliver "something" within the deadline.

The politicization of training can also be seen in an episode reported by a trainer in a new department. In a former position, this
trainer's tasks frequently required library research. Faced with a
problem for which she felt a need for more information before reaching a decision, she went to the nearby university library. She was
reprimanded when the department head telephoned and the secretary reported she was out. She explained her whereabouts but, when
a similar situation recurred, the secretary complained that "some
people get to take time off during the workday." The supervisor
asked her to remain in her office during working hours in the future.
The political symbolism of learning as a reward or even a vacation did
little to encourage real learning in this instance.

Training is learning

An alternative view is not found in these data, but can be constructed
from the action science perspective. Training can be looked at as
learning. Learner-centered models are espoused in the literature
(Knowles, 1984; Brookfield, 1986), yet trainer-directed models appear to prevail in practice. Moreover, the political climate of most

training departments is highly reactive. This is so much so that it is often conveyed in training department goals. "The training department will be highly responsive to organizational needs." Of course, there is nothing sinister or wrong in such goals. A training department focused on learning is also responsive to organizational needs but might go about it in a different way.

A learning-oriented department actively seeks ways to enhance and define learning in the organization. Such trainers seek to create an organization that functions like a learning system, emphasize a vision of a learning organization, and teach people to learn how to learn. In order to teach people to learn how to learn, they must model these skills by engaging in continual learning themselves, reflecting on what they have learned, surfacing tacit incidental learning, and using their own learning experiences almost like scientific experiments that can be publicly verified and replicated. In a learning organization, human resource developers are both guides and co-learners. When learning is a mutual task, both learners and trainers are empowered.

Argyris's (1982) Model II or double-loop learning orientation provides an alternative professional framework for human resource developers. The section which follows further explores the theory-of-action perspective that enables individuals to reframe their orientation from a control orientation to a learning orientation.

Theory-of-action perspective

According to Argyris and Schön (1974), a theory of practice is a set of interrelated theories of action that specify what actions, given a particular situation, will yield desired results. They distinguish between espoused theories, or intentions, and theories-in-use, or actions. This theory-of-action perspective has been developed in sociology, organizational learning, and education.

The action science perspective is like the action frame of reference in modern social theory. Writers such as Max Weber, Irving Goffman, and Berger and Luckmann have all contributed to this perspective. In this view, organizations are the outcome of the interaction of motivated people attempting to resolve their own problems (Silverman, 1970). Meanings come to us from society and become institutionalized as shared orientations which are then passed on to later generations as fact. People also define society by reaffirming meanings in everyday actions. To understand human action, we must determine the meanings that individuals assign to their acts.

194

The fundamental argument of this frame of reference is that individuals are constrained by the way they socially construct reality. Cohen (1968) suggests that social action takes place when other actors are present and are taken into account when the action is performed. It is assumed that these others have the capacity to influence the actor, and that the actor shares some expectations and possibly also values, beliefs, and symbols with these others.

This perspective sheds light on incidental learning by explaining what individuals may learn indirectly from experience. Complicating this even further is the problem of an individual's attributions about the meaning and motives of others. The individual's perception of the experience as important or significant determines whether or not learning takes place. From a theory-of-action perspective, this assignment of meaning to experiences is also a social artifact. Incidental learning, possibly because it is often not perceived as important, may lead to tacit, taken-for-granted assumptions which may increase the potential for error in learning. At the level of professional learning, this learning is influenced by assumptions about the meanings of clients, actions or practice of either the client or the professional, and of professional codes, standards, and literature.

Drawing on the work of Jurgen Habermas, Hart (1985) notes that "all human action is guided by norms which take the form of reciprocal behavior expectations. The force of norms governing human action derives from an underlying taken-for-granted consensus about the validity of those norms" (p. 121). Hart goes on to discuss the way in which action or speech, that is guided by norms not accessible to human consciousness, functions much like lying. Thus, "compulsive action based on unconscious intentions is a form of deception and self-deception" (p. 129). This shows the impact of oppression.

Changing oneself after a critical self-examination, a process of emancipatory education, involves dissolving and reconstructing everyday experience. Weick (1986) describes changing or redesigning oneself or one's organization as essentially the changing of one's commitments. This process involves changing one's choices, making these changes visible to others, and *reconstructing irreversibility*. What was formerly perceived to be irreversible is now seen to be reversible, while one's new choices are now seen to be irreversible. Benveniste (1987) points out that critical reflection on these tacit norms is a basic requirement of professionalism. For Benveniste, inculcating an attitude of professionalism is the best way to enhance the organization's overall learning capacity.

One's capacity for reconstructing experience-based knowledge characterizes critically reflective learners. This chapter illustrates this process of reflective learning. Kelly (1955) differentiates between learning that enhances or modifies an individual's existing constructs, or ways of seeing the world, and learning that reframes these constructs. Reflective learning may depart from that which is merely additive, and affirm that which is transformative and emancipatory. As our culture moves into a new era, learning which merely embellishes existing frameworks is hardly likely to produce the knowledge needed to transform people and organizations.

Rethinking the nature of learning from a sociological perspective leads to different assumptions about the nature of learning and about the extent to which individuals, acting alone, can in fact make major changes in their view of their world. The theory-of-action perspective emphasizes the need for dialogue in producing more critically reflective informal and incidental learning.

The process of learning about one's dysfunctional theories-in-use (those which are inconsistent with espoused theories, or ineffective) is a process Argyris and Schön (1974) cast in Kelly's (1955) terms. Kelly defines learning as the "psychological reconstruing of life" (p. 187). Kelly's reconstrual would be most like double-loop learning since it involves a reframing of one's personal constructs or ways of seeing the world. Kelly's theory rests on the fundamental assumption that "A person's processes are psychologically channelized by the ways in which he anticipates events" (Kelly, 1955, p. 46). People's frames on an event predict how they experience it. Determining an individual's expectations and retrospective rationalizations about events may provide a window into that individual's "constructs" of the world – or in Argyris and Schön's terms, their theories of action.

Argyris and Schön (1974) engage practitioners in reflection on their theories of action by looking at overall internal consistency (the absence of self-contradiction), congruence between espoused theories and theories-in-use, the effectiveness of the action strategies used to implement their theories, and whether or not they value the behavioral world created by their theories and actions. In order for practitioners to alter their behavior, they will first have to identify the deep structures that currently hold them paralyzed in inconsistency or in double binds (Argyris *et al.*, 1985) and confront the defensive routines that enable them to remain blind to their own inconsistency (Argyris, 1985). The intervention theory and method developed by Argyris to enable individuals to do this is now called action science.

Implications

This chapter alerts human resource development professionals to unconscious beliefs they hold that impede their effectiveness. These professionals can learn a great deal about what learners want by reflecting on their own learning preferences. The contrast between what they espouse for others and what they actually do as learners may lead trainers to challenge the validity of many of their current assumptions.

Professionalism

Human resource developers need a sense of professionalism. Although the nature of their work remains highly non-routine, human resource developers can ensure a threshold of comparatively predictable practice by developing facility in available technologies e.g. program design, action science, or cost-benefit analysis. They can also research their own practice by routinely collecting directly observable data using video or audio tapes of their teaching, inquiring into the thoughts and feelings of learners about their actions, and systematically following up on learners to determine effects of training. They can thus reduce the distortion common to subjective private reflections on practice. Typing transcripts of their practice, human resource developers have found that things they were sure had happened in a particular sequence often happened in a very different sequence, one that often leaves them in a less favorable light. If even the events of a learning experience are so readily distorted, how then can trainers reconstruct what they and others actually said or did to make their practice observable to them? Trainers can improve their practice considerably if they merely commit themselves to formal learning about training and informal reflective learning on their practice.

An experimental attitude

Incidental learning is also learning from covert interpersonal experiments. For example, one person said that "when I get a new boss, I go in and ask for things to see what gets turned down. In this way, I can find out what my parameters are." Asked if he had ever directly inquired into the new manager's policies, he responded, "No, that wouldn't be appropriate." Another individual described one of his first training assignments. He was asked to work with a senior trainer to design a training program for a new technical product. He recalled that he had made several assumptions that later proved false: that the senior person was there to help groom him, that the senior person was not confrontable and was more powerful than he, and that the senior person was probably "right" about what the training department would want. In their planning sessions, the junior trainer discovered that the senior trainer's technical information was outdated and sometimes wholly inaccurate. Further, they did not agree about how to teach the course. When the junior trainer "pointed out twenty-five ways that his approach was right, the senior trainer would say 'It just feels wrong to me.'" The two ended up dividing the course in half and each did his half his own way. When they presented it for the first time, the participants confirmed what they had suspected all along – that the senior trainer's portion was technically wrong. Paradoxically, in not giving each other direct information about his negative perceptions of the other's approach and allowing the negative feedback to come from the participants, they may have impaired each trainer's credibility.

This covert interpersonal experiment left considerable latitude for error. There is another potential paradox in this situation. If the new trainer valued technical expertise over training expertise and the senior trainer valued training skill over technical expertise, both individuals had only part of what was needed to do this task well. By placing a high value on only one aspect of their work, each may have demonstrated a high level of professionalism that nevertheless inadvertently threatened their credibility with learners. Had they approached the design problem with a more experimental attitude, perhaps they would have felt freer to play around with alternative possibilities without focusing on the "twenty-five ways" the other person was wrong.

Incidental learning

In management, it is almost axiomatic that what a manager does is not as important as how he or she does it. Similarly, what a human resource developer does may not be as important as how he or she does it because *how* it is done will convey an implicit learning message of its own which, as can be seen in these examples, may sabotage the explicit learning goals. Nowhere is this more apparent than in the lack of training that trainers get or seek. In Watkins and Wiswell's (1987) research, human resource developers completed a questionnaire, the Learning Practices Audit. Responses indicated that these trainers spent an average of 14 hours per week in work-related learning, only 3.9% of it in internal training sessions. Like the shoeless shoemaker's children, there is a paradox in that those who provide learning for others overlook learning for themselves. One possible consequence of this is that trainers may find their long term competence jeopardized and the training department will not have a self-renewing capacity, since it cannot train its own staff to higher levels of competence. Moreover, trainers may unintentionally model to others in the organization that they too do not really need much training. Observing the lack of training for trainers might also suggest to potential clients that it does not take any special training to educate others, a supposition supported by the fact that less than 10% of human resource developers are actually trained in the field, or that trainers see themselves as less in need of training than their clients. Each of these possible interpretations has the potential of undermining learning in the organization.

Because incidental learning is largely tacit and taken for granted, strategies for surfacing unspoken attributions and assumptions are needed. In this study, this was accomplished by observing contradictions, determining paradoxes and double binds which might paralyze or undermine actions, and inferring possible unintended consequences of actions, particularly by weighing the possible effects of actions on clients. Incidental learning is also a byproduct rather than an intentional learning activity. By intentionally reflecting on both what one learns incidentally and how one learns incidentally, human resource developers can enhance their overall critical reflection skills by interrupting their natural tendency to make incorrect attributions (especially that others have nasty motives or are resistant to change) or to frame problems based on their personal, subjective (and therefore limited), experience-based frame on those problems.

In conclusion, incidental learning is embedded in the beliefs which inform future actions. In order to transform professional practice, it is essential that professionals examine the nature of those beliefs and the validity of the learning which formed those beliefs about their practice. Action science is one approach to guide reflection on those beliefs.

Part four

Implications for practice

We began this book with a conceptual framework, the human resource learning cone, which we used to define and distinguish informal and incidental learning from formal training activities in organizations and to lay out the various levels at which learning, both formal and informal, takes place: the individual, group, organization, and profession. In these chapters, we use the human resource learning cone, the Johari Window, and problem-solving models as frameworks for summarizing what we have learned from our research, to elaborate upon the theory behind informal and incidental learning, to recommend strategies for enhancing informal and incidental learning, and, finally, to look at ways in which formal learning can be linked with informal and incidental learning.

The rationale for the human resource development profession's focus on formal learning is clear: training is more visible, definable, predictable and controllable. While human resource professionals often battle to prove their worth, tangible, visible activities and outputs make the profession more defendable – or so it seems. However, training has often been isolated from other functions within the organization and, since it is ultimately very difficult to prove results from training because of the many variables that influence transfer of learning to the job, training has been more susceptible to cuts when times get tough. We argue in Part Four that the changing times and the need for human resource professionals to be in the forefront of change require that human resource professionals re-evaluate their position on informal and incidental learning. While informal and incidental learning are much more difficult to facilitate because they take place outside of controlled circumstances, we believe that learning outside the classroom poses a challenge to human resource development that the profession cannot afford to define as something outside its purview.

In these chapters, we spell out a rationale for our emphasis on informal and incidental learning and offer some suggestions on how the profession can rise to the challenges we have identified. As we explore the strategies that will enhance informal and incidental learning, we return to the analysis in Chapter One. We have seen that informal learning at the individual, group, organizational and professional levels may be capacity-enhancing, or dysfunctional. When it is dysfunctional, some aspect of the situation is either blind or hidden from the key person or persons' view. In order to create the conditions for learning, feedback and disclosure are needed. The aim of the strategies at each level is the same – to increase the accuracy of the information available to guide action and to encourage openness to learning through reflection.

To pull together the findings on informal learning, we refer again to a diagram used in Chapter Five, the learning loop (Figure 5.1), based on Schön' (1983) and Simon (1965), that represents steps in problem setting and solving. Figure IV.1 reproduces this figure, but added are what we believe to be key processes for effective informal learning in these stages.

Chapter Ten suggests strategies for enhancing informal and incidental learning. Implications for changing the field of human resource development are presented in terms of changing paradigms, changing skills, and strategies for linking training as it is now to informal and incidental learning approaches.

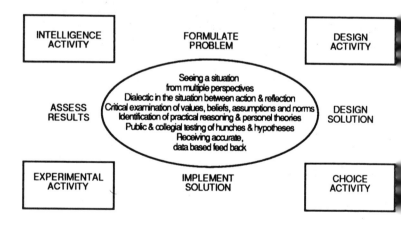

Figure IV.1 Informal learning processes in the learning loop

Chapter nine

Conclusions and implications for informal and incidental learning

In this chapter, we revisit the theoretical framework for informal and incidental learning we developed in Chapter One in light of the case studies in Parts Two and Three. We begin with our rationale for an enhanced focus on informal and incidental learning, building on the literature we reviewed on training in Chapter Two. This rationale grows out of human capital theory which posits that education is a major means for increasing the value of people in the workplace. Their vision calls for retraining of the entire adult population – a task that would be impossible if we were to rely solely on formal training methods. Researchers who examine the differences between learning in and out of school also find a need for the skills of reflection and problem setting we emphasize here. Their research is reviewed next. We also compare our work on informal and incidental learning with other work on experiential and self-directed learning. Finally, we summarize our findings regarding informal and incidental learning.

A rationale for informal and incidental learning

Human capital theories

Human capital theorists present what may be the most compelling argument for a focus on informal learning in the workplace. Human capital theory refers to "the productive capabilities of human beings that are acquired at some cost and that command a price in the labor market because they are useful in producing goods and services" (Parnes, 1986, p. 1). Thinking in terms of value as a return on investment in a cost-to-benefit ratio, education is seen as a major means for organizations (and individuals) to increase the net worth of the worker's skills and abilities. Using econometric modeling, Carnevale (1984) found that workplace learning and formal education accounted for more growth in economic output than employee health, capital, the composition of the workforce, population size, or resource adaption. In fact, he found that workplace learning accounts for 85% of the variance in lifetime earnings.

This finding is similar to that of Lillard and Tan's (1986) Rand Study which was based on measures of reported training from the current Population Survey, three cohorts from the National Longitudinal Surveys, and the Employment Opportunities Pilot Projects Survey. The study sought a broad picture of who gets private sector training and what its effects are on long-term earnings and employment. Lillard and Tan found that, overall, employer-sponsored training had the most significant and persistent impact on increasing individuals' earnings; an effect that persisted for over 13 years (ibid., p. 69). But these effects vary for different groups. Women receive disproportionately less company training than men and the economically disadvantaged receive the least training, especially from employers. Informal training is significantly more available (as is formal training) in high technology industries. This latter group is also more likely to report that prior on-the-job training experiences were needed to secure their current jobs. This training is offered in-house more than in other industries, a factor which seems to increase as the rate of technological change quickens.

The themes in Lillard and Tan's research are that company training makes a clear and significant difference in an employee's earnings and employment prospects, but access to that training may be discriminatory. It is possible that older workers are retrained only when there is a high national rate of unemployment, when it may be cheaper to retain an older worker than to train a new employee. Finally, those who work intermittently or frequently change jobs receive less training over the life cycle. Even (1987) has suggested that women's career interruptions following childbirth explain the differential in earnings between men and women. It is not only the employer-sponsored training that women miss, but also the informal learning from experience that comes from taking on increasingly challenging job tasks, or learning to work with different peers and supervisors. It is clear that the human capital benefit of employee training is enormous. Equally clear is the cost to a vast segment of the workforce who are denied access. For them, informal learning represents an alternative delivery system which may help them compete more successfully.

Critics of human capital theory see this last finding as an inherent flaw in our capitalist economic structure with its built-in class structure. They suggest that these inequities may lead to lower morale and thus lower productivity. This may result whether or not workers have access to training. They see collusion on the part of training in the sense that training is often used as a vehicle for "cooling out" the aspirations of the disenfranchised (LaBelle, 1988). These attitudes on the part of workers about training constitute a kind of incidental learning that is highly tacit. In effect, it is the internalization of capitalism in trainers and learners that is the issue.

Carnevale (1984) found that employers spend 210 billion dollars per year on training, including a full 180 billion dollars on informal training or on-the-job training. The task for learning in the workplace is to develop new strategies for enabling workers to use job experiences more effectively for learning (Watkins, 1989; Marsick, 1988c). Perhaps the most eloquent call for a human capital understanding of the need for an alternative to adult learning in the workplace is that offered by Perelman (1984):

Unless we in America greatly increase the flexibility of our human capital, the economic transition threatens turbulent, even violent, social upheaval as the economic ambitions of a major portion of the working population become increasingly frustrated.... Learning by the mainstream of workforce adults will be essential to resolve this crisis.

Virtually the entire adult population needs retraining and new learning to be economically productive. A fifth of the present adult population is functionally illiterate. Most of the rest – including skilled workers, managers, and professionals – have knowledge and skills that technological change is rendering obsolete.... The emergence of a knowledge based economy requires a new synthesis of the functions of training, education, and other forms of communication and learning under the single umbrella of the learning enterprise."

[Perelman, 1984, pp. xvi–xvii]

"Schooling" perspective: in or outside the classroom

One reason many offer for this enormous emphasis on retraining is the failure of the schools to instill adequately a lifelong capacity to learn. Others suggest that schools provide general skills and corporations provide more specific job skills which become quickly obsolete. By examining mental activity in and out of the classroom, Resnick (1987) concludes that there are differences, but these differences are disappearing as schools move to a greater emphasis on cognitive skills and training settings continue to separate learning from work experiences. She outlined four broad characteristics of mental activity outside of school that contrast with typical school work. First, in school, the emphasis is on individual cognition and achievement. Yet work, recreation, and one's personal life all take place in a social context. Each person's ability to function depends on what others do and on getting all of these individuals' mental and physical efforts to mesh. Thus, the emphasis outside of school is on shared cognition.

Second, schools emphasize pure thought, but out-of-school learning emphasizes tool manipulation. Tools shape cognitive activity. They enable the less well-educated to participate in complex activities and the highly educated to work well beyond their own individual capacities. The computer is a recent example of this phenomenon.

Third, contextualized reasoning, in which people connect actions with surrounding objects, replaces the symbol manipulation found in school. Perhaps the best example of this practical reasoning is found in the work of Scribner (1984), who found that dairy workers used the context, dairy case sizes and physical space, to work more efficiently. They would visualize the space available, use their knowledge of how many cases fill that space, and add whatever number of cases remained. In this way, they used objects within the context rather than abstract mathematical symbols to solve problems. Actions are thus "grounded in the logic of immediate situations" (p. 15).

Fourth, in school, the prime objective is to teach generalized, widely usable skills, while outside of school, people must develop situation-specific competencies. Resnick (1987) cites Morris and Rense (1985), who found that training in electronics theory ill-prepared workers for electronic troubleshooting. Resnick concludes that "very little can be transported directly from school to out-of-school use. Both the structure of the knowledge used and the social conditions of its use may be more fundamentally mismatched than we previously thought" (p. 83). She also notes, however, that those with situation-specific skills do less well than educated generalists when the situation changes. Yet, we suggest that corporate classrooms also do not typically use the workplace itself as a learning environment, so they share the same problems of school classroom-based learning.

Resnick calls for "bridging apprenticeships" that use computer simulation, tutoring, coaching, and case-based teaching methods. In addition, out-of-school learning calls for special skills in learning when optimal instruction is unavailable. Work requires people to adapt when routines break down. To do this, they must step outside the situation and reason above it. Individuals need mental models of how the whole system works to respond appropriately when the system breaks down. Schools can teach people to be adaptive learners.

In adult learning, the differences between in and out-of-classroom learning are critical. Usher (1985) echoes Resnick in noting that out-of-school learning, or learning from life, is different from formal learning and that it is heavily dependent on context. Important differences follow in the conception of learning and the use of experience. Learning from life is thematized rather than reproductive, which Usher defines as the memorizing and reproducing of facts or a body of knowledge. When learning is thematized, the emphasis is on reflection and awareness borne out of active interaction with a situation. It is perspective-dependent. In reproductive learning, experiences are anecdotes, surface-level examples of some aspect of the body of knowledge. In thematised learning, experiences are deep sources of productive learning. They are differentiated and problematized. In both Usher's and Resnick's work, there is a call for incorporating out-of-school learning into formal classrooms, to make experiences deep sources of productive learning.

Necessary conditions for learning from work experiences

Collaborative learning

Boydell (1976) identifies self-actualization as the core of experiential learning, whether inside or outside the classroom. He suggests that learners are "responsible for [their] own learning" (p. 42), much as described by advocates of self-directed learning, but they are linked with a social network in that they cooperate with, help and are helped by one another. A critically reflective stance – such as the one that we call for in this book – requires that self-actualization be redefined to include a willingness to identify and challenge many of the blind spots that lead to gaps between our espoused theories and theories-in-use. Brookfield (1987) notes that "challenge is central to helping people think critically....Challenge prompts self-scrutiny, consideration of alternatives, and the taking of action" (p. 90). Action science and our research suggest that, for learning to occur, challenges must include an illustration of the attribution, judgment, or evaluation with directly observable data and an invitation to inquire mutually into the assertion.

Self-actualization, as espoused in the culture of the United States, is highly oriented to individual achievement as is the concept of self-directed learning. Informal and incidental learning must take place with the collaboration and joint inquiry of others in the workplace who form a learning community. Learning from experience involves other people. It is not enough that other people are drawn upon as resources, as is often advocated in self-directed learning theory. If

Conclusions and implications

that were the case, the focus would still be on individual achievement. As we discuss later in regard to organizational learning, the learning of one person is inextricably intertwined with the learning of others in natural work groups. As Boot and Reynolds (1983) point out, from one perspective, others are valuable because they provide feedback or shape another's behavior; but they can also be seen as "negotiators in the construction of social reality" (p. 8), which is the stance we also take.

Developing a learning community

Smith (1987) points out that "when organizational structure maximizes participation, human interaction, and flexibility in carrying out roles, the possibilities for learning through day-to-day activity are maximized" (p. 40). The climate and organizational policies must also permit learning. Smith notes, "As they think and decide and act, organization members are guided by principles, rules, understandings, and norms" which can support or discourage learning (p. 41).

This finding is reinforced by Davies and Easterby-Smith (1984) in a study of managers who learned from work experience. The managers described "confrontations with novel situations and problems where their existing repertoire of behaviours are inadequate and where they have to develop new ways of dealing with these situations" (p. 180). In all such cases, however, managers were encouraged by the organization to learn. Davis and Easterby-Smith note that "organizations have many filters which reduce the impact of change on managers within them" (ibid.) and can thus reduce the managers' willingness to experiment and change. Thus, a second critical component is a "developing culture," that is, "support for the managers who are prepared to develop new ways of dealing with problems, and who do not see themselves being bound entirely by existing rules and procedures" (p. 181). When learning is in the workplace, the organization is the defining environment for learning.

The organizational context

Mocker and Spear (1982) also found that context was a key ingredient in the learning experience. Our research strongly concurs with Mocker and Spear's findings on "the organizing circumstance," that is, that the learner's environment is the major determinant in organizing a learning project. Drawing on Kurt Lewin's conception of the individual's life space, Mocker and Spear define the organizing circumstance as those elements in the adult's life space that provide motivation, resources, activities, and overall direction to the planning of a learning project. Through content analysis of learners'

210

descriptions of their learning activities, they identified four types of organizing circumstances: (1) Single Event / Anticipated Learning; (2) Single Event / Unanticipated Learning; (3) Series of Events / Related Learning; (4) Series of Events / Unrelated Learning. This typology reflects the emphasis on intentionality and goal-directedness of their four types of adult learning. It is unfortunately still focused on what learners control rather than the role of the environment. We could suggest that their category of unintentional learning *is* environmentally induced learning. This would fit our examples of incidental learning. Growing up with an alcoholic parent, for example, certainly is an environment which triggers considerable incidental and tacit learning, and is yet also an environment that a child is hardly likely to choose *intentionally*.

Mocker and Spear conclude that, unlike the artificial environment in institutionally sponsored learning, self-directed learning takes place in natural, everyday settings. It is the individual's perceptions of, and interaction with, that environment that give meaning to experience. This also contrasts with formal learning situations since, in them, authorities often control salience and interpretation. Of course, the sociological perspective offered in Chapter Eight ratifies these conclusions, but we would also further suggest that individuals' perceptions of formal settings give them meaning. Few would argue that the characterizations of institutions as "artificial" or instructors as "authorities with prerogatives" are themselves interpretive.

What we do question in this volume is the explicit and implicit advocacy of self-directed learning that implies there is something better or more adult in learning on one's own. Brookfield (1986) also raises issues with the self-directed learning credo and notes that most self-directed learning includes peer and group learning as well as formally tutored learning. He wonders if there is not considerable virtue in the opportunity for reflection which is a byproduct of listening to lectures.

Our concern is less with method, however, than with the effectiveness of this learning. We do not deny that much useful learning is acquired in autonomous learning projects, but we *are* concerned that misinformation and unintentional learning are also learned this way. The organizational context is a powerful mediator of an individual's learning. In organizations, learning typically occurs in groups who have a life together outside of the classroom, one which is continuous over a long period of time. These people share norms, a culture, and meanings that are so mutually reinforced that individuals may seldom consider the possibility that other meanings are thinkable. The relationships between the people in organizations is role-bound and hierarchically accountable. There is an unspoken exchange process

211

operating that asks individuals to perform "for their supper" and silently threatens to let them go without supper if they do not perform. There is no doubt that these consequences are real. Although we could argue that many, if not most of these dynamics are present in school, the contractual relationship between learners and teachers is different, and the consequences of violating it, though in reality possibly more dire and long-lasting, seldom appear to be so immediately disastrous.

Informal learning

Figure 9.1 is a summary of the steps that learners, described in Chapters Three, Four, and Five, took to learn informally from experience in non-routine situations. The reader will note that the sequence of steps is slightly different in each case. In the MiL projects, more time is spent in problem framing than in solving the problem. While managers often act to begin to implement solutions they propose, the experimentation in these projects is focused on identifying the right problem by testing out different alternatives and using the information that is generated to re-examine and reformulate the problem. Thus, at the end of the project, the team makes its recommendations on choices, based on successive stages of solution testing.

The Philippines program follows the same sequence as does MiL. The difference is that MiL participants are working on a temporary project, whereas Philippines participants look at their real-life experience to set up educational programs. Another difference, difficult to illustrate in this summary, is the relative emphases placed on problem framing and formulation. This step is closer to a simple kind of problem identification in the Philippines program. The village leaders seem to accept the staff's framing of the problem, based on the trust they have in their judgment. In the Nepal program, learning begins with an experimentation phase in the villages as a prelude to problem framing. The field workers start by living with clients so that they can begin to see their point of view. They use this new perspective as a basis for problem formulation. As in the Philippines program, problem framing and formulation is more guided than in the MiL program. In Nepal, the trainers focus on predefined objectives.

The sequence for professional trainers in the minicases examined in Chapter Four follows the four stages, as outlined, more sequentially. However, as was pointed out in that chapter, the lines are frequently blurred between stages and, at times, professional trainers seem to be engaging in several stages simultaneously.

Intelligence	Design	Choice	Experimentation
MiL Projects I. Managers examine context from many perspectives to frame problem & plan action.	III. After successive stages of framing & testing hunches, they give feedback to host.	IV. The team helps host look at feedback. While host makes decision, all discuss situation.	II. Managers take action to generate information & examine group dynamics.
Nepal Training II. Workers reflect on their experience & analyze client views to frame problems.	III. Workers design & try out interventions in villages. They assess results.	IV. Workers choose strategies, but continue testing ideas & examining results with team.	I. Workers live in villages to experience client viewpoint & observe behaviors.
PRRM Program I. Staff meet village leaders & help them frame problem as amenable to change.	III. Staff help Councils design educational program & develop criteria for workers.	IV. Councils test ideas with villagers & recruit Technicians who continue cycle with others.	II. If village leaders frame the problem as educational, they talk & form Council.
Trainers I. Trainers begin with task that is ambiguous, surprising or that creates dissonance.	II. Trainers examine context, formulate hypotheses, talk with others, & experiment.	III. Trainers act based on hunches & beliefs, whether or not these are examined.	IV. Trainers test ideas & stay open to feedback, but may not see blind spots.

Figure 9.1 Comparison of informal learning from experience in non-routine situations

Conclusions and implications

While this diagram is useful as a conceptual framework, it is likely that people do not always move sequentially through stages when they learn informally even though they might engage in more or less of a certain kind of activity at different times during their learning. We might envision informal learning as an iterative process over time in which people use all four stages as they move continually through a process of problem framing, problem formulation, solution finding, solution testing, reframing, and reformulation of the problem. A person might draw on elements of intelligence, design, choice, or experimentation as he or she goes through each stage of this cycle. The last stage in the sequence usually leads to a further cycle of learning until the person has met his or her criteria for satisfactory learning.

Self-directed learning in organizations

In these studies, we differentiate our findings from the self-directed, informal learning described by Tough (1979) who reported on a study of informal adult learning projects outside the classroom. Two criteria are used for our differentiation: degree of intentionality of the change, and individual vs. collective dimensions of informal and incidental learning in organizations.

Tough focused on "episodes in which a certain *intention* (gaining and retaining certain knowledge and skill) accounts for more than half the person's motivation" to learn (p. 13). Tough (1982) also emphasized intentionality in a second study of 330 men and women in England, Canada, and the United States. Tough focused solely on what he defined as "*highly* intentional" changes (p. 20), a self-defined, successful series of activities to achieve a goal, which excluded self-initiated change processes that were not successful or that, after a period of thought and experimentation, were abandoned. He wrestled over the definition of "*highly* intentional":

> First, the change must be deliberately chosen and intended. That is, the person clearly makes a decision to change in a particular direction. Second, the person then takes one or more steps to achieve the change. The person does something specific, rather than passively letting the change occur with no effort at all. Choosing and striving are the two key elements: the person chooses a particular change and then takes action to achieve it.
> [Tough, 1982, p. 20]

Tough's concept of self-directed learning fits ours in that people learn from experience, the situation is often defined by them as non-

214

routine, and people can be proactive in their learning. However, Tough is concerned with planned events to reach a goal that leads his subjects to exclude other kinds of informal and incidental learning. For example, he describes a trip he took to India as highly intentional because of a desire to learn about that country. Tough's interest began with a vague, undefined interest but once in India, he quickly framed the problem to focus more specifically on poverty in India. Tough notes that he would exclude something he learned from his definition that we would include in our definition:

> The other major impact of my two months abroad was a sharp awareness of the importance to me of my family. I do not count this as intentional because I had not anticipated nor chosen it.... I count a change as intentional...only if the person expects and definitely seeks the approximate sort of change that does occur.
>
> [Tough, 1982, p. 21]

Tough's definition effectively excludes much of the learning that we talk about in this book. Informal learning, as we use it, can be planned, but includes learning that is not designed or expected. Incidental learning, by definition, includes the unexpected. Moreover, we are talking about learning that is prompted, at least in part, by the needs of the organization and sometimes by the direct command or request of others. By contrast, Tough emphasizes the voluntary, purposeful nature of self-directed learning in his studies. Our studies emphasize the unintentional, unanticipated learning that is *often* influenced or triggered by a chance encounter with a person or event or by a need imposed on the person by the organization.

We include a further dimension to our studies: the collective dimension of learning in organizations. People do pursue their own learning, but our research shows that the natural work groups through which they learn influence the learning process and outcomes. Thus, we believe we should talk about two different kinds of self-directed learning, which probably are somewhat interdependent, when we talk about learning in group or organizational settings: learning directed at one's own self-development, and learning by an individual in the pursuit of collective needs within a group or organization.

In a study by the Center for Creative Leadership on how managers learn from experience (McCall, Jr. *et al.*, 1988, p. 139), a framework is developed for the individual, self-directed learning of managers that meets the needs of the first kind of learning. It is based on choice points, oriented to either action or avoidance, arranged in three phases: awareness of one's shortcomings, acceptance of responsibility and diagnosis of deficiencies, and remediation. Awareness can occur by default, by waiting for a crisis or a negative consequence such as a missed promotion or job loss, or the manager can seek out information about him or herself from situations, feedback from others or self-analysis. If he or she decides to change, a detailed diagnosis is needed that looks at shortcomings of knowledge, experience and skills, as well as personal and situational limitations. Four avenues are then available if he or she decides to act: building new strengths, anticipating what will be needed for new situations, compensating for one's own weaknesses, or changing oneself.

The MiL data suggests that managers are directed to pursue their own *individual* needs in tandem with *collective* needs within a group or organization. It may be that the consensus-oriented values of Swedish society, discussed earlier, point MiL staff more in this direction. However, many U.S. organizations have renewed their interest in a team orientation because they see other companies gaining a competitive edge when they capitalize on the synergy of groups. Examples in this book reinforce the fact that people in organizations naturally work and learn in groups, and that much of this learning takes place on the job. While not intentional as in Tough's studies, this group learning is equally as important as individual self-directed learning and may be more relevant to both the individual's and the organization's needs. In the MiL study, for example, managers became aware of their own needs, as in the first phase of the Creative Leadership framework, through all three routes: unfamiliar problems and circumstances that pushed the manager to act in new situations where his or her shortcomings were revealed, along with the feedback of others in the program and self-analysis activities. However, managers focused on their relationship to a group context: their own, both in work and at home with family and friends, that of the host company, and that of their own company. They looked at patterns in their relationships within those contexts, and at the patterns of relationships of those involved in dealing with the problem. Awareness, diagnosis and action thus went beyond the individual, although the individual learned much about him or herself as well, and involved others in the person's environment – at home, on the job, or in the project – in the learning cycle.

We highlight the step of "awareness" in the Center for Creative Leadership model because of what we know about informal and incidental learning. In Chapter Six, Watkins and Rogers compared three transformative learning theories (Table 6.1). Awareness bears a strong relationship to the early stages of reflective learning as depicted in their Table 6.1. Boyd and Fales (1983), for example, speak of a sense of inner discomfort that something does not fit or when

216

there is "unfinished business." Watkins compares this stage with "unfreezing," the concept from Lewin (in Argyris, 1975) that is also reflected in the "taking over" process in the chapter on the Nepal and Philippines programs. "Unfreezing" is the stage in which our pictures of the world crumble so that new pictures can emerge. This step of awareness leads to a willingness to reframe the problem.

While it is true that individuals can and do learn on their own, managers in the MiL study gained far more by learning with peers in teams. Relationships are the nexus of organizational life and the medium through which managers succeed. Leadership necessarily involves relationships with others. In groups, managers can examine how they interact with others and get valuable feedback. They can challenge their own expectations about "the way things are done around here." Groups allow multiple perspectives to be brought to bear on a situation, so that managers can alter their interpretations of a situation.

Is there also a collective dimension to the learning of professionals? Both Chapters Four and Five address this question in part because of the *professionalism* of the people studied. The paraprofessionals in both the Nepal and Philippines programs were intentionally being trained to think and act like professionals even though their jobs would not be defined as professional. The trainers in the adult educator study did not necessarily identify with the field of adult education but did illustrate many of the characteristics and attitudes of professionals. We can see that both the Nepal and Philippines programs fostered a collective dimension to learning as a strategy to build professionalism. Benveniste (1987) described professionals as "cosmopolitans, committed to a larger good" (p. 49). In the minicases in Chapter Five, this good was in line with the goals of the organizations described. In other examples cited in Chapter Five, we also saw times where higher-order principles were invoked that caused people to leave jobs and organizations rather than continue to work in the service of values or practices in line with "the larger good" with which they could not agree.

The process of self-directed learning, when in pursuit of collective rather than individual goals, differs from the process described by McCall, Jr. *et al.* (1988, p. 139) because the professional works with others to set and achieve collective goals. In the process of seeking answers to collective problems, other people learn along with the person initiating the action.

Conclusions and implications

Enhancing informal learning

Another facet of informal learning that shows up clearly in the analysis of programs in Chapters Three, Four, and Five is the value of the three enhancing conditions identified in Chapter One: proactivity, creativity, and critical reflection. These conditions seemed to be related. Proactive learners got more out of their experience because they were attuned to opportunities. These proactive learners also seemed ready to explore many creative avenues to deal with the situations they faced. And finally, in doing so, these learners were often open to critical reflection on the underlying causes for something they were experiencing.

Proactivity

When people were not proactive, they could easily adopt what Jarvis (1987) calls a non-learning stance. One of the clearest findings in the study of the Nepal and Philippines programs, for example, is that people do not necessarily learn from their experiences when they learn informally. Programs were set up because it was considered unlikely that people, under ordinary circumstances, would encounter the innovations promoted by these programs or that they would necessarily see themselves as sufficiently in charge of their destinies to initiate change if they did encounter it. As Jarvis points out, people can act habitually on presuppositions, not consider the situation as an opportunity for learning, or reject the possibility of something new because it is not meaningful. All things being equal, it seems easier for people to interpret a situation using existing mental frameworks. People thus fit the data to their own preconceptions rather than develop new mental frameworks; they see the routine in an event rather than the non-routine and interpret it accordingly. When people see situations as routine, they seem less likely to pay attention to what is unique, surprising or unexpected about a situation, reflect on the new dimensions of the situation, and respond through learning.

According to Jarvis, a variable needed to change a situation from nonlearning to learning is that it be meaningful to the person. It may be that learners become more willing to pay attention proactively to what might otherwise be taken-for-granted as routine or be rejected as unimportant when they see the meaning in the situation for themselves. Mezirow's notion of meaning schemes and meaning perspectives is helpful in examining this variable. Mezirow (1985) suggests that people interpret situations through meaning schemes, "sets of related expectations governing cause–effect relationships" that "guide the way in which we experience, feel, understand, judge and act upon our situations" (pp. 21–22). People can learn within the same meaning scheme, acquire new meaning schemes, or transform their meaning schemes. Meaning schemes fit together within meaning perspectives, integrated psychological structures with dimensions of thought, will and feeling which represent the way a person looks at him or herself and relationships. When people achieve a higher-order meaning transformation, they do not typically revert to prior meaning perspectives. Mezirow calls this perspective transformation.

The managers in the MiL study, for example, experienced significant changes in the meaning schemes by which they saw themselves, their relationships with others in both their personal and work lives, and their role as leaders. Perspective changes, if not transformations, typically accompany learning in programs of planned change such as those in Nepal and the Philippines because these programs introduce a world view radically different from that held by the learners. Without a perspective change, it is highly unlikely that people will even pay attention to data in their experiences and, if they do, they will interpret it using schema that are often inadequate.

Creativity

Creativity showed itself in several ways in the informal learning of people in these studies. First, there were deliberate attempts to bring creativity into programs, particularly in the MiL program where journeys into the world of the arts were used to see things from different points of view and in the PRRM program where Srinivasan's self-actualizing method was used. As discussed in Chapter Four, Srinivasan designed programs to release the creative potential of learners and materials that would stimulate novel ways of thinking about reality. Second, many of the adult educators studied in Chapter Five had creative hobbies (music, painting, writing) or considered themselves creative entrepreneurs or intrapreneurs. They valued this creativity and sought opportunities to express it in their work. The creative dimension, however, that is highlighted here relates directly to the step in informal learning that Schön (1983) called a reflective conversation with the situation. In this conversation, people creatively connect ideas that might otherwise be considered quite dissimilar. This requires a willingness to suspend judgment and try out new ways of seeing and doing things which do not always come naturally.

Critical reflectivity

One of the key factors for successful learning was critical reflection that enabled people to challenge norms and examine assumptions that lay behind their reasoning and actions. Frequently, critical reflection led people also to question the collective assumptions of the organization, program, group, or other unit in which they worked. People learned best when they were able to ask questions about why they saw the world as they did, whether their thinking was true, or how they came to believe a perceived truth that they held sacred. There was no systematic method in any of these studies for double-loop learning, as there is in action science. Success frequently depended on the assistance of other people whom they consulted – facilitators, mentors, colleagues, family, or friends – who were able to give them feedback that opened them up to another point of view.

Incidental learning

Findings about incidental learning are examined at each of the levels discussed in Chapter Two, followed by an overview of the nature of incidental learning as it relates to Argyris's problem-solving model.

At the individual level

In Chapter Six, individuals reflected on the ways in which their beliefs influenced their actions, critically examined whether or not those beliefs were a byproduct of their childhood in an alcoholic family, and determined whether or not they were no longer valid guides to their present behavior. The process itself was an exploration of the incidental learnings of adult children of alcoholics (ACOA) about how to act and how to survive in an unhealthy situation.

The interventionist's beliefs, as evidenced in her actions, also led to incidental learning about the nature of intervention. The ability to make judgment calls about whether to intervene in a therapeutic or an educational way, or both, requires not only refined judgment in action, but also the *capacity* to intervene competently in both ways. The findings from this study affirm the complexity of professional practice in non-routine situations.

The study produced numerous illustrations of the tacit beliefs about intervention in both the interventionist and the group. These beliefs guided action and often misguided perceptions about the intentions of others. One example was an individual's belief that a redesign of the case would mean a cure for dysfunctional ACOA behaviors. This mixture of an educational intervention – in other words, how do we redesign what the person should do in this case, what should he or she say or do – with a therapeutic outcome illustrates the internalization in the group of the confusion of educational and therapeutic interventions. Yet, this mixture often produced potent interventions such as when one individual attempted to reframe the dilemma in another person's case in terms of the common roles found in alcoholic families. This captured a very subtle aspect of the other person's practice that may not have been evident without the analytical framework provided by the literature on alcoholic families. By critically examining these tacit beliefs in the context of the results they produced and their desirability, individuals were able to determine whether or not to rethink their assumptions.

Related to this is the finding that what an individual does is interlocked with what others do. As we saw in Chapter Six, when individuals change themselves, as the interventionist did in her "moments of surrender" of a frame on the problem or on the group, the group had to change as well. This basic law of systems (that a change in any part of the system will affect the whole) applies to human systems as well as mechanical systems. Yet, individuals also found that all constraints were not surmountable, nor all people tractable. Even when individuals attempted to surface tacit beliefs and tacit knowing or to inquire into others' reasoning, they were not necessarily able to bring about the changes they sought. In the case of the human resource developers in Chapter Eight, repeated attempts to get longer time frames for training and repeated denials of these requests led to their unwillingness to engage in dialogue with management on this issue. Yet, our research suggests that conditions change any time one member of the group leaves or changes. Therefore, we would argue that these human resource developers need to continue to test their attribution that the system will not change. What they have learned incidentally about their system and culture is "true" but their system and culture is constantly in motion and in flux.

What people learn incidentally is not inherently correct, nor will it always lead them to produce error. In fact, much that people learn in dysfunctional families may be very useful, effective survival strategies. The process of surfacing these tacit learnings is one of reflecting first on what they are, and then on whether or not they lead to desirable results in the here-and-now. This process of discovering what one believes "below the surface" and examining automatic actions is part of learning how to learn. If what people have learned incidentally is outside of their conscious awareness, yet evident in their actions, learning to recognize the message in their actions allows them to rethink beliefs and thereby to choose whether or not to change their actions. This is indeed empowering and potentially transformative.

Conclusions and implications

At the group or project level

Chapter Seven reported a study of the roles and concerns of managers of change projects. These projects were selected because they were highly unusual, non-routine changes which therefore demanded considerable trial-and-error and learning-by-doing on the part of users and change facilitators. In the process of bringing about change in their institutions, these leaders developed attributions or frames about the nature of the change and their role in managing it. These role frames had a significant impact on the nature of their managerial functioning. Yet, there also appear to be features intrinsic to some changes that make demands on change facilitators. The incidental learning that results from the interaction of a manager's frame on the change process and the nature of the change is evident in the manager's actions and in the project's history. The need for a process of mutual inquiry was acknowledged in these complex changes, but seldom enacted. A long-term perspective was needed to institutionalize the change, but long-term use of the change to solve an organizational problem did not appear to be the primary goal of one or more of the change facilitators. Once again, individuals' beliefs shaped their actions. But because many people were now involved and affected by those actions, problems involved in achieving shared meaning escalated exponentially.

Incidental learning at this level is influenced by the situation, people's frame on that situation, and the number of people involved. As with incidental learning at the individual level, the key issue is to surface tacit beliefs and to examine the embedded logic in action that produces intended and unintended consequences. The more people that are involved, the more complex is this task.

At the professional level

Professionals are characterized by an explicit code of ethics. Yet, their practice can also be a template for discovering their *implicit* code of ethics. Perhaps the most interesting finding in Chapter Eight is that, although we often enact a code of ethics that differs from our professional codes, we can use the strategies offered here to inquire into the nature of the unintended consequences produced by the gap between what we believe we should do and what we actually do. We can begin to alter our practice to align it with our own beliefs.

The individuals described here were highly competent, concerned professionals. Poignantly, their good intentions often led to actions that produced the opposite result from those intentions. Professionals in human resource development will quickly recognize the binds and dilemmas in the stories reported in Chapter Eight as typical of those they too face. By reflecting on the long-term consequences of continuing to act as they have in the past, these professionals may elect to take some risks and negotiate more acceptable conditions for learning within their organizations and with their learners. Ultimately, they may create a learning-oriented environment for themselves and their organizations.

Overview

Figures 9.2–9.4 illustrate the nature of incidental learning and potential sources of error therein. Incidental learning is part of informal learning from experience and learning from problem solving. It is learned from taking action, and from reflecting on that action and on the problem it was intended to solve. In the figures that follow, Argyris's problem-solving cycle is used to highlight those components that involve tacit or inferential reasoning, and the way in which the process can be distorted by errors in either the incidental learning or the initial problem solving. Argyris suggests that problem solving is a cycle that moves from diagnosis of the problem to the invention of a strategy for solving it, to producing that strategy, to drawing evaluations and generalizations from the consequences of what was produced. Errors occur because there is often an interruption between the invention and the production stage. Individuals can invent strategies that they cannot produce either because they do not have the necessary skills or because assumptions and defensive routines, that are outside of their conscious awareness, lead them to produce behavior that is different from that which they intended.

Figure 9.2 presents Argyris's problem-solving model. People who continually recycle between the invention and production stages are caught in a single-loop. They see that their inventions are not working and therefore try to produce another strategy. Or, they see that they are not enacting their strategy, so they may experiment with many alternative actions. Double-loop learning occurs when the individual or system begins to question the initial diagnosis. When this occurs, the person can question the underlying values or assumptions that are guiding their actions and can reframe the problem.

In Figure 9.3 Watkins depicts the incidental learning that is subsumed in the problem-solving process. Behind a diagnosis is a way of framing the problem. As individuals develop a strategy or invention for solving the problem, they view solutions through the lens of the context, assessing the constraints and limitations of that context against the feasibility of each solution. Once a strategy or invention is formulated, they may need to learn how to produce that strategy.

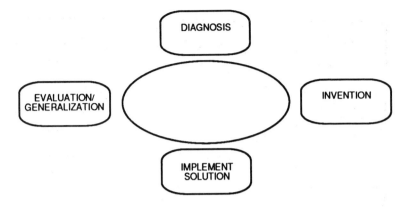

Figure 9.2 Argyris's problem-solving model

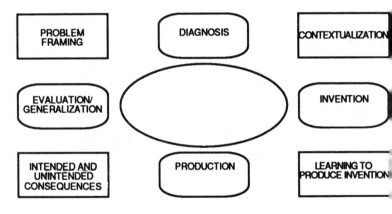

Figure 9.3 Incidental learning as part of problem-solving

This phase may look like trial-and-error experimentation or learning from mistakes, a form of incidental learning. At this point, the strategy is implemented and the production leads to some consequences. These may include both what the person intended and some effects he or she did not intend. Individuals then embed into their con-

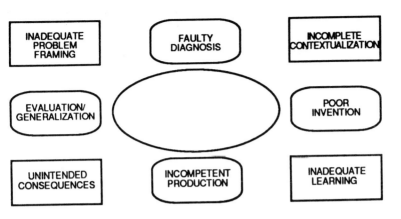

Figure 9.4 Potential for error in problem-solving

sciousness assumptions or generalizations about whether or not the strategy worked.

Finally, in Figure 9.4 Watkins shows that individuals may make errors at any point in this cycle. Moreover, an error in an earlier stage almost guarantees errors in later stages. Because this problem-solving so often occurs as an automatic process and because so much of the process is tacit or unexamined, the potential for error is great. Clearly, when problems are ambiguous and complex, there is a great need to surface these incidental learnings attendant to the problem-solving process to increase our effectiveness.

Chapter ten

Challenges to human resource development

This chapter offers ideas for enhancing informal and incidental learning at the individual, group, organizational, and professional levels. These strategies represent special challenges for human resource developers. At their most basic, they demand a broadened conception of the field and a professionalization of the practice of human resource development. Implications for practitioners which conclude this volume and this chapter include a change in thinking, skills, and an integration of informal and incidental learning with training.

Strategies for enhancing informal and incidental learning

There is considerable overlap among strategies that are useful at the individual level and those useful at the group, organizational, and professional levels. Strategies are separated here in order to stress the usefulness of particular approaches for meeting the special needs of each level. Human resource developers will find it useful to think of these strategies as forming a *gestalt* of expert professional practice.

At the individual level

Action science is a science of interpersonal action which includes use of the strategies listed here. It is the most comprehensive approach we have seen for enhancing informal and incidental learning for individuals. We especially recommend the following six strategies.

1. Surface tacit theories. Gareth Morgan (1986) said that our images and our metaphors are our theories of practice. By learning to explore the theories embedded in these metaphors, and by learning to discover the logic or causal reasoning implied by our actions, we

can make explicit what is now tacit and automatic. Once surfaced, we can make a decision about whether or not to change these theories.

2. Identify attributions that we have made about others or about situations and look for confirming and disconfirming illustrations. Making quick intuitive analyses of situations is a hallmark of expert practice. Yet, if these judgments are not supportable by the data in the context, then a habit of making routine responses to non-routine situations may have undermined that expertise.

3. Problematize situations. Jarvis (1987) finds that many situations evoke non-learning responses, such as the automatic judgments alluded to in the previous paragraph. By taking familiar situations and looking at them as though they were problematic or unfamiliar, individuals can reframe situations and consider alternatives.

4. Engage in deliberately reflective, transformative learning. Many theorists have described transformative learning as a process that is catalyzed by a significant event such as a loss of a job. But individuals can also elect to enter transformative learning processes, such as when they enter therapy or self-help groups. Individuals might therefore choose to enter learning groups with a transformative intent.

5. Seek public confirmation and disconfirmation of private theories. Developing skill in reflecting on one's practice requires finding ways to get feedback on how others see that practice, and ways to disclose to oneself and to others what one actually said or did, along with the underlying reasoning. Work groups can use action science in this way to debrief one another after critical events.

6. Try to take a "big picture," long-term view of the learning task. When individuals pursue a natural learning progression (Tough, 1979), they tend to learn about one aspect of a problem, which then leads them on to other areas suggested by what they learned about the first aspect. This chain of learning works well enough when each link is large enough and actually connected to the other links. Yet, if we do not know what we do not know, the size and shape of the links and their interrelationships may be dimly outlined, if grasped at all. By looking for the broadest possible view of the problem and viewing it from many disciplines and many angles, the aspect of the problem that is most relevant to the current situation is more likely to emerge.

At the group level

In this work, we cited some of the ways in which role and hierarchical power relationships in groups and organizations influence informal

227

and incidental learning. To facilitate learning on this level, groups need to find ways to reflect on the tacit or hitherto undiscussible meanings they have inferred about the group and its members. Given the tendency of groups to agree overtly while disagreeing privately (Harvey, 1988) and to align around "party line" interpretations, this will not be easy.

Kurt Lewin (in Argyris, 1952) originally developed action research to help groups resolve social conflicts. Kemmis and McTaggart (1988) define action research as a form of "collective self-reflective enquiry undertaken by participants in social situations in order to improve the rationality and justice of their social or educational practices and the situations in which these practices are carried out" (p. 5). They see action research as a continually renewing spiral of reflection, planning, acting and observing. The process must be collaborative and participatory and aimed toward improvement. Kemmis and McTaggart use the participants' own understandings and contradictions between their actions and their intentions to develop areas of improvement.

The theory of change inherent in these models, then, is that groups should act consistently with their intentions. Since groups have many intentions, and these intentions are often at odds with one another and may also demand contradictory actions, this theory may be of limited utility in complex social settings such as corporations. Double-loop learning, through which groups reassess the assumptions and goals on which they base their actions, may be more helpful. It focuses on broader goals and values that may subsume contradictory intentions. The cyclic nature of action research recursively feeds back information about results to guide future action.

At the organizational level

Considerable interest in the last few years has been engendered by a metaphor: "organizational learning." Many have sought to define this elusive metaphor in the belief that it holds a key to operationalizing lifelong learning in the organization. We too believe that the creation of a learning organization is achievable and a logical extension of the ideas presented here. If we attempt to institutionalize, credential, or codify informal and incidental learning, we may simply recreate formal learning dynamics and lose the essential qualities of learner autonomy and artistry. It may be better to teach others how to be critically reflective and how to learn more effectively, while institutionalizing more routine opportunities for proactive on-the-job learning and challenging organizational norms which suppress learning.

To the extent that organizational norms suppress learning, designed learning systems are often less effective. DeGeuss (1988) said that "institutional learning begins with the calibration of existing mental models" (p. 74). He believes that the only competitive advantage organizations of the future will have is their managers' ability to learn faster, to revise continually their mental models of the world. His view is similar to that of Argyris and Schön (1978) who define organizational learning as that which occurs when:

> members of the organization act as learning agents for the organization, responding to changes in the internal and external environments of the organization by detecting and correcting errors in organizational theory-in-use, and embedding the results of their inquiry in private images and shared maps of organization.
> [Argyris and Schön, 1978, p.29]

Organizational learning, then, might be defined as the organization's capacity to create, diffuse, and use knowledge in response to non-routine events. It consists of the intentional and unintentional processes of the formal and informal learning systems of the organization, including the organization's learned responses to environmentally-induced change. Garratt (1987) sees the learning organization operating on two levels – an operational level, and a re-framing level that responds to disruptions or threats from the external environment. This idea – that organizational learning includes both maintenance and transformative processes – is consistent with the transformative learning theories we have emphasized to augment formal learning systems. Learning must occur at both levels.

Designing an organizational learning system

An organization must thus reframe current maintenance practices to support organizational learning, as well as develop transformative learning processes that address the underlying shared values and norms of the organization. The organization's learning system should enable it to observe itself and to use its slack resources to adapt (Acebo and Watkins, 1988). The capacity to observe itself, the disclosure process in the Johari Window, is normally accomplished through management information systems that monitor data about organizational performance. Benveniste (1987) suggests that slack does not necessarily refer to financial resources. Slack can involve available skills or knowledge and the *willingness* to use those untapped skills. Knowles (1985), for example, asks about all of the resources available in the system to support human growth and development. Framed in this way, the formal and informal learning systems come together under one heading.

Two comprehensive approaches to reframing the maintenance level of the organization's learning system are the Swedish Work Environment Fund Program (1988) and the Work in America Institute's continuous learning model (Rosow and Zager, 1988). Sweden has been engaged in a sustained national effort to introduce new technology, while upgrading worker skills and job content, in which training has become a continuous part of everyday life. They concluded that the workplace *should* be a learning system since "a natural condition of people is to be active, to look for solutions to problems, to learn, and to seek greater understanding" (p. 13). Rather than changing workers to promote learning, they assumed that workers naturally learn all of the time. Instead, the *work* should be changed so that it will motivate continued learning. Work should be varied, independent, worthwhile, and based on feedback. Organizations were also reorganized to promote learning. Saab, for example, used training and rotation among tasks to help people learn more than one job. Other strategies include expanding job content, giving work teams responsibility for developing skills, using data-based information systems for better feedback, and employee contacts with customers and suppliers. A holistic approach is fostered through study visits, projects that demand creative and analytical abilities, job exchanges, and helping people see "the big picture" and see through others' eyes. Many of these characteristics are found in the Action Learning programs discussed in Chapter Three.

The continuous learning model developed by the Work in America Institute is similar and also emphasizes "starting with the shop floor." Learning is also considered an everyday part of the job, but it is institutionalized through a series of requirements. Employees are to learn the skills of others in their work unit, and see how their work fits into the organization as a whole and its goals. Active interaction among employees, work teams and managers is institutionalized. Finally, employees are required to transmit their knowledge to other employees and to learn from them. It is interesting that this model seeks to build a learning organization by requiring what the Swedish program assumes is a natural tendency of people. It is unclear whether the American program, which is designed to change the worker, will be effective if it does not also emphasize changing the work.

Morgan (1988) also suggests that, in an information society, people are the key resource, and education is the key to enhancing and maintaining that resource continually. But educational needs will quickly outstrip available time and money, so organizations must make strategic educational investments. Continuous on-the-job informal learning is one cost-effective approach to institutionalizing learning.

McCall, *et al.* (1988) list strategies to enhance on-the-job learning. Their strategies emanate from a development framework that includes three choice points, as discussed earlier in this chapter in regard to the collective nature of self-directed learning in organizations. Organizations can help promote learning by helping first-time managers make role transitions, by consciously timing job enlargements or promotions for optimum growth, by helping with critical transitions – especially in dealing with complexity and increasing scope – and by making corrections. McCall, Jr., *et al.* conclude that an effective system for developing executives is opportunistic, individualistic, long term, self-motivated, and on-line – i.e., it deals with real people and real consequences. As have we, they too see the need for organizations to set aside time for reflection and analysis. When that reflection is about on-line events, the consequences can be observed and people's understanding of those actions discovered. Feedback and disclosure can enhance productive work and personal effectiveness. An organization that routinizes these processes for its people and itself has a healthy learning system.

At the professional level

Informal and incidental learning can help professionals develop from novices to experts. By attending to the lessons of experience, professionals evolve from simple, programmed actions to a kind of fluid artistry. They reach expert status when they have opportunities that enhance their breadth of experience and their work capacity. Their ability to both do a task and reflect on it permits them to extrapolate the consequences of their actions out over time and to simultaneously consider the impact on the different parties affected by their actions.

McCall, Jr., *et al.* (1988) suggest that this breadth of experience can be consciously extended. They found that managers learned most from hardships, challenging assignments, and other people. In our research, mistakes were especially potent learning experiences, as were novel or unique experiences. On the other hand, when experiences looked or felt like previous experiences or childhood memories, learning was often supressed and automatic: "Here we go again" responses were triggered. Strategies to enhance informal and incidental learning should expand the breadth of work experience by letting people take on difficult projects or systematically widening and deepening their personal network. Strategies should also create low threat opportunities for using mistakes as learning and interrupting the "Here we go again" response through the use of peer groups who come together to inquire mutually into the effectiveness of their practice.

Benveniste (1987) suggests that professional learning requires public reflection on the ethical implications of one's work and on the errors and compromises professionals have made. This enables self-monitoring along with an opportunity to learn ways to improve and upgrade the profession. This professional "conscience-raising" is risky and threatening to many individuals. But without it, learning at this level will not influence the profession as a whole. At a time when professions are under attack for unethical and unprofessional practice, the need for this critically reflective learning in the field is great. For human resource developers whose work is still quasi-professional, this learning can contribute to the professionalization of practitioners.

New challenges for human resource developers

We have outlined specific strategies for enhancing informal and incidental learning, based on our research. In this concluding section, we look at new challenges posed by our perspective. What implications does this work have for the way in which we conceptualize the field? If learning is everyone's responsibility, including that of the worker and the line manager, do we need "trainers" and courses? What competencies should human resource developers bring to the learning organization that make them uniquely valuable? Given the strategic value of informal and incidental learning, how can formal, informal and incidental learning be integrated?

A broadened conception of the field

Over time, an emphasis on informal and incidental learning will lead to a redefinition of the professional field of human resource development. In our experience, high-level human resource developers in large corporations already have a broader view of their role. In their practice, the ten roles discussed in Chapter Two merge into one expanded role. They have a strong sense of ethics and of professionalism. Their practice, like that of the expert professionals in Schön's (1983) work, already embodies a new vision for the field. A definition that captures such a vision for the field of human resource development is found in Watkins (1989):

> Human resource development is the field of study and practice responsible for the fostering of a long term, work-related learning capacity at the individual, group, and organizational levels. As such, it includes but is not limited to training, career development and organizational development.
>
> [Watkins, 1989, p. 427]

Using this definition, the range of activities in which human resource developers might engage is vast. They should facilitate or monitor all types of learning in the workplace – formal, informal, and incidental. The learner or client will vary, be it individuals, groups or departments, the organization, or professions. But the professional mission will not. Human resource developers should focus on enhancing learning capacity and learning-how-to-learn skills.

A case example

A case may illustrate the range of this definition. The director of training for a defense contractor was given the task of designing ethics training for the entire corporation to comply with federal mandates. Two months were allotted to develop a corporate-wide program that would not only explain the new federal regulations to every single employee who would ever touch a part or product that was to be sold to the federal government, but that would also encourage ethical practice in a broader sense. The training director called every major defense contractor that he knew as well as a number of consulting firms who specialized in ethics training. He also interviewed managers throughout the organization. Using sample materials from other programs and from extensive reading, he developed a three-inch notebook of color-coded materials.

The training director took his materials to the vice-president for human resources to present what he believed was the best ethics training program in the defense industry. The vice-president took one look at it, did not even flip through the pages, and asked, "Is that it?" The vice-president went on to ask other questions. What about all of the other things that we need? What policies will you recommend to the president to encode the ethical practices that you suggest in this training notebook? What about a director of ethics to implement and watch over the organization's compliance with this federal mandate? How will you get the executive officers involved? What about a steering committee for oversight of the ethical aspects of this contract that would include the president and her immediate subordinates?

The training director was chagrined that, having interviewed managers up and down the line, he had not interviewed his own supervisor. And yet he was also miffed to think that he would be asked to write policies and to suggest the creation of a new position. Is not that what managers do? He had been asked to design a training program and felt he had designed a superb one within an unrealistic time frame.

This case illustrates the problem of narrow role definition. If the training director had been given the task of enhancing the *organization's* responsiveness to federal ethical mandates, would he have conceived of the task as only the design of a training program? From a strategic perspective, change of this magnitude would require not only legally-trained personnel assigned to the task of helping people think through difficult ethical issues but also some enforcement of the organization's commitment to compliance. Who could better write this policy than the person who had been examining the literature on ethics in the defense industry? Moreover, a training program would give people information but would not necessarily lead to a change in their behavior. Seeing the executive office of the organization committed and actively engaged in inquiry about the ethical practices of the organization through participation on a steering committee might encourage commitment at all levels of the organization.

In this instance, it was not that the training director could not appreciate the strategic thinking of the vice-president of human resources but that he was not given a strategically framed task. He also did not see that these suggestions were his to suggest or implement, given his position in the hierarchy. One could see this case as an interpersonal problem rather than a definitional one: each person has a different picture of the task in mind, and each assumes the other person shares his picture. Or one could view it hierarchically, i.e., the picture in one's head is a function of where one sits. Yet it is also clear that this is a matter of problem framing. The vice-president's reaction indicated that he did not perceive any hierarchical barrier to prevent the training director from taking a more strategic approach. Further, it is precisely because the training director also thought only in terms of *training* that other forms of learning did not suggest themselves.

It is clear that enhancing an organization's resources is much more than merely training people to do specific tasks. Individuals and organizations must learn how to adapt to a changing environment. Professionals in this field will need high levels of skill in creating opportunities for learning and in removing barriers to learning.

Emotions and adult learning

Adult educators write that we cannot separate emotional from cognitive learning (Boyd and Myers, 1988; Brookfield, 1986; Marsick, 1990; More, 1974). Our research supports this assertion. Yet participants continue to anticipate primarily cognitive, rational learning. If a transformative experience is triggered, involving emotions, they define it as therapy, not adult education. Further, when they think of therapy, they often also think "That's for people who are sick." But even coolly rational subjects such as mathematics may inspire strong emotions and good teachers "respond to students' needs" – a feeling for and insight into their learners (More, 1974).

Experiences produce emotional responses. We have already noted that experiences may or may not trigger learning and, if they do, it may be first-level learning rather than Kelly's reconstrual. But when double-loop learning is triggered, an individual experiences the "agonising grief of colluding in the death of someone who he knows was himself" (More, 1974, p. 69). As old ways of framing the world give way to new, individuals experience a sense of loss; grief work at some level may be needed if the individual is to move on (Boyd and Myers, 1988).

We believe the cutting edge of professional practice for adult educators and human resource developers is the successful integration of the affective with the cognitive in adult learning. An example is the interventionist in Chapter Six who learned that she could not manage or control the emotional and still produce learning. Likewise, we need to develop responses that enable us competently to "go with" the powerful emotional currents attendant to reflective learning experiences. We see the same phenomenon in Chapter Three when Action Learning advisors guide managers through both cognitive and affective dimensions of their learning. To be effective in this role, we need some mixture of artistry and expertise.

Expertise in interpersonal helping may include a background in counseling, action science, or other transformative learning approaches. These "technical" skills assist facilitators in recognizing normal learning fits and starts, and the message behind the words as adults struggle to accept new meanings. These skills are not intended to drag people kicking and screaming into unwanted insights. Rather, they can be used to help individuals who want to grow beyond their present state or who find themselves in the midst of a

235

transformative learning process and seek the help of human resource developers.

Artistry is essential. It is that blend of learning-by-doing and sensitivity that tells a facilitator that a person may need therapy, not education; that a person will respond to a little nudging; or that a person simply needs to be left alone. Jerry Harvey (1988) wrote that some techniques can "break the human prayer." Harvey tells the story of a therapist and management consultant, who is also quite religious. Harvey asked him how he would respond to a client who was in great difficulty and considerable emotional turmoil, and who asked the therapist to pray with him. The therapist responded that he would not, because it would "break the prayer." The misuse of techniques, or even their use *as* techniques rather than as part of a fluid learning process, can indeed do more to disrupt than to facilitate transformative learning.

Human resource developers may be wary of these approaches. Caution seems appropriate. This area is at the cutting edge and not a starting place for novices. Each of the approaches requires considerable effort and "time on task" to learn. As Marsick (1990) suggests, if a trainer is working with relatively normal people, some simple skills and attitudes will take the trainer a long way toward dealing well with emotions in learning. Yet, it is unfortunate that many human resource developers shy away from learning that involves emotions. Learners in the workplace are often left on their own, experiencing strong emotions, while facilitators are unable to respond appropriately to these learners' needs. Learning in the workplace may bear little similarity to therapy, but we would be insensitive if we did not think that adults sent to retraining because their jobs were being phased out have strong feelings. Or that managers sent to mandatory interpersonal skills training by top executives, who themselves lack interpersonal skills, will not have feelings that affect the learning process. Or that individuals entering a team-building session, who are asked to share their criticism of one another when this has hitherto been undiscussible, will be able to pick up on Monday as though nothing had happened. Trainers need skills for dealing effectively with these situations. Perhaps the most important skill is to recognize that trainers themselves collude in engendering these strong feelings when they accept dysfunctional conditions for learning – such as short time frames, norms for training that undermine people's ability to work together after training, and the use of training as punishment.

Trainers have also engendered strong emotions inadvertently through instruments and exercises that are either manipulative or intrusive. The most well-known example of this was the Pacific Bell case. Employees company-wide were required to attend seminars based on the teachings of Russian mystic George Gurdjieff. He and many others are part of the New Age Movement which stresses human potential and draws on a combination of Eastern mysticism, the occult, and a Norman Vincent Peale-style of positive thinking. Employees appealed to the California Public Utilities Commission charging the training department with mind control (Lindsey, 1987).

It seems clear to us that trainers need to be professional enough not to use a test or instrument that they have not been certified to interpret, or which is not valid and reliable. Nor can they use these tests on "human subjects" unless those individuals have first given informed consent. Similar standards should attend the use of exercises and prepackaged training programs. The National Diffusion Network established a kind of Good Housekeeping seal of approval that certified educational innovations through rigorous experimental research. Prepackaged training programs should meet a similar test.

Professional expertise is needed to integrate affective aspects of learning into one's work and to develop the skills to do this. With this comes a recognition that some training is now far from professional. This is not to say that trainers do not have good intentions, nor that they do not work hard to be as competent as they can be. Yet, few trainers are themselves trained before taking their positions, or even while in them. This research highlights some of the potential hazards of such real time, on-the-job learning. When strong emotions are present, the situation is non-routine and automatic, and preprogrammed responses are not likely to be functional. At these times, trainers need considerable skill in thinking on-their-feet and in doing the kind of unprogrammed work we discussed in Chapter One. Professionals specialize in non-routine work. As more and more demands are placed on trainers and the workplace becomes more complex and fluid, more and more of their work will become non-routine. Learning how to learn from and through emotions requires a high level of mastery.

Changing thinking

We have suggested that human resource developers move toward reflective, transformative learning. We have called for an expanded role definition from trainer to one who enhances the learning capacity of individuals, groups, and organizations. We have said that trainers will need to make explicit their tacit theories-in-use and to reframe their existing theories to more consistently learning-oriented theories. We have called on human resource developers to take a human capital perspective on their task so that they can recognize and take a helpful role in meeting the dramatically changing needs of the workforce.

These are substantive shifts in thinking. We recognize that there are inherent dilemmas in what we ask of human resource professionals. On the one hand, we value informal learning from work experiences, learning that goes on without the help of human resource developers. On the other, we call for a dramatically enlarged conception of the role of human resource developers. In a field that already feels vulnerable to cuts, "the first to go when there's a budget cut," asking human resource developers to encourage more effective learning on one's own may appear to make human resource developers even more vulnerable. Moreover, asking them to enlarge their scope when they already feel overburdened may seem to be asking too much. But we think that the key to the future of this field is not in credentialing and institutionalizing the training/education function, as Scott (1988) has suggested, but rather in the professionalizing of human resource developers. They need to think strategically first, as Knowles (1985) said, about all of the learning resources already in the organization, and then, about what learning resources *could* be in this organization. When human resource developers frame their role in this fashion, they will be more like developmental coaches than performance trainers whose task is to teach people to make better use of their experiences for learning. Many human resource developers do this now.

Watkins spoke to a seasoned veteran trainer who works for a *"Fortune* 100" high technology company. She is responsible for a staff of seven who serve the learning needs of 1000 supervisors. She views those supervisors as her "clients." She described an interaction she had with one new supervisor who was quite young (the average age of supervisors at this division is 30) who was having trouble getting her older employees to listen to her or to share important information. The trainer said, "Go talk to them. Find out the names, birthdays, and current concerns of their kids." The supervisor demurred at first, pointing out that she did not have kids yet; she would not know what to say. Reluctantly, she tried it and came back enthusiastically describing how well it worked. The older workers were talking to her now, not only about their kids but their work as well. The trainer said, "Yes, you have to connect with people where they are. You don't have to have the same experiences (have kids, longevity on the shop floor) as your employees, you just have to acknowledge the importance of that experience and of the person who had it." This was a trainer who knew how to design proactively developmental experiences for her clients, as well as how to help the client learn the "lesson" of that experience.

Human resource developers may also begin to see a role for themselves as developers of the organization's learning system. A senior trainer for a multi-million dollar service industry described his role as "internal marketer." He said his role was to "sell" the organization's mission to the employees, to interpret and to help to operationalize the chief operating officer's visions and dreams, and to embed the norms and values that characterize his organization's unique culture. He developed a video sharing the organizational saga – the critical turning points in its history, the vision of the founding fathers, and the current heroes who now carry the torch that was lit the day the organization was founded. He worked with top level staff to develop corporate vision and mission statements. And his primary training function was new employee orientation. In many training departments, new employee orientation is the least preferred task and it is often relegated to new trainers. This trainer saw that new employee orientation was the pressure point for embedding the organizational culture. Done well, it could produce employees who know from the start what the organization stands for and how they can contribute to its mission. It can give them a sense of being part of something larger than themselves that is worthwhile, something worthy of their loyalty. It can also allow them to make an informed choice about whether or not this organization is one to which they want to make a long-term commitment. In this organization, new employee orientation became more than a means to share rules and procedures. It enhanced the long-term learning capacity of the organization by producing employees who knew how to focus their learning and work on the organizational vision. Potentially, orientation also reduced turnover so that the wisdom accumulated by these employees stayed in the organization and the organization grew as they did.

Changing skills

We noted earlier that we believe that human resource developers need to upgrade their technical skills so that they can accurately negotiate more effective learning conditions in their organizations. We suggested that they should be able to engage learners in deliberately transformative, critically reflective learning. We said that they should develop skill in integrating emotional and cognitive learning. All of this should lead to a professional expertise that is more artistry than rote performance. Once again, we have asked a lot. Yet, it seems to us that human resource developers have either moved in this direction or have become, as Knowles (1985) predicted, logistics arrangers; scheduling conferences, handling outside consultants who can do these things, or managing resources such as film libraries or packaged courses. Why would we expect that training would be immune to the paradigm shift attendant on a society as a whole moving into an information age?

One way of characterizing the types of skills needed is by thinking again in terms of the Johari Window presented in Chapter Two. The fundamental strategies for enhancing learning at each level are feedback and disclosure. Table 10.1 illustrates this concept. Several of the strategies in this table can be useful at several levels, but are shown here where they are particularly useful in bringing to light that which was hidden to consciousness and that to which we are blind.

Torbert (1972) suggests that feedback has long been taken for granted, to the extent that feedback is very often useless. It is either too bland, general, distorted, or softened to guide action. We have few skills in voicing difficult information. It is a cliché that bad news travels down the organization, and good news travels up. Not surprisingly, trainers are called in to teach managers to "be positive Pygmalions," to "catch employees doing something good." And management information systems analysts design support systems to capture the "bottom-line" data. Torbert says that effective feedback is "first-hand, unconceptualized, self-acknowledged, authenticity-enhancing, non-evaluative, descriptive, and non-controlling" (1972, p. 11). Feedback that does not meet these specifications produces "noise" in the system. Torbert introduces Deutsch's three orders of feedback – first-order feedback that is goal-directed and redirects a system toward a goal as it is being affected by its environment; second-order feedback, or learning, that alerts a system to changes it needs to make within its own structure to meet its goal (leading, at times, to goal redefinition); and third-order feedback, or consciousness, that serves as a system-environment scanner "to maintain a sense of the overall, lifetime, autonomous purpose and integrity of the system" (p. 14). Effective feedback is undistorted feedback at all three levels.

Torbert says that there is an interplay among feedback, attention, and consciousness. With Polanyi, he sees an inseparability between people's inner and outer worlds. He points out that if we lose touch with our acts of choice-making, we will make choices as a result of pressures of which we are unaware. Attention, what we attend to, also involves three levels of experience: focal attention (what we see or perceive), subsidiary presence (our bodily sense of perceiving it), and a thread of intentionality (our perception of the meaning of what we see).

Torbert suggests that people reject feedback that does not fit or reinforce their internalized meanings and interpretations of the

240

Table 10.1 Feedback and disclosure strategies

Feedback	Disclosure
Individual Level *Action Science:* Group reaction to data, other relevant actors' reactions to one's theories in action	Collect directly observable data on practice, disclose underlying thoughts, feelings, assumptions
Group Level *Action Learning:* Group shares its results, reactions and recommendations	Group observes actions, discloses reactions, takes action, designs tests of those actions
Organization Level *Organizational Learning Systems:* People share with others what they learn about the flaws in the organization's learning system; develop ways for the organization to learn about itself and to communicate this information	People collect information about all of the resources in the organization that support learning about all of the forces which constrain learning; they determine the organization's theories-in-use, its ability to correct and detect errors
Professional Level *Professionalism:* Professionals have routine ways to share what they have learned, to reflect on their own and others' errors; they systematically obtain client feedback in terms of concerns, results, etc.; they certify competent practice and censure incompetent practice	Professional peer groups share errors, ethical concerns; they publish an ethical code of conduct; they make their results public

world. Openness is needed for people to receive feedback without distortion. People need to see that their selective attention and interpretations are not facts, but inferences, and that others' inferences may also be valid. Thus, feedback on the level discussed here will require considerable skill both from those who give it and from those who receive it. Torbert also identifies three types of experiential learning: (1) learning that is a result of external conditioning; (2) problem-solving; (3) self recognition. Learning in the first case may require disclosing tacit, incidental theories; in the second, disclosing and learning from mistakes; and in the third, disclosing personal theories about who one is and engaging in transformative learning processes. Each requires different strategies for facilitating disclosure. Human resource developers need to guide learners through each type of learning.

Linking training with informal and incidental learning

Training has increasingly grown away from a reliance on formal classroom activities. Our work suggests that this is a healthy direction, but one that will demand more of trainers. Earlier we reported that training has been found to produce long-term gains in employability and income, but that training was considerably less available to minorities and women. Unskilled employees receive fewer training hours than technical and professional employees. Watkins (1988) suggested that formal and informal training such as apprenticeships could help address the earnings gap for women following career interruptions. Perhaps one way in which training could integrate informal and incidental learning – while also better serving women and minorities – is by developing ways to encourage and support more such apprenticeships and self-directed learning among unskilled and semi-skilled employees. Among technical and professional workers, critical reflection on challenging work experiences could be facilitated by developing peer self-help groups. By strategically and proactively supporting informal and incidental learning, the training function can extend its impact while also increasing the learner's effectiveness. Whether one adopts the American continuous learning model and decides to change the worker, or the Swedish model and seeks to change the work, rapid changes in technology will drive a massive retraining effort (Watkins, 1989).

Learning how to learn

Cheren (1987) introduces a new term for developing learning skills, "learning management," which he distinguishes from self-directed learning. The former involves other people, whereas the latter is often seen as an individual, isolated activity. Cheren argues, as do we, that the information age makes it impossible for organizations to supply all needed learning opportunities, even if they so wished, because of rapid change. Cheren offers a checklist of competencies for learning management that cover the following tasks: orienting staff to learning management, building these skills into all programs, creating a learning resource center, developing self-instructional materials and problem-based learning modules, running a supervisory training program that helps managers help their staff to learn, keeping records on development projects, and creating a climate that fosters active and self-conscious learning.

It is tempting to solve the problem of integrating formal learning with informal and incidental learning by designing courses on the subject. We think this is a mistake, if relied upon as a *primary* strategy, because courses easily become substitutes for the more difficult effort of creating an organization where learning is integrated with daily work experiences. There are problems with the separate course approach, even though it is one vehicle for developing learning-how-to-learn skills. In this approach, learning is artificially separated from experience as it is in many other courses. In order to make the learning meaningful, experience can be brought into the course through simulations, practice sessions, case studies, critical incidents from participants, and action plans that bridge the gap between simulations and real life. But the problem in such cases is that many people do not take the learning seriously or, if they do, the real difficulties start when they try to implement the skills outside the classroom without the kind of support they had in the classroom. However, we do believe that formal learning can be integrated with informal and incidental learning in the following ways: courses with learning skills as a primary focus, enhancement of learning skills in existing courses, and the design of Action Learning programs that integrate learning skills with other kinds of learning as people solve real life problems.

The starting point for learning to learn seems to be the desire to solve problems, whether those problems are clearly identified by the organization or whether they begin with a vague sense that something is wrong. Smith (1987), gives the example of an hourly machine operator who could not think of any learning projects in which he engaged at home.

> Eventually, he enthusiastically described a part-time job in which he and another man dismantle and move heavy machinery. As he talked, the problem-solving nature of this work and its learning component began to emerge. He described in detail how the two of them had devised a way to move, with a minimum of equipment, a very heavy obsolete electrical generator from the basement of an old building. It must have been a formidable and dangerous task, and was clearly accomplished through creativity and trial and error. "Figuring out" how to do such tasks obviously appealed to him even more than his regular job, company-provided training, or the job-related courses he periodically takes at his local community college, although he expressed no dissatisfaction with these activities.
>
> [Smith, 1987, p. 42]

243

This description is strongly reminiscent of Scribner's (1986) dairy workers and well illustrates Resnick's (1987) out of school learning described in Chapter Nine. However, we would add that, when people learn informally and incidentally, much more can be learned that falls outside the person's original problem orientation, and that may lead to problem reformulation. If people only focused on what they thought was the original problem, they would ignore what they could learn incidentally and might also exclude much informal learning. Boydell (1976) takes the same view in describing a concept associated with learning how to learn, that is, meta-goals or "any goal which is about learning to learn" (p. 66). Drawing on Harrison and Hopkins (1967) who introduce this concept, Boydell points out that "meta-goals [which are also called 'values' by Schein and Bennis (1965)] are learnings and values that are picked up, almost coincidentally, by the learner as a result of the way he is taught" (ibid.). As such, meta-goals have much in common with incidental learning and the gap discussed in action science between espoused theories and theories-in-use:

> The crux seems to be in the notion of learning in addition to the content; learning caused by the nature of the process, rather than the content message.... At another level, if I shout at my daughter that people shouldn't shout, the content goal is "shouting is wrong"; the meta-goal (or meta-learning would be a better word) is "Daddy shouts so shouting is OK".
>
> [Boydell, 1976, p. 67]

Integrating learning skills into courses

A second option that alleviates some of these difficulties is integrating learning skills into all existing courses, whatever the topic. In this way, the organization would send a message to its staff that learning skills are valued since they would be taken as seriously as the topic-related content. Some learning skills are generic and could be integrated into all courses, e.g. making tacit reasoning explicit to open joint inquiry and publicly testing one's beliefs and assumptions.

There are many advantages to this approach. Courses are always being given. By integrating learning skills into them, participants simultaneously learn what they need in order to do their jobs and how to go about continually acquiring new information or skills about a specific job. There should be less difficulty in transferring what is learned to the job because participants would also know how to modify the prescriptive solutions they have acquired in courses to new circumstances "back home." By taking the time to learn these skills on-the-spot, participants are more likely to see the relevance of the skills to what they need to know or do.

However, there may be difficulties in implementing this approach. The organization, the trainer, and the participants may have less control over the content when they engage in exercises to enable individuals to reflect on related work experiences. In a short time, participants are expected to achieve many measurable objectives. If they also learn how to learn, they will take some time away from these course objectives. Further, while it is possible to predesign some activities on learning skills, they are more effective when they arise from the participants' experience. This places demands on the skills of the facilitator. When fragments of experience are divorced from one's own reality, they are not representative of real life. Yet we know that people learn best when dealing with problems they see as real.

Building learning skills around experience

The strategy we recommend for integrating formal with informal and incidental learning is Action Learning, or some variation of that. Action Learning, as described in Chapter Three, builds learning modules around experience modules. People work on projects that are real, preferably in teams in an environment outside their immediate work group so that they can question taken-for-granted norms and protocols, and so they are not constrained by habitual status, power, or other interpersonal patterns.

There are three main components to Action Learning: a project (experience), seminars in which participants reflect on both content (the problem) and process (learning skills), and back-home experience. All three segments run parallel; participants and the facilitator build linkages among them since the problems encountered in training or real life are often the same. The principles of Action Learning can be used in many different formats. They are: (1) that learning be built around experience through a combination of action and reflection; (2) that learning is developmental, and therefore, takes place over time and involves the whole person (and in organizations, the entire system); (3) that people can learn from one another by working together on real problems in collaborative work teams; (4) that personal, implicit assumptions and beliefs must be examined as critically as "objective" reality encountered; (5) that learning is best facilitated by an outside process consultant who can raise difficult issues and ensure that the learning group will get the most out of their experience.

Action Learning does not encourage faddish solutions, which we believe leads us away from learning. Learning – a long-term developmental process – is not as "sexy" as many of the one-minute solutions available in the management training market. A Swedish colleague, Lars Cederholm, observed that principles of yoga, a lifelong health-oriented discipline, are the basis of many of the television-based exercise workouts popular in the United States. However, yoga's slow stretches, which orient a person to deep breathing and reflective meditation, are transformed in the United States into quick, rapid movements accompanied by rock and jazz music. Learning can be viewed through the same lens. We are discussing lifelong learning habits that do not take place en masse in highly visible training centers. Learning can be ambiguous, diffuse, centered around experiences wherever they happen, and not dependent on the instructor.

Some possible versions of Action Learning include "sandwich" courses in which classes are alternated with experience, internships, and cooperative work-study programs. However, these formats leave a wide divide between what is taught formally in the classroom and what learners experience in their projects or back-home work situations. Action Learning requires that some portion of the formal classroom activity be devoted to reflection in groups on the experience so that lessons can be drawn that are more generic than the specific project.

We believe that Action Learning is a highly effective format for integrating formal learning with informal and incidental learning, but it is not always easy to implement. A key problem is that people do not always recognize learning from experience as legitimate. While often criticizing the halls of academia, the workplace often looks to experts to provide solutions. The United States has a cookbook approach to learning that requires short, prescriptive statements about what a worker should do, even though studies on the increasingly educated workforce tell us that workers are capable of far more judgment and intellectual involvement in problem solving. Action Learning requires time, and businesses frequently want short, quick answers. If training cannot be done in three days, it often cannot be done.

Action Learning also requires trainers to reexamine their beliefs about learning because they must act as learning consultants, not classroom delivery specialists. Trainers, and the clients they serve, may bring with them perceptions of learning as passive, instructor-dependent, and classroom-oriented. People want to be told what to do in the classroom, a desire that can be reinforced in organizations by authoritarian managers or cultures where people are not allowed to make mistakes or not encouraged to learn from experience. Instructors, like managers and others hired for their expertise, feel that they lose credibility when they do not have all the answers. Trainers are rewarded in the classroom and the organization for having the right answer even if an easy answer is not available. Trainers are thus not invited by line managers to consult with them about difficult learning problems not amenable to easy training solutions.

Conclusion

Perceptions of learning and of the trainer's role, held both by trainers and the clients they serve, are particularly critical for informal and incidental learning because perceptions currently held exclude much concern with informal and incidental learning. The first step toward change is for trainers to transform these perceptions. As such, we start at the top of the Human Resource Learning Cone, at the level of transforming the training profession itself. This, then, is the challenge we would make to the field of human resource development – to transform itself into a professional field of practice by adopting a broadened conception of the field, by acquiring expertise and artistry in facilitating reflective action learning, and by developing an enhanced capacity to observe and examine one's own practice critically. These skills must be coupled with efforts to promote and enhance the learning capacity of their organization and of their profession.

Research notes

Chapter three

This chapter is based on qualitative research done in 1987 and 1988 on programs conducted by the Management Institute, Lund, Sweden (MiL). Designers of Action Learning programs in MiL do not just "add" knowledge and skills to those already possessed by managers; they set out to change the frameworks by which managers understand their experience, their roles, and themselves. While it is not always easy to explain *how* managers change after a MiL program, there is little doubt that they *have* changed in some fundamental way. This study was conducted to find out more about the nature of these changes and how they were facilitated by the program.

This study was based on open-ended interviews and observation. This exploratory, descriptive research builds rather than tests hypotheses (Glaser and Strauss, 1967). The research documented "stories" of what people did in the program and how they managed differently after the program. A total of 36 people were interviewed. The first phase of the research involved 20 interviews, informal discussions, participation in several staff meetings, and observation of three different MiL programs: the opening day of a Swedish MiL program, the middle "project revision" sessions of an internal program, and the closing day of a shorter program for senior executives.

The second phase of the research involved five more interviews and a presentation of preliminary findings at Mil's tenth anniversary, a three-day reunion, conference and celebration. The final phase involved eleven interviews with managers conducted by a Swedish research assistant, Camilla Sternberg, who serves as an administrative assistant in the MiL programs. She conducted the interviews in English, based on an interview schedule, but, as necessary, clarified questions in Swedish before recording them in English. All interviews were tape recorded and transcribed, and then content analyzed.

248

Of the twenty-one managers interviewed, only three were women. This is fairly representative since few women in Sweden hold senior management positions. Nine of the group were in their thirties, seven in their forties, and five over fifty years of age. Six had participated in multi-company Swedish MiL programs, one in an international program, three in the Senior MiL program, two in some kind of partnership program, and the remainder in one of three internal programs (a shipping company, a power company, and a bank). All staff members interviewed were male, which is also representative for this group. The Contact Person interviewed, however, was female. Most staff members worked part time with MiL, since this is how MiL operates, and worked as well either at the University or in consulting groups. Staff were professionally trained in different disciplines, most commonly in psychology, organization development or business, but also in professions such as medicine or law. Some staff were participants in early programs, and began working as project advisors after leaving their companies.

Chapter four

This study was conducted in 1977 through 1979 in Nepal, the Philippines and Taiwan to document and analyze the way in which educational field workers learned from their experience so that they could assist clients, primarily in the rural area, to understand and adopt changes oriented to health, family planning, and other related development concerns. The study was called "training for taking over" because it centered around training for empowerment: of the workers and ultimately the clients with whom they worked.

Grounded theory was also used in this study (Glaser and Strauss, 1967). Data were collected in two stages, with intervening periods used to analyze and discuss findings with colleagues in preparation for the second round of data collection. The researcher was living and working in Bangladesh for two years during the study period.

The combined data base included 40 interviews in the Philippines, 42 in Nepal, and 59 in Taiwan with administrators, trainers, trainees and a few clients. Five formal and numerous informal interviews were also conducted with representatives of other agencies involved in this kind of training. Finally, observations were done of several training programs in each country. The researcher also had extensive experience with at least six similar training programs in other countries in Asia. Precautions were taken for cross-cultural bias and unfamiliarity with the the local languages by using multiple interpreters at each site and cross-checking perceptions and interpretations with interpreters and colleagues during the analysis phase.

Chapter five

This chapter reports on the first phase of an ongoing study, begun in 1988, to determine whether or not there is a common professional identity embraced by adult educators and, if so, how this identity is shaped by the life experiences of those in the profession. Finger (1988) has raised similar questions about the formative experiences of adult educators in Europe where professional identity is unclear and formal preparation absent. Finger suggests that the answers to such questions are best found in the self-described accounts of adult educators themselves, identified through life history research.

The life history method, itself somewhat controversial but increasingly popular (Marsick, 1989, March), and the first phase of the study (Marsick, 1988b) are discussed elsewhere. This life history research is more limited in its scope than many studies. It is based on a three-week, eighteen-hour course with 28 new doctoral students in adult education who enrolled in a special professional development program called AEGIS (Adult Education Guided Independent Study). This chapter focuses on the life stories of a subsample of 14 doctoral candidates who also work full-time in some way with staff development and training – in an organization, whether private or non-profit, or in a college that works in partnership with business and industry – or who are concerned with issues of workplace learning in their administrative roles in organizations. This subsample is contrasted with the total sample of 14 males and 14 females who work in a broader range of adult education settings. The subsample consists of seven males and seven females; of this group, three were people of color. Ten of the larger group were people of color. The sample is not necessarily representative nor is it random.

The specific question posed to students was: "What life experiences have influenced your formation as an adult educator and your practice?" Students first analyzed their life histories in groups of four. The remaining time was spent in plenary or in different subgroupings looking at common themes and patterns. Students also wrote short papers on their life histories. Written and oral data were later analyzed, written up, and checked with the class. Subsample students were also later asked for critical incidents involving informal learning that they could relate to their life histories. Information was also drawn from "think pieces," short papers in which students explored ideas with respect to various topics, written for another class.

Chapter six

A group of six self-identified adult children of alcoholics met with Renee Rogers once a week for sixteen weeks in the conference room of a hospital. There were two males and four females: a public school administrator, an internal management consultant at a municipal utility, two public health nurse practitioners, a director of nursing at a metropolitan hospital, and an administrative aide at a state agency. Participants wrote cases of an interpersonal interaction in their workplace. These cases became the focus of group diagnosis and reflection in order to explore the limits of self-understanding and to discover self-sabotaging behavior that undermined inter- and intrapersonal functioning. In this sense, the group had an explicitly critical intent – to discover and change dysfunctional interpersonal functioning.

The group met for approximately two and a half to three hours each week. Meetings were tape recorded and transcribed before the subsequent session. The facilitator met almost weekly with her co-researcher, Karen Watkins, and a consultant who had been trained in action science methodology at Harvard University. These two individuals read the transcripts each week or excerpts of interactions that the facilitator highlighted. This group served two important functions: they provided peer debriefing (Guba, 1981) where the facilitator could test her interpretations and be exposed to searching questions and alternative interpretations; and they confronted and encouraged her to try interventions with participants that she would have avoided.

Chapter seven

A descriptive study was designed and conducted using the case study method. The unit of analysis for each case was the innovation project. All projects were selected from among those funded by the Fund for the Improvement of Postsecondary Education (FIPSE) from 1975–1979 in three innovation categories: peer tutoring or counseling, competency-based education, and basic skills enhancement. Dimensional sampling was used to select the final sample for this study. With dimensional sampling, projects and respondents are selected on the basis of their ability to represent the critical variables reflected in the problem statement. Respondents were the FIPSE project directors and the top-level administrators they nominated as their Organizational Sponsors. Cases were selected from among those private liberal arts colleges and community colleges funded by FIPSE who were persisting and at either the implementation or the institutionalization stage in the project's development. These cases were further classified into routine, non-routine continuous, and non-routine discontinuous projects. FIPSE was used for this study because of their emphasis on funding non-routine projects and because of the high rate of persistence of their projects (Bunting, 1980).

Data collection procedures included completion by both respondents from each site of the Change Facilitator Stage of Concern Questionnaire developed by the Research on Concerns-Based Adoption project (Hall *et al.*, 1977) and the Tasks to Support Innovation Questionnaire developed by Watkins (1981). Each questionnaire yielded a categorical profile of responses. Further, an open-ended interview reflecting similar content was conducted. Finally, project documents were examined.

Profiles developed from questionnaire responses (both individually and by variable groupings) were analyzed. Project documents were examined for information on project history and on the nature of the innovation. Interview responses were examined for confirmation or lack of confirmation of questionnaire responses and for supporting details. This analysis led to the development of seven case descriptions and a set of findings relative to each of the research questions in this study.

Chapter eight

This study examined the beliefs of human resource developers about their own learning and training practices. Argyris's theory-of-action framework was used to identify potential dysfunctional, unintended consequences of these professionals' beliefs, which were then examined in light of the stages of consciousness identified by Freire (1970). The consequences of these beliefs were illustrated using the mapping technique described by Argyris (1983). Interviews with 47 human resource developers at three separate sites were used to collect stories of these individuals' learning practices and workplace incidents involving their human resource development practice.

This study was designed to answer the following question: what are the dysfunctional causal patterns of reasoning about learning and about their practice that characterize human resource developers across three different organizational settings?

As part of a larger study of the learning practices of human resource developers, data collected by Watkins and Wiswell (1987) from interviews were transcribed and analyzed. The sample was drawn almost equally from three different types of organizations: a research hospital, a high technology corporation, and a government agency. For this portion of the study, the research procedure involved 30–60 minute interviews based on five open-ended questions with extensive probing for critical incidents reported in retrospective accounts. To the extent that it was possible, individuals were asked to recapture actual dialogue to illustrate key events following the critical incident technique of Flanagan (1954). Questions sought individuals' beliefs and perceptions about barriers to their learning in the organization, a critical incident which illustrated a recurring problem in their practice and another of a learning project, and the characteristics of exemplary learners in their organization.

Bibliography

Acebo, S. and Watkins, K. (1988) 'Staff Development in the Community College' in Marsick, V. J. (ed.) 1988c.

Ackerman R.J. (ed.) (1986) *Growing in the Shadow*, Pompano Beach, FL, Health Communications Inc.

American Society for Training and Development (ASTD) (1987) *Facts about Retraining America's Workforce*, Alexandria, VA, ASTD Press.

Argyris, C. (1952) *An Introduction to Field Theory and Interaction Theory*, Labor and Management Center Monograph, New Haven, CT, Yale University.

Argyris, C. (1965) *Organization and Innovation*, Homewood, IL, Richard R. Irwin Inc.

Argyris, C. (1968) 'Conditions for competence acquisition', *Journal of Applied Behavioral Science*, vol. 4, pp. 147–177.

Argyris, C. (1970) *Intervention Theory and Method*, Reading, MA, Addison-Wesley.

Argyris, C. (1982) *Reasoning, Learning and Action*, San Francisco, CA, Jossey-Bass.

Argyris, C. (1983, November) 'Making Social Science Research more Usable: Maps for Action', presentation to Center for Effective Organizations, University of Southern California, November.

Argyris, C. (1985) *Strategy, Change, and Defensive Routines*, Cambridge, MA, Pitman Publishing.

Argyris, C. and Schön, D. A. (1974) *Theory in Practice: Increasing Professional Effectiveness*, San Francisco, CA, Jossey-Bass.

Argyris, C. and Schön, D. A. (1978) *Organizational Learning: A Theory of Action Perspective*, San Francisco, CA, Jossey-Bass.

Argyris, C., Putnam, R. and Smith, D. M. (1985) *Action Science*, San Francisco, CA, Jossey-Bass.

Ashby, W. R. (1952) *Design for a Brain*, New York, NY, John Wiley.

Astin, A. (1977) *Four Critical Years*, San Francisco, CA, Jossey-Bass.

Baldridge, J.V. and Tierney, M. (1979) *New Approaches to Management*, San Francisco, CA, Jossey-Bass.

Bandura, A. (1977) *Social Learning Theory*, Englewood Cliffs, NJ, Prentice-Hall.

Bateson, G. (1972) *Steps to an Ecology of the Mind*, New York, NY, Ballantine Books.

Bennis, W. G. (1965) 'Theory and Method in Applying Behavioral Science to Planned Organizational Change', *Journal of Applied Behavioral Science*, vol. 1, no. 4, pp. 337–359.

Bennis, W. G., Benne, K. D. and Chin, R. (eds) (1969) *The Planning of Change*, 2nd. edn, New York, NY, Holt, Rinehart and Winston Inc.

Benveniste, G. (1987) *Professionalizing the Organization: Reducing Bureaucracy to Enhance Effectiveness*, San Francisco, CA, Jossey-Bass.

Berg, B. and Ostergren, B. (1979) 'Innovation Processes in Higher Education', *Studies in Higher Education*, vol. 4, no. 2, pp. 261–269.

Berman, P. and McLaughlin, M. (1976) 'Implementation of Educational Innovations', *The Educational Forum*, vol. 40, no. 3, pp. 345–370.

Bion, W. R. (1961) *Experiences in Groups*, New York, NY, Basic Books.

Boot, R. and Reynolds, M. (1983) *Learning and Experience in Formal Education*, Manchester Monographs, Bournemouth, U.K., Direct Design Ltd.

Boyd, E.M. and Fales, A.W. (1983) 'Reflective Learning: Key to Learning from Experience', *Journal of Humanistic Psychology*, vol. 23, pp. 99–117.

Boydell, T. (1976) *Experiential Learning*, Manchester Monographs No. 5, Dorset, U.K., Direct Design (Bournemouth) Ltd.

Brookfield, S. D. (1986) *Understanding and Facilitating Adult Learning*, San Francisco, CA, Jossey-Bass.

Brookfield, S. D. (1987) *Developing Critical Thinkers*, San Francisco, CA, Jossey-Bass.

Brookfield, S. D. (ed.) (1985) *Self-Directed Learning: From Theory to Practice*, New Directions in Continuing Education, No. 25, San Francisco, CA, Jossey-Bass.

Bruner, J. (1962) *On Knowing*, Cambridge, MA, Harvard University Press.

Bunting, C. (1980) 'Funding Quality Improvement: Lessons from the FIPSE Experience', *Current Issues in Higher Education*, vol. 2, no. 2, pp. 1–11.

Burgoyne, J. G. and Hodgson, V. E. (1983) 'Natural Learning and Managerial Action: A Phenomenological Study in the Field Setting', *Journal of Management Studies*, vol. 20, no. 3, pp. 387–399.

Byrne, E.T. and Wolfe, D. E. (eds) (1980) *Developing Experiential Learning Programs for Professional Education*, New Directions for Experiential Learning, No. 8, San Francisco, CA, Jossey-Bass.

Carlaw, R. W. (1970) 'The Development of Interaction as an Approach to Training', *Public Health Reports*, vol. 85, no. 9, pp. 754–759.

Carlaw, R. W. (1978) 'Training for Nutrition and Education', unpublished paper prepared for His Majesty's Government, Nepal.

Carnevale, A. (1984) *Jobs for the Nation: Challenge for a Society Based on Work*, Alexandria, VA, American Society for Training and Development.

Cell, E. (1984) *Learning to Learn from Experience*, Albany, NY, State University of New York Press.

Cermak, T.L. and Brown, S. (1982) 'Interactional Group Therapy with Adult Children of Alcoholics', *International Journal Group Psychotherapy*, vol. 32, pp. 375–389.

Chené, A. (1983) 'The Concept of Autonomy in Adult Education: A Philosophical Discussion', *Adult Education Quarterly*, vol. 32, no. 1, pp. 38–47.

Cheren, M. E. (ed.) (1987) *Learning Management: Emerging Directions for Learning to Learn in the Workplace*, Information Series No. 320, Columbus, OH, ERIC Clearinghouse on Adult, Career, and Vocational Education, Ohio State University.

Cohen, P.S. (1968) *Modern Social Theory*, London, U.K., Heinemann Educational Books Ltd.

Collins, J. H., Estes, N. and Walker, D. (eds) (1989) *Proceedings of the Sixth International Conference on Technology and Education*, Edinburgh, U.K., CEP Consultants Ltd.

Coombs, P. and Ahmed, M. (1974) *Attacking Rural Poverty: How Nonformal Education Can Help*, Baltimore, MD, Johns Hopkins University Press.

Comstock, D.E. (1982) 'A Method for Critical Research' in Bredo, E. and Feinberg, W. (eds) *Knowledge and Values in Social and Educational Research*, Philadelphia, Temple University Press.

Copar, H. (ed.) (1987) *Proceedings of the Human Resources Management and Organizational Behavior Western Regional Conference*, Virginia Beach, VA, The Association of Human Resources Management and Organizational Behavior.

Cotton, N.S. (1979) 'The Familial Incidence of Alcoholism', *Journal of Studies on Alcohol*, vol. 40, pp. 89–116.

Craig, R. L. (ed.) (1987) Training and Development Handbook, 3rd. edn, New York, NY, McGraw Hill.

Cross, P. (1988) 'In Search of Zippers', AAHE Bulletin (June), pp. 3–7.

Danchak, M. (1987) 'Knowledge Maintenance for the Professional', Challenges for Continuing Higher Education Leadership: Corporate Campus Collaboration, Washington, D.C., National University Continuing Education Association.

Davies, J. and Easterby-Smith, M. (1984) 'Learning and Developing from Work Experiences', *Journal of Management Studies*, vol. 21, no. 2, pp. 167–183.

Davies, S. (1979) *The Diffusion of Process Innovations*, London, U.K., Cambridge New Press.

DeGeuss, A. P. (1988) 'Planning as Learning', *Harvard Business Review*, vol. 66, no. 1, pp. 70–74.

DeGreene, K. (1973) *Sociotechnical Systems: Factors in Analysis*, Design, and Management, Englewood Cliffs, NJ, Prentice-Hall.

Dewey, J. (1938) *Experience and Education*, New York, NY, Collier Books.

Dreyfus, H.L. and Dreyfus, S.E. (1986) *Mind Over Machine: The Power of Human Intuition and Expertise in the Era of the Computer*, New York, Free Press.

Emrick, J., Peterson, S. and Agarwala-Rogers, R. (1977) *An Evaluation of the National Diffusion Network*, Vol. I: Findings and Recommendations, Washington, D.C., U.S. Office of Education.

Eurich, N. (1985) *Corporate Classrooms: The Learning Business*, Princeton, NJ, The Carnegie Foundation for the Advancement of Teaching.

Even, W. (1987) 'Career Interruptions Following Childbirth', *Journal of Labor Economics*, vol. 5, no. 2, pp. 255–277.

Feuer, D. (1988) 'Training Magazine's Industry Report 1988', *Training*, vol. 25, no. 10, pp. 31–34.

Fiol, C.M. and Lyles, M. (1985) 'Organizational Learning', *Academy of Management Review*, vol. 10, no. 4, pp. 803–813.

Finger, M. (1988) 'The Process of Becoming an Adult Educator' in Proceedings of the Twenty-Ninth Annual Adult Education Research Conference, Calgary, Canada, The University of Calgary, May 6–8, pp. 127–132.

Flanagan, J. (1954) 'The Critical Incident Technique', *Psychological Bulletin*, vol. 51, no. 4 (July), pp. 327–358.

Freire, P. (1970) *Pedagogy of the Oppressed*, trans. M. Bergman, New York, NY, Seabury Press.

Freire, P. (1973) *Education for Critical Consciousness*, New York, NY, Seabury Press.

Fund for the Improvement of Postsecondary Education (1975–1979) *Resources for Change*, Washington, D.C., The Office of Educational Research and Improvement.

Garratt, B. (1987) *The Learning Organization*, London, U.K., Fontana.

Getzels, J. and Guba, E. (1957) 'Social Behavior and the Administrative Process', *School Review*, vol. 65, pp. 423–441.

Glaser, B. and Strauss, A. (1967) *The Discovery of Grounded Theory*, Chicago, IL, Aldine Publishing Co.

Goodwin, D. (1978) 'The Genetics of Alcoholism: A State of the Art Review', *Alcohol Health and Research World*, vol. 2, pp. 1–12.

Goodwin, D. (1985) 'Alcoholism and Genetics: The Sins of the Fathers', *Archives of General Psychiatry*, vol. 42, pp. 171–174.

Gordon, J. (1988) 'Who is Being Trained to do What?', *Training*, vol. 25, no. 10, pp. 51–60.

Gravitz, H. and Bowden, J. (1985) *Guide to Recovery: A Book for Adult Children of Alcoholics*, Holmes Beach, FL, Learning Publications.

Grene, M. (ed.) (1969) *Knowing and Being: Essays by Michael Polanyi*, Chicago, IL, University of Chicago Press.

Gross, N., Giacquinta, J. and Bernstein, M. (1976) *Implementing Organizational Innovations*, New York, NY, Basic Books.

Guba, E. (1981) 'Criteria for Assessing the Trustworthiness of Naturalistic Inquiries', *Educational Communication and Technology: A Journal of Theory, Research, and Development*, vol. 29, pp. 75–91.

Hall, G. (1974) 'Phases in the Adoption of Educational Innovations in Teacher Training Institutions', Austin, TX, Research and Development Center for Teacher Education of The University of Texas.

Hall, G. (1978) 'Concerns-Based Inservice Training: An Overview of the Concepts, Research and Practice', Austin, TX, Research and Development Center for Teacher Education of The University of Texas.

Hall, G. and Hord, S. (1987) *Change in Schools*, New York, NY, Suny Publications.

Hall, G., George, A. and Rutherford, W. (1977) *Measuring Stages of Concern About the Innovation: A Manual for Use of the SOC Questionnaire*, Austin, TX, The Research and Development Center for Teacher Education of the University of Texass.

Harvey, J. (1988) *The Abilene Paradox and other Meditations on Management*, La Jolla, CA, University Associates.

Hart, M. (1985) *Thematization of Power*, The Search for Common Interests, and Self-reflection: Towards a Comprehensive Concept of Emancipatory Education', International Journal of Lifelong Education, vol. 4, no. 2, pp. 119–134.

Havelock, R. (1971) *Planning Innovations*, Ann Arbor, MI, Institute for Social Research.

Hofstede, G. (1980) *Culture's Consequences: International Differences in Work-Related Values*, Beverly Hills, CA, Sage.

Inkster, R. P. (1987) 'How Do You Know? Michael Polanyi and Adult Education', *Proceedings of the Twenty-Eight Annual Adult Education Research Conference*, Laramie, University of Wyoming.

Janis, I. (1972) *Victims of Groupthink*, Boston, MA, Houghton-Mifflin.

Jaques, E. (1988) 'Development of Intellectual Capability' in Link, F. (ed.).

Jarvis, P. (1987) *Adult Learning in the Social Context*, London, U.K., Croom Helm.

Kaij, L. and Dock, J. (1975) 'Grandsons of Alcoholics: A Test of Sex-linked Transmission of Alcohol Abuse,' *Archives of General Psychiatry*, vol. 32, pp. 1379–1381.

Kast, F. and Rosenzweig, J. (eds) (1973) *Contingency Views of Organization and Management*, Chicago, IL, Science Research Associates.

Keen, P. and Scott-Morton, M. (1978) *Decision Support Systems: An Organizational Perspective*, Reading, MA, Addison-Wesley.

Keeton, M. and Associates (1976) *Experiential Learning*, San Francisco, CA, Jossey-Bass.

Kelly, G. (1955) *The Psychology of Personal Constructs*, Vol. 1, New York, NY, Norton and Co.

Kemmis, S. and McTaggart, R. (1988) *The Action Research Planner*, 3rd. edn, Victoria, Canada, Deakin University Press.

Kern, J. (1986) 'Adult Children of Alcoholics as Professionals in the Alcoholism Field' in Ackerman, R. J. (ed.).

Kerrigan, J. and Luke, J. (1987) *Management Training Strategies for Developing Countries*, Boulder, CO, Lynne Reinner Publishers.

Knight, K. and McDaniel, R. (1979) *Organizations: An Information Systems Perspective*, Belmont, CA, Wadsworth Publishing.

Knowles, M. (1950) *Informal Adult Education.*, New York, NY, Association Press.

Knowles, M. (1985) 'Shifting to an HRD Systems Approach', *Training and Development Journal*, vol. 39, no. 5, pp. 24–25.

Kolb, D. A. (1984) *Experiential Learning*, Englewood Cliffs, NJ, Prentice-Hall.

LaBelle, T. (1988) 'Nonformal Education for Industrialization in Latin America: The Human Capital Approach', *The Alberta Journal of Educational Research*, vol. 34, no. 3, pp. 203–214.

Lee, C. (1985) 'Trainers' Careers, *Training*, vol. 22, no. 10, pp. 75–80.

Levine, A. (1976) *Why Innovation Fails: The Institutionalization and Termination of Innovation in Higher Education*, unpublished doctoral dissertation, State University of New York at Buffalo.

Lewin, K. (1947) 'Frontiers in Group Dynamics', *Human Relations*, vol. 1, pp. 5–41.

Lewis, L. (ed.) (1986) 'Experiential and Simulation Techniques for Teaching Adults', *New Directions for Continuing Education*, no. 30, San Francisco, CA, Jossey-Bass.

Lewis, L. (ed.) (1988) 'Addressing the Needs of Returning Women', *New Directions for Continuing Education*, no. 39, San Francisco, CA, Jossey-Bass.

Lillard, L. and Tan, H. (1986) *Private Sector Training: Who Gets It and How Much?* Santa Monica, CA, Rand Corporation.

Lindemann, E. (1926) 'To Discover the Meaning of Experience', *Survey*, vol. 55, pp. 545–546.

Lindemann, E. (1961) *The Meaning of Adult Education*, originally published in 1926 by New York, New Republic Inc., reissued by Montreal, Harvest House, Ltd.

Lindsey, R. (1987) 'Gurus Hired to Motivate Workers are Raising Fears of Mind Control', *The New York Times*, April 17, vol. 136, col. 1, pp. 8 and 10.

Link, F. (ed.) (1988) *Essays on the Intellect*, Alexandria, VA, Association for Supervision and Curriculum Development.

Lufts, J. and Ingram, H. (1961) 'The Johari Window', *Human Relations Training News*, Washington, D.C., National Education Association, vol. 5, no. 1.

Marsick, V. J. (1979) 'Training for "Taking Over": Three Asian Models for Educational Fieldworkers', unpublished doctoral dissertation, University of California, Berkeley.

Marsick, V. J. (ed.) (1987a) *Learning in the Workplace*, London, U.K., Croom Helm.

Marsick, V. J. (1987b) 'UNICEF: A Children's Program with High Adult Education Impact' in Rivera, W. and Walker, S. (eds).

Marsick, V. J. (1988a) 'Action Learning: A Transformative Experience for Managers?' in Zukas, M. (ed.), pp. 283–288.

Marsick, V. J. (1988b) 'Becoming Adult Educators: A View from Within', manuscript submitted for publication.

Marsick, V. J. (ed.) (1988c) 'Enhancing Staff Development in Diverse Settings', *New Directions in Continuing Education*, no. 38, San Francisco, CA, Jossey-Bass.

Marsick, V. J. (1988d) 'Entering a New Era' in Marsick, V. J. (ed.) 1988c.

Marsick, V. J. (1989, March) 'Learning to Be: Life History and Professionalization', paper presented at the annual meeting of the American Educational Research Association, San Francisco, CA.

Marsick, V. J. (1990) 'Action Learning in the Workplace' in Mezirow, J. D. (ed.).

Marsick, V. J. and Cederholm, L. (1988) 'Developing Leadership in International Managers – An Urgent Challenge', *The Columbia Journal of World Business*, vol. 23, no. 4, pp. 3–11.

Marsick, V. J. and Smedley, R. R. (1989) 'Education for Health' in Merriam, S. and Cunningham, P. (eds).

Maslow, A. (1971) *The Farther Reaches of Human Nature*, New York, NY, Viking Press.

McCall, M. W., Jr., Lombardo, M. M. and Morrison, A. M. (1988) *The Lessons of Experience: How Successful Executives Develop on the Job*, Lexington, MA, Lexington Books, D. C. Heath and Co.

McCarthy, B. (1987) *The 4 Mat System*, Barrington, IL, EXCEL, Inc.

McClellan, J. (1983) 'Toward a General Model of Collective Learning: A Critique of Existing Models of Specific Social Systems and a Sketch of a Model for Social Systems in General', unpublished doctoral dissertation, University of Massachusetts.

McDaniel, R. and Morris, S. (1978) 'Effective Use of Personnel in Human Service Systems', a working paper, Austin, TX, Bureau of Business Research of The University of Texas.

McGeoch, J.A. (1942) *The Psychology of Human Learning*, New York, NY, Longmans Green and Co.

McLagan, P. (1983) *Models for Excellence: The Conclusions and Recommendations of the ASTD Training and Development Competency Study*. Washington DC, ASTD Press.

Merriam, S. and Cunningham, P. (eds) (1990) *1990 Handbook of Adult Education*, San Francisco, CA, Jossey-Bass.

Meyer, J. (1982) 'Adapting to Environmental Jolts', *Administrative Science Quarterly*, vol. 27, no. 4, pp. 515–537.

Mezirow, J. D. (1981) 'A Critical Theory of Adult Learning and Education', *Adult Education*, vol. 32, no. 1, pp. 3–27.

Mezirow, J. D. (1985) 'A Critical Theory of Adult Learning and Education' in Brookfield, S. D. (ed.).

Mezirow, J. D. (ed.) (1990) *Developing Critical Self-Reflection: Tools for Transformative Learning*, San Francisco, CA, Jossey-Bass.

Miller, V. A. (1987) 'The History of Training' in Craig, R. L. (ed.).

Mintzberg, H. (1973) *The Nature of Managerial Work*, New York, NY, Harper and Row.

Mitroff, I. (1983) *Stakeholders of the Organizational Mind*, San Francisco, CA, Jossey-Bass.

Mocker, D. W. and Spear, G. E. (1982) *Lifelong Learning: Formal, Non-Formal, Informal and Self-Directed*, Columbus, OH, ERIC Clearinghouse on Adult, Career and Vocational Education.

More, W. (1974) *Emotions and Adult Learning*, Westmead, Farnborough, Hants, U.K., Saxon House.

Morgan, G. (1986) *Images of Organization. Beverly Hills*, CA, Sage.

Morgan, G. (1988) *Riding the Waves of Change: Developing Managerial Competencies for a Turbulent World*, San Francisco, CA, Jossey-Bass.

Mowday, R. and Steers, R. (eds) *Research in Organizations: Issues and Controversies*, Santa Monica, CA, Goodyear Publishing Co.

Nadler, L. (1980) *Corporate Human Resource Development*, NY, Van Nostrand.

Nadler, L. (1982) *The Critical Events Training Model*, San Francisco, CA, Jossey-Bass.

Nadler, L. (1983) *Human Resource Development: the Perspective of Business and Industry*, Information Series no. 259, Columbus, OH, ERIC Clearinghouse on Adult, Career and Vocational Education.

Neumann, A. (1988, April) 'Making Mistakes: Error and Learning in the College Presidency', a paper presented at the American Educational Research Association Annual Conference, New Orleans, LA.

O'Connell, J. (1968) *Managing Organizational Innovation*, Homewood, IL, Richard R. Irwin Inc.

Parnes, H. (1986) *Developing Human Capital*, Columbus, OH, The National Center for Research and Vocational Education, Ohio State University.

Perelman, L. J. (1984) *The Learning Enterprise: Adult Learning, Human Capital and Economic Development*, Washington, D.C., The Council of State Planning Agencies.

Perrow, C. (1967) 'A Framework for the Comparative Analysis of Organizations', American Sociological Review, vol. 32 (April).

Pfeiffer, J. W. and Jones, J. E. (1983) 'Design Considerations in Laboratory Education', *Reference Guide to Handbooks and Annual*, 1983 Edition, San Diego, CA, University Associates.

Pincus, J. and Williams, R. (1979) 'Planned Change in Urban School Districts', *Phi Delta KAPPAN*, vol. 60 (June).

Polanyi, M. (1962) *Personal Knowledge*, corrected edn, Chicago, IL, University of Chicago Press.

Polanyi, M. (1967) *The Tacit Dimension*, New York, NY, Doubleday and Co.

Polanyi, M. and Prosch, H. (1975) *Meaning*, Chicago, IL, University of Chicago Press.

Poortinga, Y. A. (ed.) (1977) *Basic Problems in Cross-cultural Psychology*, Amsterdam, Swets and Zeitlinger.

Postman, L. and Senders, V. (1946) 'Incidental Learning and Generality of Set', *Journal of Experimental Psychology*, vol. 36, pp. 153–165.

Postman, N. and Weingartner, L. (1971) *Teaching as a Subversive Activity*, New York, NY, Penguin.

Pressman, J. and Wildavsky, A. (1973) *Implementation*, Berkeley, CA, University of California Press.

Reischmann, J. (1986, October) 'Learning "En Passant": The Forgotten Dimension', presentation at the annual conference of the American Association of Adult and Continuing Education, Miami, FL.

Resnick, L. (1987) 'Learning In School and Out', *Educational Researcher*, vol. 16, no. 9, pp. 13–20.

Revans, R.W. (1971) *Developing Effective Managers: A New Approach to Business Education*, New York, NY, Praeger and London, Longman.

Revans, R. W. (1982) *The Origin and Growth of Action Learning*, Bickly, Kent, Chartwell-Bratt and Lund, Sweden, Studenlitteratur.

Rivera, W. and Walker, S. (eds) (1987) *Lifelong Learning Research Proceedings*, College Park, University of Maryland, Department of Agriculture and Extension Education.

Rogers, C. (1961) *On Becoming a Person*, Boston, MA, Houghton Mifflin.

Rogers, C. (1965) *Client Centered Therapy*, Boston, MA, Houghton Mifflin.

Rogers, R. P. (1989) *Reflective Learning About the Workplace: An Action Science Study with Adult Children of Alcoholics*, unpublished doctoral dissertation, The University of Texas at Austin.

Rosow, J. and Zager, R. (1988) *Training: The Competitive Edge*, San Francisco, CA, Jossey-Bass.

Ross, D. *et al.* (eds) (1951) *Administration for Adaptability*, Vol. II: The Agencies and Processes of Change in Schools, New York, NY, Columbia University Press.

Russell, M., Henderson, C. and Blume, S.B. (1985) *Children of Alcoholics: A Review of the Literature*, New York, NY, Children of Alcoholics Foundation, Inc.

Schaef, A.W. and Fassel, D. (1988) *The Addictive Organization*, San Francisco, CA, Harper and Row Publishers.

Schein, E. H. (1969) 'The Mechanisms of Change' in Bennis, W. G. *et al.*, (eds).

Schön, D. (1967) *Technology and Change*, New York, NY, Delacorte Press.

Schön, D. A. (1983) *The Reflective Practitioner*, New York, NY, Basic Books.

Schön, D. A. (1987) *Educating the Reflective Practitioner*, San Francisco, CA, Jossey-Bass.

Scott, W. Richard (1988) 'The Organization of Training', speech presented at The Texas Conference on Organizations, Lakeway, Texas, April.

Scribner, S. (1986) 'Thinking in Action: Some Characteristics of Practical Thought' in Sternberg, R. J. and Wagner, R. K. (eds).

Senge, P. (1988) 'Systems Thinking: Notes Prepared for Union Carbide', Framingham, MA, Innovation Associates Inc.

Shor, I. and Freire, P. (1987) *A Pedagogy for Liberation*, Smith Hadley, MA, Bergin and Garvey Publishing.

Shrivastava, P. (1983) 'A Typology of Organizational Learning Systems', *Journal of Management Studies*, vol. 20, no. 1, pp. 7–28.

Silverman, D. (1970) *The Theory of Organization*, Aldershot, Hants, Gower Press.

Simon, H.A. (1965) 'Administrative Decision Making', *Public Administration Review*, vol. 25, no. 1, pp. 31–37.

Skruber, R. (1987) 'Organizations as Clarifying Learning Environments' in Marsick, V. J. (ed.) 1987a.

Smith, R. M. (1987) 'Learning to Learn in the Workplace' in Cheren, M. E. (ed.).

Srinivasan, L. (1977) *Perspectives on Nonformal Adult Learning*, third printing, New York, NY, World Education.

Staw, B., Sanderlands, L. and Dutton, J. (1981) 'Threat-Rigidity Effects in Organizational Behavior: A Multilevel Analysis', *Administrative Science Quarterly*, vol. 26, no. 4, pp. 501–524.

Sternberg, R. J. and Wagner, R. K. (1986) *Practical Intelligence: Nature and Origins of Competence in the Everyday World*, Cambridge, Cambridge University Press.

Stokes, L. and Pankowski, M. (1988) 'Incidental Learning of Aging Adults via Television', *Adult Education Quarterly*, vol. 38, no. 2, pp. 88–100.

Sutherland, J. (1975) *Systems: Analysis, Administration, Architecture*, New York, NY, Van Nostrand Reinhold Co.

Swedish Work Environment Fund (1988) *Towards a Learning Organization*, Stockholm, The Swedish Work Environment Fund.

Terreberry, S. (1973) 'The Evolution of Organizational Environments' in Kast, F. and Rosenzweig, J. (eds).

Thompson, J.D. (1967) *Organizations in Action*, New York, NY, McGraw Hill.

Torbert, W. (1972) *Learning From Experience: Toward Consciousness*, New York, NY, Columbia University Press.

Tough, A. (1979) *The Adult's Learning Projects*, 2nd edn, Research in Education Series No. 1, Toronto, The Ontario Institute for Studies in Education.

Tough, A. (1982) *Intentional Changes: A Fresh Approach to Helping People Change*, Chicago, IL, Follett Publishing Co.

Usher, R.S. (1985) 'Beyond the Anecdotal: Adult Learning and the Use of Experience', *Studies in the Education of Adults*, vol. 17, no. 1, pp. 59–74.

Usher, R. (1988) 'The Practical and the Critical in the Study of Adult Education' in Zukas, M. (ed.), pp. 243–437.

Vorapipatana, K. (1975) 'The "Khit-Pen" Man', *World Education Reports*, vol. 8 (January), pp. 1–5.

Watkins, K. (1981) *Managing Change: Roles and Stages of Concern for Three Higher Educational Innovations*, unpublished doctoral dissertation, The University of Texas at Austin.

Watkins, K. (1988) 'Supporting Women's Re-entry to the Workplace' in Lewis, L. (ed.) (1988).

Watkins, K. (1989) 'Human Resource Development' in Merriam, S. and Cunningham, P. (eds).

Watkins, K. (1989) 'Technology, Training, and Obsolescence' in Collins, J. *et al.* (eds).

Watkins, K. and Wiswell, B. (1987) 'Incidental Learning in the Workplace' in Copar, H. (ed.).

Watzlawick, P., Weakland, J. and Fisch, R. (1974) *Change: Principles of Problem Formation and Problem Resolution*, New York, NY, W.W. Norton.

Weick, K. (1984) 'Small Wins: Redefining the Scale of Social Problems', *American Psychologist*, vol. 39 (January), pp. 40–49.

Weick, K. (1986, August) 'The Demystification of Organizing: Discovered Threads', paper presented at the Academy of Management Conference, Chicago, IL.

Whitfield, C. (1980) 'Children of Alcoholics: Treatment Issues', *Maryland State Medical Journal*, vol. 29, pp. 86–91.

Whitfield, C.L. (1987) *Healing the Child Within: Discovery and Recovery for Adult Children of Dysfunctional Families*, Pompano Beach, FL, Health Communications Inc.

Witkin, H. A. (1949) 'The Nature and Importance of Individual Differences in Perception', *Journal of Personality*, vol. 18, pp.145–170.

Witkin, H. A. (1950) 'Individual Differences in Ease of Perception of Embedded Figures', *Journal of Personality*, vol. 19, pp. 1–15.

Witkin, H. A. (1977) 'Theory in Cross-Cultural Research: Its Uses and Risks' in Poortinga, Y. A. (ed.).

Witkin, H. A. and Goodenough, D. R. (1977) 'Field Dependence and Interpersonal Behavior', *Psychological Bulletin*, vol. 84, pp. 661–689.

Woititz, J. (1986) 'Common characteristics of adult children of alcoholics' in Ackerman, R. J. (ed.).

Woititz, J. (1987) *Home Away from Home*, Pompano Beach, FL, Health Communications Inc.

Woodside, M. (1986) *Children of Alcoholics on the Job*, New York, NY, Children of Alcoholics Foundation.

Work in America Institute (1985) 'Training For New Technology, Part II: Toward Continuous Learning', A Work In America Institute Policy Study, Scarsdale, NY, Work In America Institute.

Zuboff, S. (1988) *In the Age of the Smart Machine*, New York, NY, Basic Books.

Zukas, M. (ed.) (1988) *Transatlantic Dialogue: A Research Exchange*, Proceedings of the SCUTREA, AERC, CASAE Conference, July 11–13, Leeds, U.K., University of Leeds, School of Continuing Education.

Index